'This book examines the essential commercial implications of the unique phenomenon of rapid ageing. As the world's population of over sixties doubles by 2030 and almost trebles by 2050, societies will need new coping mechanisms, and companies will need to adapt to a big shift in the structure of their consumer markets. Dick Stroud and Kim Walker take an important and innovative approach to show why and how.' **George Magnus**, Senior Economic Adviser, UBS Investment Bank, London

'This book informs brand owners on how to grow value by opening up to new audiences, an absolutely essential strategy in saturated markets. *Marketing to the Ageing Consumer* looks at the positives that marketing to an older consumer can bring to brands. Stroud and Walker's debate around age-friendliness adds a very fresh perspective to the age debate.' **Jo Rigby**, Global Insight Director, Omnicom Media Group

'*Marketing to the Ageing Consumer* isn't just about age-neutral marketing in the mode of the brilliant Apple case. It goes way beyond that and powerfully points out the lost profit opportunities for companies that fail to appreciate the enormous purchasing power of older consumers and to understand their needs.' **Professor Malcolm McDonald**, Emeritus Professor, Cranfield School of Management

'We are getting old – and we are all in a state of denial about the physiological and practical impact. Large and easy-opening containers are never sexy topics but organisations, private and public, that want to grasp the opportunities that demographic change represents, have an essential tool in the "age-friendliness" framework outlined in this book. Read it and prepare your organisation for the future.' **Alex Batchelor,** Chief Operating Officer, BrainJuicer

'The commercial world has belatedly woken up to the need to address the 50+ population respectfully and strategically. Dick Stroud and Kim Walker's work is thorough, insightful and backed by both empirical evidence and an instinctive understanding of the various types of characters in this age group. This book proposes an important, ambitious and practical new metric to help businesses address what is without question one of the biggest issues of the 21st century.' **Neil Barrie,** Global Planning Director, TBWA\Chiat Day Los Angeles

'Kim Walker and Dick Stroud say: "Population ageing will soon equal sustainability as a global trend that the corporate world must understand and devise policies to embrace." I agree – and I would further argue that age-friendliness is inextricably linked to sustainable development and therefore to corporate sustainability. Happily, becoming age-friendly makes business sense *and* is the right thing to do too.' **Prof David Grayson CBE,** Director of the Doughty Centre for Corporate Responsibility, Cranfield School of Management

'*Marketing to the Ageing Consumer* is a timely offer not to be missed. The approach, the first of its kind, is firmly based on the latest scientific insights on the physiology of ageing, which the authors then translate into practical marketing knowhow needed to create an age-friendly business. Their work is an indispensable business guide to marketing to the ageing consumer.' **Professor Yuwa Hedrick-Wong**, HSBC Professor of International Business, University British Columbia, Global Economic Advisor, MasterCard Worldwide

'The populations of Asia Pacific, Europe and the US are getting older. The physical effects of ageing mean that companies must adapt their products and re-invent the customer experience. This book is a handbook to help executives navigate this future.' **David Sinclair,** International Longevity Centre (UK)

'The older consumer population is in growth globally and our collective understanding in how to best engage with this audience is decades behind where it needs to be. Read this book now if you want real expertise and actionable insight on how to build an effective strategic approach.' **Orlaith Blaney,** CEO, McCann Erickson Dublin

'With its informative and straightforward approach to understanding older people, this book has wide relevance to people working across the creative industry. A timely and much-needed publication.' **Rama Gheerawo,** Deputy Director, Helen Hamlyn Centre for Design, Royal College of Art

'All good marketers need to be able to look into the future and anticipate business opportunities. Few aspects of the future are as certain as the ageing of individuals and populations. The authors are unusually perceptive guides on how to prosper in this different world.' **Hugh Burkitt,** Chief Executive, The Marketing Society

'The authors provide a very practical guide as to how to cater for the requirements of the huge segment of the consuming population that is ageing, that is open to change and willing to embrace new channels and technologies, but only when these are designed to take account of their particular physical and emotional requirements.' **Richard Webber,** Visiting Professor Kings College London, Former Director, Experian Ltd

'The authors are knowledgeable and perceptive commentators at the interface between ageing and marketing. Their latest book is essential reading for those involved in businesses that aspire to grow in a world in which the ageing of the population is becoming a defining feature.' **David Metz,** Visiting Professor, University College London and author of *Older Richer Fitter*

'What I found most valuable and unique about this book is that it gives the reader a deep insight into the physiology of ageing and draws out the implications of the ageing process for the products and services that older consumers need. It's effectively a crash course for executives who need to evolve their companies to meet the opportunities and challenges of global population ageing.' **Anne Connolly,** Executive Director, Ageing Well Network

'Forget the "problem" of ageing, embrace the reality of longevity – for us, for our services, for society. This book confirms the case and provides the tools to make that shift.' **Jane Ashcroft,** Chief Executive, Anchor

'This compelling book provides a crash course for executives who need to evolve their companies to meet the challenges and opportunities of such global population ageing. The authors have systematically interpreted the physiology of ageing into a manual for 21st-century business transformation.' **Professor Adrian Done,** IESE Business School, author of *Global Trends: Facing Up to a Changing World*

'This book is potentially revolutionary. Because population ageing is a global phenomenon, it is a book most businesses would be well advised to read.' **Dr. Florian Kohlbacher,** German Institute for Japanese Studies, author of *The Silver Market Phenomenon: Marketing and Innovation in the Aging Society*

'Through the development of the concept of age-friendliness they demonstrate the necessity to touch all aspects of entrepreneurship and company management, from product development to marketing and sales, and even HR Management. A highly recommendable book for all managers who want to keep their business sustainable.' **Luc Willemyns,** Director Responsible and Engaged Bank Platform BNP Paribas Fortis

Marketing to the Ageing Consumer

The Secrets to Building an Age-Friendly Business

By

Dick Stroud
Kim Walker

First published 2013 by
PALGRAVE MACMILLAN

Palgrave Macmillan in the UK is an imprint of Macmillan Publishers Limited, registered in England, company number 785998, of Houndmills, Basingstoke, Hampshire RG21 6XS.

Palgrave Macmillan in the US is a division of St Martin's Press LLC, 175 Fifth Avenue, New York, NY 10010.

Palgrave Macmillan is the global academic imprint of the above companies and has companies and representatives throughout the world.

Palgrave® and Macmillan® are registered trademarks in the United States, the United Kingdom, Europe and other countries.

ISBN 978–0–230–37819–3

This book is printed on paper suitable for recycling and made from fully managed and sustained forest sources. Logging, pulping and manufacturing processes are expected to conform to the environmental regulations of the country of origin.

A catalogue record for this book is available from the British Library.

A catalog record for this book is available from the Library of Congress.

10 9 8 7 6 5 4 3 2 1
22 21 20 19 18 17 16 15 14 13

Printed and bound in Great Britain by
CPI Antony Rowe, Chippenham and Eastbourne

We dedicate this book to the 1.5 billion consumers over 50 who currently occupy this planet and the millions who will soon follow. Our hope is that some of the thinking from this book will make life easier for them and deliver profits to companies that adapt to serve them better.

CONTENTS

LIST OF FIGURES AND TABLES

Figures

Tables

ACKNOWLEDGMENTS

Our sincere thanks to Suzanne Arnold for helping us make sense of our words and to Vishesh Mittal for his help in solving our technology puzzles. Thanks to our families and friends for tolerating a Brit and an Aussie who, for the past year, talked of little other than physiological ageing and marketing.

Finally, thanks to the numerous marketers and scientists who have contributed to the body of knowledge about ageing that we were able to access and build upon.

Without Google, this book would not have been possible!

Introduction

A quarter of a century ago Charles Scheme published a journal paper titled *Marketing to our Aging Population: Responding to Physiological Changes*. The paper outlined the implications for marketers as the senses, minds and bodies of their customers age.

Since then, very little else has been researched and written about the subject. This is surprising because the median age of consumers in the USA has increased by 16 per cent since its publication.[1]

Much has been written about the psychological effects of ageing and the mechanics of segmenting and communicating with older consumers. Even more has been written about the apparent differences in attitudes and behaviours between the generations.

Yet the most basic of questions has been largely ignored: 'How do companies adapt to the relentless ageing of their most important asset – their customers?' How could such a basic issue be ignored?

The answer lies in the mindset of marketers who pigeonhole products into a very small group that are sold to 'old people' and the vast majority that are consumed by everybody else.

Clearly physiological ageing is important if you produce products that ameliorate the effects of ageing (for example, spectacles, hearing aids, anti-ageing cream) and the medical products that repair failing bodies (for example, hip and knee replacements). Until recently, if your company didn't cater to these specialist sectors, then there appeared few reasons to be concerned about the ageing issue.

Where marketers have considered the issue the perception is that the effects of ageing only manifest towards the end of life. This is not true. Eyesight, hearing and mobility problems start during a person's 40s and 50s. The more we learn about cognitive ageing points to this changing even earlier in life.

The simplistic model of the world has been exploded by the financial convulsions that have affected Europe and the USA. Policy makers and business leaders are being forced to confront a series of trends that have long existed but that could be ignored during the past two decades of unrelenting economic growth. The USA, Europe and increasingly Asia Pacific are rapidly ageing at a time when the finances of the western world are least able to cope with the resulting implications.

For many years the subject of 'sustainability' was of interest to a dedicated group of activists on the fringe of the business world. In a matter of five years it became the subject that dominates much of government and corporate decision-making. A similar change is taking place with the subject of 'population ageing', which has moved from an academic debate between demographers and gerontologists to become a mega-issue that affects companies, large and small, whether they are based in China or the USA.

Population ageing will soon equal sustainability as a global trend that the corporate world must understand and devise policies to embrace.

Our experience is that companies that are attempting to respond to the population ageing issue have difficulty in knowing where to begin. For the small group of brands that are already targeting the older cohort, the challenge is one of marketing tactics and execution.

For the majority of companies, which have not perceived themselves as being dependent on older consumers, the challenge is much harder to define. Older consumers in Asia Pacific are very different from those in Europe. The poorest of older consumers have radically different needs and aspirations from the wealthiest. Older women have very different behaviours from older men. It appears that a company's response is totally dependent on the profile of its customers.

There is one factor that is common across all of the geographies, and all of the social and economic classes, and is shared by men and women. With a few small exceptions, the changes to consumers that result from their physical ageing are universal, as are their implications for companies and governments.

It was not difficult for the authors to see that a topic of such importance that was so lacking in understanding was a perfect subject for a book and the creation of tools that translate the nebulous issue of population ageing into insights and metrics that companies can action. This was our rationale for writing *Marketing to the ageing consumer.*

The book's story is told in four parts.

History and scope

The first two chapters summarize how the discipline of marketing to older people has evolved and the scope and magnitude of the economic changes that population ageing creates. Our objective is to distil a complicated subject so that readers understand the 'big issues' that govern how companies market to the older demographic and to explain the potential problems and opportunities that population ageing creates.

Often the facts of population ageing are presented to show either a catastrophe resulting from there being too few young and too many old people or a business bonanza from satisfying evolving consumer demands as Baby Boomers desperately attempt to retain their youth. The reality is far more complex and lies somewhere between these two extremes.

Touchpoints and physiological ageing

The purpose of this part is to explain the intricacies of physiological ageing from the perspective of their impact on a company's products, services, distribution infrastructure and support and communication channels. There is no point in a company trying to understand and respond to the psychological issues of ageing if the foundations of its products and supply channels are not fit for purpose for this age group.

Sophisticated theories about the generational cohort effect and developmental relationship marketing will founder if the customer cannot use the product or see and hear the advertising.

This requires an understanding of the details of cognitive, sensory and physical ageing and how these conditions affect an organization's touchpoints with its customers.

The five chapters of this part explain these issues from the business standpoint, not the scientific theory of ageing. The primary objective is to ensure the reader has the knowledge to understand the changing demands of an ageing customer base and the tools to exploit the business opportunities this creates.

Age-friendliness – what it is and how it is measured

The authors' definition of age-friendliness is an environment in which the unique physical needs of older people are satisfied in a way that is natural and beneficial for all ages.

The three chapters in this part explain in detail the concept of age-friendliness and how it is measured. The authors have audited the age-friendliness of many global brands and explain what good (and bad) lessons can be learnt from their experiences. The final chapter in this part considers the practical issues of how companies overcome the internal and external obstacles of creating and implementing an age-friendly strategy that becomes part of their corporate culture.

Making age-friendliness a way of life

Population ageing affects much more than the relationship between the company and its customers. Older customers are also older employees; they are also older citizens. The book's final part explains how the concept of age-friendliness and the techniques that have been developed to improve customer touchpoints can be applied to helping companies use their ageing workforce and governments to best serve an ageing citizenry.

The final chapter in the book looks to the future and considers how new technologies and evolving social attitudes will change the corporate and government response to demographic change.

Marketers continually have to acquire skills and knowledge to cope with opportunities provided by new technologies and the ever-changing needs and wants of consumers. The authors hope that *Marketing to the Ageing Consumer* provides the knowledge and techniques to help marketers benefit from a new dimension of change that will progressively affect all areas of their work.

CHAPTER 1

The ageing consumer – a historic perspective

The importance of older consumers and the techniques employed by marketers to capture their spending power are not new subjects.

As far back as 1991, a front cover of *Business Week* was devoted to: 'Those aging Baby Boomers and how to sell to them'. A decade and a half later (2005), *Business Week* returned to the same subject with another edition and a front cover devoted to the year in which the USA's Baby Boomers celebrated their 60th birthday.

Twenty years ago, the American academic George P. Moschis published the book *Marketing to Older Consumers*, followed a decade later by the French marketer Jean-Paul Treguer and his book *50+ Marketing*.

The joint author of this book (Dick Stroud) added to the body of knowledge with the publication in 2005 of the marketing textbook *The 50-Plus Market*.

Virtually all of the hundreds of thousands of words that have been written about older consumers have focused on their behaviour; how they can be segmented, the metrics of their purchasing power and their changing demographics.

Surprisingly, little attention has been given to the universal issue affecting all consumers – how their ageing bodies create marketing challenges and opportunities.

Before discussing the implications of physiological ageing it is worthwhile summarizing what we know (and don't know) about the marketing factors affecting older consumers. The starting point for this summary is an attempt to resolve the paradox of why such a large group of wealthy people attracts so little attention from the marketing community.

Myths, stereotypes and inertia

Much of the thinking that still permeates the culture of marketing comes from an era when the youth population was growing rapidly. Employment levels were high and expanding the customer base was the number-one priority. This invariably meant focusing on the young rather than the old.

For as long as this subject has been studied, there has been a set of arguments about why it is too difficult or even dangerous to focus overtly on older consumers. These arguments are heard less often but they have not disappeared.

Older people don't change brands

This argument assumes that once buying preferences are established, during a person's 20s or 30s, they are difficult and expensive to change. The corollary to this assumption is that by the time a person reaches their 50s their 'shopping basket for life' is fixed and hence it is worthwhile spending a disproportionate amount of marketing resources on young people to 'capture them young'.

Undoubtedly, there is a relationship between brand preferences and age but, as the recent rise in popularity of supermarket own-brands proves, they are far from fixed (in both the USA and Europe). If this argument had any validity, the older population would still be watching their TV using VHS videotape rather than Blu-ray players. This argument means older people would have rejected e-book readers rather than accounting for a third of users in the USA.[1]

Explicit advertising to the old alienates the young

As with so many of these myths, there is a grain of truth in this argument. Clearly, it would be silly to target a fashion campaign at 20-year-olds showing the clothes modelled by people looking like their parents or grandparents. However, the corollary of this is not that older people should be banished from advertising to avoid alienating their children's generation.

World-class companies such as Apple and Marks & Spencer have shown that it is possible to create successful advertising that can appeal across the age spectrum. Both companies have run successful advertising campaigns featuring a mix of imagery to appeal to three generations of customers.

We get them anyway

The basis of this argument is that marketing communications that are created to appeal to the 18–35 cohort will also be seen by and influence their parents and grandparents. Why bother to appeal overtly to older consumers when they are already being reached by the primary communications aimed at the young? This is probably the silliest of all of the myths.

If the marketing communications are optimized to appeal to a younger person, then it doesn't matter how much they are seen by older people – they will instinctively be labelled as 'not being meant for me' and ignored. Studies in Asia Pacific, the USA and Europe all conclude that older people believe that many marketing communications are not intended for them – and they are right.

When older people are the largest buyers in many product categories, such as luxury cars, it seems odd to optimize the marketing communications for an age group that can't afford to buy the product.

Older people are stuck in their ways

This argument assumes that the spirit of change, adventure and experimentation is solely the province of the young. Research conducted by the media agency OMD and Dick Stroud showed that in some European countries (especially France) ageing did result in a loss in the desire to experiment; however, in other countries (especially Australia) the reverse was true. In these countries the desire to try new things increased with age, as did the ability to pay for them.

Older people are technophobic

Again, there is some truth to this argument but the reality is far more complex. A cursory study of the statistics on Internet use shows that nationality, education and socio-economic group are major influencers of online use. In the USA, the richest 18–24-year-olds are 30 per cent more likely to own a smartphone than the poorest. For the 45–54 age group, that difference rises to 230 per cent.[2]

These myths and stereotypes partially explain marketers' reluctance to spend the time and budget on older consumers that is warranted by those consumers' spending power.

Most corporate cultures are resistant to radical change. The pressures to satisfy shareholders each quarter and the short tenure of senior marketing staff, less than 24 months, discourage out-of-the-box thinking and the adoption of new strategies.

There are two other, more important reasons why attitudes have been so slow to change. The very obvious one is the youthfulness of most marketers, especially agency staff. In the UK the average age of agency staff has been approximately 33 years old for the past three years.[3] There are no reasons why young marketers cannot excel at understanding and appealing to consumers of their parents' and grandparents' generation. This requires skill, determination and above all an unconventional approach. But, the path of least resistance is to approach the market by extrapolating the needs and wants of your peers or basing your insights on the peculiarities of your older relatives.

The final and by far the most important reason why marketers have been so slow to change is the depressingly conservative culture in which they work. This syndrome is best described as: 'being youth-centric has done us OK for the past decade, so why change now?'

Wally Olins, the co-founder of the branding agency Wolff Olins, is harsher in his use of words:[4] 'Marketers are lazy and will take the easy option. It is much easier to keep doing what you know rather than moving out of your comfort zone.'

Many years ago there was a saying that: 'Nobody ever got fired for buying IBM.' This was when IBM ruled the computer industry. The reason we are still talking about the aversion that marketers have for older consumers is the assumption that: 'Nobody ever got fired for targeting the young.'

Trends go on until they stop. In IBM's case, the business came very close to bankruptcy and with its downfall the old certainties of IT investments disappeared. At some stage, the behaviour of marketers will have to catch up with reality and reflect the importance of the older consumer's spending power.

What we have learnt

As marketers, we all like to have a complex subject reduced to a list of 'dos and don'ts' or a set of 'the top five things you need to know'. Unfortunately, the subject of marketing to older people doesn't lend itself to this type of simplistic summary.

During the past decade, our knowledge of older people has improved, as has our portfolio of useful marketing techniques. The following are the most important elements of knowledge that we can use with confidence.

Demographics

Most regions of the world have a wealth of data about the age and geographic profile of all their citizens. The UN is one of the best sources of this information.[5] We know that in nearly all regions the median age is increasing; the only differences are the starting point and the rate of change. Allied to this is our understanding of the declining birth rate in most countries. The relationship between these two factors results in one of the most significant social and economic upheavals affecting the planet.

Wealth

In the USA and most of Europe (and many countries of the Asia-Pacific) older people own the largest percentage of wealth. This is not surprising because the components of wealth are residential property and pension investments. Both of these are financial instruments that increase in value with age. There are many marketing opportunities resulting from the conversion of this wealth into income to support older people in their retirement.

Lack of uniformity

Whichever prism you use to view older consumers (for example, economic, social, educational, technological literacy) there is little consistency in their behaviours and personal circumstances. The wealthy, healthy and well-educated 65-year-old professional lady has very little in common with the poor and unemployed manual worker with failing health. Age is a poor proxy for predicting behaviour.

Unreadiness for retirement

Very few governments are adequately prepared to manage the fiscal and social changes resulting from the ageing of their populations. A recent report from the OECD concluded that: 'The demographic transition – to fewer babies and longer lives – took a century in Europe and North America. In Asia, this transition will often occur in a single generation.'[6] Like their governments, most citizens, approaching retirement, are financially unprepared to maintain their quality of life once they leave employment. This situation has been made worse, in Europe and the USA, by the financial effects of the recession.

Figure 1.1 shows research from Saga of the perceived change in the quality of life of older people in the UK at the end of 2011, compared with a year ago.[7]

That the perception of quality of life varies by age illustrates two important points. Not surprisingly, the older the person the more important is their state of health in determining their quality of life. What is not

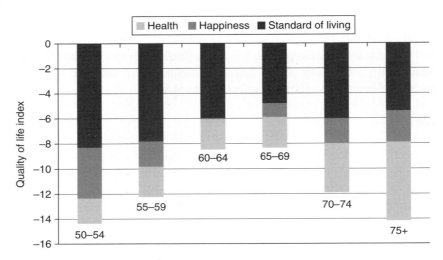

Figure 1.1　Annual change in the quality of life index for six age groups

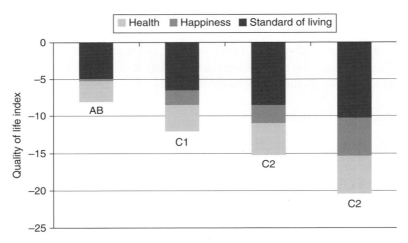

Figure 1.2　Annual change in the quality of life index for four socio-economic groups

so obvious is that people in the mid- phase of ageing, between 60 and 69 years, feel they have a better quality of life.

People who have retired and secured their pensions are faring far better than those approaching retirement and who are exposed to the dual issues of reduced employment security and falling investment returns. In Europe and the USA, the fall in housing values has had a disproportionate effect on the younger-old.

Older people, in Europe and the USA, who are in the lower socio-economic groups have suffered far worse than their richer peers. Using research from Saga, the diagram in Figure 1.2 illustrates this by showing that in the UK the annual decline in the standard of living of the lowest group is twice that of the most affluent.

In those countries that have experienced and are still experiencing the recession, we can be confident in predicting that older consumers are going to fragment into the 'haves' and the 'have-nothings'. The split between these two will not be as extreme as the 'We are 99%'[8] movement maintains, but it will result in the majority of older people having to reappraise how they live the last quarter of their lives.

Types of marketing

When marketers refer to 'marketing to older people' they invariably mean 'marketing communications' rather than all of the facets of marketing (that is, the product, product offer, pricing, communications, sales channels and support).

The other distinction that is rarely made is the interrelationship between the product design and the focus of the marketing activities. These differences are best illustrated using the age/marketing matrix shown in Figure 1.3.

Silo marketing, represented in the bottom left-hand corner of the matrix, is where products are designed for older people and marketed exclusively to older people. Examples of such products are retirement housing, drugs for age-related medical conditions and housing, care and financial products for retirees. This is the most common form of marketing to older consumers.

The diametric opposite of age-silo is age-neutral marketing. In this case, the products are bought by all ages and marketed across the age spectrum. Examples of age-neutral products are white goods, hospitality and travel services, cars and consumer packaged goods. The range of products and the business potential of age-neutral products are far larger than those in the silo category, but so is the difficulty of marketing that they demand.

The matrix contains other variants, including products that are neutral in design but with specific marketing propositions for older people. Examples of this variant, called targeted marketing, are age-related discounts on products such as spectacles or the use of older celebrities to promote products that are bought by all age groups (for example, computer games consoles, destination holidays).

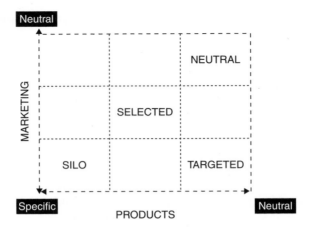

Figure 1.3   The age/marketing matrix

The final category is selected marketing, in which both the product and the marketing campaign are modified to relate to the older shopper. Products appealing to the health concerns of older people (for example, cholesterol reduction) and products with modified packaging that help those with eyesight or strength issues are in this category.

If there is a single lesson that marketers have learnt about the relationship between marketing and the age of the customer, it is that marketing should be 'age blind'.

There are no fundamental differences between marketing to the young and marketing to the old. Like all good marketing, the starting point is getting inside the customer's head and understanding their motivations and attitudes. The challenge for marketers has been (and still remains) abandoning the stereotypes and myths about older people and focusing on evidence-based knowledge.

What we don't know

At the core of successful marketing to older people are two questions:

- How do you segment the older market?
- What are the needs, wants and behaviours of older consumers?

New product development, communications and channel strategies are easy to devise once you are confident about your answers to these questions.

During the past decade a range of theories has purported to answer these questions. Some of them are useful theoretical constructs; some have direct relevance in refining marketing campaigns.

The difficulty in applying these theories is managing the interrelationship between them and recognizing the circumstances in which one technique is better used than another.

In addition to using chronological age as a predictor of behaviour, a dozen other factors claim to decide why older people behave the way they do. These are the most commonly used.

The zeitgeist effect

This is also known as the cohort or generational effect. The concepts are based on the ideas of the sociologist Karl Mannheim, who theorized that generations have a collective set of outlooks, tastes and desires. Understanding these formative experiences provides insights that can be used to define marketing strategies. This technique is intellectually appealing but difficult to apply.

Lifestyle

This is a collective description for the economic, educational, social and cultural factors that influence how older people behave. These factors can be aggregated into geodemographic segments, such as those used by Experian and CACI. In this case, geographic location and housing type are used as a proxy to predict the lifestyle factors. Alternatively, the segments might be bespoke lifestyle groups such as the ones created by the media agency OMD.[9] In addition to behaviour, lifestyle influences practical characteristics such as life expectancy and healthiness.

Lifestyle can be effective and simple to use for tangible variables such as financial factors, but is harder to apply for aspirational factors.

Lifestage

The transitions from work to retirement, from living in multi- to single-generation households and crossing the threshold to assume responsibility for parental care are three of the major lifestage events that older people experience. All of these can have a significant impact on behaviour.

George Moschis' work on lifestage segmentation theory has been important in the understanding of lifestage and how it can be applied by marketing practitioners. Dr. Mochis showed how the factors that make older consumers receptive to marketing offerings result from their changing life events. These events might be physiological, such as the onset of chronic conditions and the menopause. Others events are triggered by such things as retirement, becoming a grandparent or losing a spouse.

The mortality effect

At the age of 65 years, a man can expect 10 more years of healthy life; a woman a year or two more. Most older people are not aware of this fact but they will be conscious of the onset of physical ageing and age-related illnesses. The youthful assumption of the unchanging nature of life is gradually replaced by the awareness of one's own mortality. The 'ticking clock' can be the initiator of major life-changing events (such as moving house, deciding to divorce). It is a very powerful influence on behaviour but difficult to apply.

Psychological

There is a collection of theories that are used to explain how ageing influences human values, self-awareness, beliefs, priorities and our very reason for being. The late David Wolfe was probably the most vocal proponent of the importance of these age-related psychological factors as the mechanism for understanding behaviour in later life. His theory of developmental relationship marketing was explained in his book *Ageless Marketing*.

Although the theory and constructs appear to be founded in academic research, the technique is difficult to translate from the theoretical to the practical applications of marketing.

Gender

There are multiple theories about the difference in the consumer behaviour of men and women but little that explains how these behaviours change as people age. The American marketers Marti Barletta and Carol Orsborn have done the most to expand our understanding of this subject. Their conclusions are that the importance of women in household decision-making increases with age.

The fact that women live longer than men is another reason why understanding their behaviour is so important. In the USA in 2010, for every 100 females aged 65–74 years there were 86 males. This age imbalance increases so that for the over-85s there are only 49 men for every 100 women. This pattern of women outliving men occurs in most geographies.[10]

The unresolved challenge is how these gender differences are combined with the other effects of ageing.

In addition to these techniques there are three others that in certain circumstances can be very important:

- Nationality – there are significant 'nationality effects' that influence the way people age. These cannot be simplified into regional categories. There is as much difference between the ageing behaviours of the English and the French as there is between Singaporeans and Malaysians.

- Sexuality – in some circumstances the sexuality of the older person is an important determinant of behaviour. Older people who are gay and lesbian and who require care home services will be influenced by the attitude to homosexuality of care providers.

- The recessionary effect – the economic upheaval of the recession has altered many of the assumptions that older people have about their lifestyle and that of their children. This can create major upheavals in priorities and lifestyle.

Each of these theories has a band of loyal supporters who believe their ideas are the best and possibly the only way of understanding the machinations that make older people behave the way they do. The most important measure about the usefulness of these theories is whether they pass the 'so what test'. The theory can be intellectually interesting, but does it enable marketers to make operational decisions about advertising, channel selection and product design?

In addition to the difficulty in combining these techniques and deciding in what circumstances they should be used, there is another issue that is not resolved. We might have a reasonable understanding of the gender differences for today's 60–70-year-olds, but how will these change for the next cohort of older people? There is some evidence suggesting that the gender differences will narrow, but that is far from certain. In truth we have little understanding of how these techniques for predicting behaviour and segmentation will change over time.

Today's state of play

There is unlikely to be a tipping point when marketers wake up, 'see the light' and start committing the marketing resources that they should to the older cohort. There appears to be a slow, probably begrudging realization that marketing to older people has to be taken seriously and become an integral part of all marketing plans.

One of the few positives that have resulted from the recession is the widespread awareness that a significant number of older people are relatively immune to the financial hardships it creates. Unlike past recessions, the one that is depressing economic activity in Europe and the USA has affected the young more than the old.

The techniques for researching and understanding older people will continue to improve, but it is unlikely there will be any major breakthroughs in our understanding of their psychological make-up. The same applies to methods of segmentation. There have been marginal improvements but no radical change.

We are entering a new era in which companies can no longer be complacent about population ageing. The single fact we know for certain is that 95 per cent of the world's population is ageing. With ageing come physiological changes that affect private and public organizations, even if they are not overtly attempting to appeal to older people.

If the past two decades of the techniques of marketing to older people were associated with responding to their psychological needs, the coming decade will be dominated by the physiological changes to their bodies and minds. These changes will be a major source of new product requirements and opportunities for organizations to compete on the excellence of their age-friendliness.

Chapter at a glance

→ Virtually all of the hundreds of thousands of words that have been written about older consumers have focused on their behaviour; how they can be segmented, the metrics of their purchasing power and their changing demographics. Surprisingly, little attention has been given to the universal issue affecting all consumers – how their ageing bodies create marketing challenges and opportunities.

→ Since the subject of marketing to older consumers was first studied, there has been a set of arguments why it was a dangerous or impossible task. For example, older people don't change brands and explicit advertising to the old alienates the young. These arguments are heard less often but they have not disappeared. The most important reason why marketers have been so slow to recognize the importance of older people is the depressingly conservative culture in which they work. This syndrome is best described as: 'being youth-centric' has done us well for the past decade, so why change now?

→ During the past decade, our knowledge of older people has improved, as has our portfolio of useful marketing techniques. We now understand their demographics, wealth and income distribution and the lack of uniformity. The widespread use of the age/marketing matrix enables the categorization of marketing to older consumers to be divided into various categories, the most important being age-silo and age-neutral marketing.

→ The key to successful marketing to older people requires knowing how they can be segmented and understanding their needs, wants and behaviours. New product development, communications and channel strategies are easy to devise once you have answered these questions. There are a range of theories that claim to answer these questions. The difficulty in applying these theories is managing the interrelationship between them and recognizing the circumstances in which one technique is better used than another.

→ If the past two decades of the techniques of marketing to older people were associated with responding to their psychological needs, the coming decade will be dominated by the physiological changes to their bodies and minds. These changes will be a major source of new product requirements and opportunities for organizations to compete on the excellence of their age-friendliness.

CHAPTER 2

Population ageing – situation analysis

This chapter explains why, for the foreseeable future, population ageing will have a profound influence on the policies and decisions of governments and businesses.

Demographic change is rapidly moving from an arcane academic debate between demographers and gerontologists to become a mega-issue that affects all types of companies, whether they are based in Europe, the USA or Asia Pacific.

Population ageing will soon equal sustainability as a global trend that the corporate world must understand and devise policies to exploit.

There was a simple reason why companies embraced the sustainability agenda – it made good business sense. A global study by Nielsen found that approximately two-thirds of consumers would prefer to buy from, work for and invest in companies that are implementing society-friendly programmes.[1]

Up until now there has not been a financial imperative driving companies to incorporate the issues of demographic change into their corporate social responsibility agenda. Attempts have been made to raise the profile of the subject – for example, the demographic change project that brought together BASF, Evonik and SAP with academia.[2] However, there is little evidence that these types of government-sponsored initiatives have either raised the profile of the subject or resulted in a lasting change in how companies behave.

This situation is about to change. Fuelled by the effects of the recession on national finances, combined with the resultant costs and repercussions of ageing, the 'do nothing' option is no longer available. The 'do something' strategy eludes most organizations but, as this chapter explains, their time to devise and implement it is running short.

Population ageing – good for some but not for others

Viewed from the perspective of the individual, the past 50 years have seen prosperity and life expectancy increase. There are parts of the world that have not been so fortunate, mainly in Africa and areas ravaged by wars, but for most the quality and length of life have improved.

Rising prosperity and life expectancy have gone hand in hand with a reduction in the birthrate. For some countries the fall has been dramatic.

Having a population that lives longer and has fewer children brings material and social benefits for a country's citizens but creates huge challenges for the government. The corporate world is somewhere between the two extremes and is trying to decide if an ageing population is an opportunity or a threat.

The last of the Baby Boomers were born in 1964. At this time, Japan was the only country with a birthrate below the replacement rate of 2.2 children per woman. In the USA, the birthrate was 3.5 and life expectancy was 70 years, but in China the birthrate was 5.7 and life expectancy was 52 years.

By the time this age group was celebrating its 45th birthday, the world's demographics had changed beyond all recognition. The birthrate in the USA, China, Russia and most of Europe was below the replacement rate. Life expectancy in China had increased by two decades to 73 years, while the birthrate had declined by a factor of 3.5. In Japan life expectancy had risen to 83 years and in the USA it had increased by ten years to 79 years.

In less than half a century, increasing longevity accompanied by falling fertility had radically changed the numbers of young and old – a process that still continues.

Table 2.1 shows the forecasted change in life expectancy and fertility until 2020. These forecasts, from the UN Department of Economic and Social Affairs, suggest that life expectancy continues increasing but fertility stabilizes and in some cases slightly decreases.[3] Such forecasts should be viewed with some scepticism.

Demographic forecasters have habitually underestimated the rate at which life expectancy extends. In 1977, the UK's Office of National Statistics believed the life expectancy at birth for males in 2011 would be 73 years. The actual life expectancy was 79 years.[4] The forecasts for fertility rates have been a little more accurate but have tended to be overestimated.

The trend in the developed and developing world for more older and fewer younger people appears set to continue. How these trends translate into the relative numbers of old and young is shown in Figure 2.1.

Table 2.1　Life expectancy and birthrate changes during the period 2010–20

	2010–15		2015–20	
	Life expectancy	**Fertility**	**Life expectancy**	**Fertility**
China	73.8	1.56	74.7	1.51
Italy	82	1.48	82.6	1.56
Japan	83.7	1.42	84.3	1.51
UK	80.4	1.87	81	1.9
USA	78.8	2.08	79.4	2.08

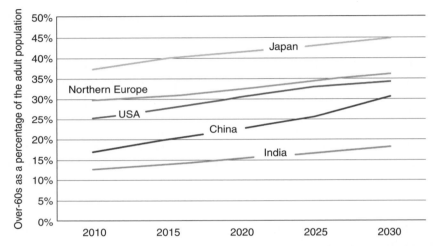

Figure 2.1　The change in the percentage of the over-60s as a percentage of the adult population (the over-20s)

By 2020, Japan will have reached the point at which over 40 per cent of the adult population, defined as those over the age of 20 years, will have had their 60th birthday.[5]

These forecasts show that as this age ratio in the USA starts to plateau, the proportion of older people in China begins to accelerate.

The longer the forecast horizon, the more pervasive the influence of population ageing becomes. The Boston Consulting Group (BCG) believes that by 2050 the population of all the Group-7 countries and the BRIC (Brazil, Russia, India and China) countries will be as old as Japan is today.[6]

In 2012 there are 20 countries whose population is shrinking. The largest are Russia, Germany and Japan. By 2050 another 25 countries will join this list, the largest and economically most important being China.[7]

The enormity of change that these trends and percentages fail to communicate is the resulting increase in the numbers of older people within the population. In 2010 there were 375 million over-60s in the five areas shown in Figure 2.1. In the next 20 years, by the end of 2030, this number will have **increased by 320 million over-60s**.

The speed and size of the demographic change is difficult to comprehend and yet these numbers omit the results of another major trend that is happening in parallel. An additional 350 million people will be added to China's urban population by 2025. This is more than the population of the USA (2009).[8]

The growth of cities at the expense of rural populations is happening in almost all geographic regions. Even the USA, a country that has already undergone dramatic periods of urbanization, is still changing. By 2050, an additional 100 million Americans will be living in cities.[9]

Young people are normally at the forefront of 'rural flight', the migration from the countryside to urban areas in search of jobs. This asymmetric change in the age of the rural population causes the density of older people to increase even further.

The importance of understanding the distribution of older people within a country has been researched by the Rostock Centre for the Study of Demographic Change, which concluded that 'regional differences within countries might be larger than between countries'.[10] The outcome of this interplay between urbanization and ageing is the formation of geographic hotspots of older people where their population density is much higher than the national norm.

The economic and social upheaval created by the combined trends of urbanization and ageing generate immense economic and social challenges. These would be difficult developments for governments to manage during benign economic times. The global economy in 2012 is anything but benign.

The USA, Japan and Europe are being forced to rapidly reduce their budget deficits and the countries of Asia Pacific need to realign their economies to reflect the new global balance of economic power.

It is very difficult to quantify the financial effects of population ageing, urbanization and economic recession. From a cursory study of the media, it is plain that they believe the economic difficulty of the USA and Europe to be the number-one issue. The International Monetary Fund has come to a different conclusion. It believes the fiscal cost of future increases in financial entitlements resulting from ageing is ten times the fiscal cost of the economic crisis.[11] When the memories of the recession start to recede, the impact of population ageing will continue.

The uncertainties of population ageing

In 2006, Ben Bernanke, the US Federal Reserve Chairman, said, in respect of the USA, that although many forces will shape society in all likelihood no single factor will be as pervasive as the effect of population ageing.[12]

The word 'pervasive' does not imply the results of population ageing will be benign or threatening. It was wise of him to use a neutral word because it is extremely hard to predict the outcome of demographic change and its economic and social consequences.

The most important of these consequences are listed in Table 2.2.

It is impossible to rank these economic and social consequences by their importance, their timing or the level of confidence we have in their effect.

We can be certain, however, that the increase in healthcare costs and the changes to GDP growth will have significant and pervasive effects. For this reason, these two factors are covered in more detail below.

Table 2.2   The economic and social consequences of population ageing

Factor	Areas affected by demographic change
Property	The price and availability of property as older people move or use the equity in their homes to fund their retirement and care.
Workforce	The dynamics of the demand and supply of young people into the workforce and the trend for older people to delay their retirement.
Investment capital	The reduction in the level of savings and the change in demand for different types of financial instruments as older people deplete their wealth to fund their living expenses.
Health and care costs	The magnitude and timing of the increase in these costs and the ability of technology, the adoption of healthier lifestyles and the establishment of new lower-cost delivery models to ameliorate the cost increases.
Gross domestic product (GDP) growth	The impact on economic growth of changes in the numbers and spending habits of the old and young.
Demographics	The likelihood and implications of forecasting errors for life expectancy, healthy life expectancy and fertility rates.
Demand for products and services	The changing patterns and levels of demand for products and services created by the changing numbers and requirements of different age groups.

Healthcare costs

According to Standard & Poor's, the combination of population ageing and the costs of new life-saving medical technologies will create a dramatic increase in the share of sovereign expenditure spent on healthcare. This increase will occur in all of the G20 countries. Table 2.3 shows the forecasted increases in sovereign healthcare expenditure, by 2050, for France, the UK, the USA and China.[13]

All of these countries will have to fund a very large increase in healthcare expenditure. China will have to double its spending. The UK will have to increase its expenditure by the same amount as it already spends on education. The USA will have to increase its expenditure by the equivalent of its existing defence budget.

The most obvious contributor to this rise in costs and the easiest to quantify is growth in the number of patients for healthcare services. The other factor, which Standard & Poor's believes represents two-thirds of the total cost increase, is the cost of new (and expensive) technology and treatments.

Technological change and its implications are much harder to quantify and forecast than demography. There is little disagreement about the latter but many opinions about the former.

The Economist Intelligence Unit (EIU) polled the views of healthcare professionals across Europe to understand their concerns about the effect of ageing on their national systems. In Spain, Germany and Scandinavia the threat was seen as minimal or non-existent. In the UK, 35 per cent of the research sample believed population ageing would threaten the viability of the health system. Health professionals in France and Eastern Europe also expressed high levels of concern.

Maybe the healthcare professionals in the UK are too pessimistic or those in Spain are being overly optimistic, especially at a time when their country is suffering badly from the effects of recession.

Table 2.3 Projected increase in healthcare spending in 2010–50 as a percentage of GDP

Country	Percentage of GDP in 2010	Increase in percentage of GDP by 2050
France	8.6%	5.8%
UK	8.0%	6.1%
USA	4.4%	6.0%
China	2.2%	2.0%

There is no doubt that increasing numbers of older people in the population will result in elevated demands for care and medical services. In the UK, 40 per cent of the National Health Service's budget and two-thirds of its hospital beds are occupied by the over-65s.[14]

In the final analysis, the effect that population ageing will have on the care and health systems is under the control of politicians and policy-makers. There is no alternative but to divert a significant amount of public expenditure from other budgets into healthcare. To date there is little evidence that governments are willing to face this challenge.

GDP growth

When commentators refer to the 'ageing problem' they invariably mean the scenario in which population ageing reduces GDP growth, which in turn destabilizes national finances.

This nightmare scenario results from the concurrence of four factors:

- There are fewer people in the workforce to fund public expenditure. *This results in* ...
- Taxation levels rising to fund healthcare and pensions with a subsequent reduction in disposable incomes to buy goods and services. *This results in* ...
- A fall in demand, which affects employment levels and the amount of tax collected and increases the demand for public services. *This results in* ...
- A fall in savings levels as older people spend their savings to fund their retirement, and the young having insufficient income to invest.

The result of these unpleasant circumstances is economic stagnation.

The likelihood and severity of this outcome is totally dependent on the level of economic activity of older people. If it is low and older people leave the workforce and consume state support, then the chances of the nightmare scenario increase. If the older population extends its economically active life, it pays more tax and reduces the period requiring state funding and sets in play a virtuous circle of rising growth.

David Bloom, Professor of Economics and Demography at Harvard School of Public Health, wrote with two colleagues a paper that questions the pessimistic views of demographic change and explains how this outcome can be averted.[15]

The core of his argument is that 'As long as the private and public sector are flexible enough to adjust to the newly emerging societal structures, aging is unlikely to have much effect on economic growth.'

He argues that as populations age, the attitudes of individuals and companies will change. The length of 'healthy life' will increase, resulting in people working longer and saving more to fund their retirement. Immigration policies will adapt to increase the numbers of younger workers. Basically, the behaviours of the state, business and individuals will adapt.

The importance of how long people remain economically active in the workforce was demonstrated in research conducted by Accenture, in association with Oxford Economics.[16] A combination of extending working life and productivity improvements was estimated to have the potential of increasing the USA's GDP, in 2020, by nearly $450 billion. Proportionally similar levels of GDP increase were thought to be possible in Germany, the UK, Spain and India.

Research funded by the UK government demonstrated that extending the working life of the population by one year increased the country's level of real GDP by approximately 1 per cent.[17]

Unfortunately, any discussion of extending the period of working life is met by two sets of arguments. Trade unionists perceive extending the time people need to work as an attack on 'workers' rights'. Commercial pressures have resulted in an extension of the working lives of employees in the private sector in Europe and the USA. It is in the public sector, where unionism is the strongest, and guaranteed pension levels are the highest, where the resistance to change is the greatest.

It was interesting (and disturbing) that one of the first actions of François Hollande, France's socialist president, was to reduce the age of retirement from 62 to 60.

The second argument, which is easy to counteract but is still growing in popularity, is the misguided assumption that retaining older people in the workforce reduces jobs available for younger workers.

Economists term this notion 'the lump of labour fallacy'; it also known as 'the zero-sum fallacy'. The fact that there is no correlation between the numbers of older and younger workers has not stopped calls for younger workers to be given preferential employment rights. The idea of 'intergenerational equity', which argues that the old have disproportionally benefited, compared with the young, has become a popular theme in the media in Europe and the USA.

If the economies of Europe and the USA grow at the levels of the 1990s, then the need to extend working life would not be an issue. However, in 2012 the growth levels in Europe and the USA are anaemic, which results in low or negative levels of job creation. At this point, the effects of population ageing and global economics become integrally intertwined.

Revisiting the original question – does population ageing result in declining GDP levels? The answer is that it all depends on the macro-economic conditions and how business and politicians behave.

The certainties of population ageing

The most certain outcome of ageing is the change it creates in the minds, senses and bodies of consumers – the subject of this book. That consumers will experience physiological ageing is a 100 per cent certainty. The uncertainty is the vigour and thoroughness with which businesses will exploit the opportunities this creates.

The other certainty, and the one that is of fundamental importance to business, is the high level of spending power of the older age group, at least for the next two decades.

Accenture, BCG and McKinsey, three of the world's largest strategic consultancies, have studied this subject and come to a similar conclusion.

McKinsey studied how French consumer spending will change in the period 2007–30 and concluded that 'The mature consumer segment, aged 55-plus, will dominate, accounting for around two-thirds of all additional consumption in the period to 2030.'[18]

Households in France, with consumers aged 65-plus are forecast to account for almost half of additional consumption during this period. The results of McKinsey's research, showing the increase in spending by the older age groups, by different product categories, are displayed in Table 2.4.

Table 2.4   Quality-adjusted volume increase in total spending by age for the period 2007–30 for different product categories

	Households aged	
Product category	**65-plus**	**55-plus**
Food at home	84%	100%
Utilities	84%	100%
Gasoline	75%	100%
Financial service fees	83%	95%
Apparel and accessories	65%	88%
Personal care	67%	84%
Alcohol and tobacco	58%	81%
Furnishings	63%	81%
Motor vehicles	57%	78%

These figures speak for themselves, with the over-65s dominating the increase in spending in many major product types.

Accenture forecasted how spending in the USA would change for the period 2009–30 by the age of consumers and concluded that: 'Between 2009 and 2030, Americans 65 and older will see their power as consumers grow more dramatically than that of other age groups.'

Accenture's forecasts are shown in Figure 2.2. The two oldest age groups are expected to have the highest growth in spending, with the 65–74 age group increasing by 87 per cent.[19]

BCG also forecasted the change in consumer spending in the period from 2008 to 2030 and concluded that in Germany, Japan and the USA the 55-plus age group would contribute over half the increase in spending. These results are shown in Table 2.5.

Forecasting until 2030 is extremely difficult, especially during volatile economic times. However, three of the world's leading strategic consultancies all conclude that the older age group will be the dominant driver of consumer spending for the next two decades.

This doesn't mean that the standard of living of all older people is set to increase – far from it.

As explained in Chapter 1, most older people are financially unprepared for retirement. The aggregate consumer demand of the older age group is and will remain high, but it is skewed so that a few are able to maintain a prosperous lifestyle while many will just be surviving.

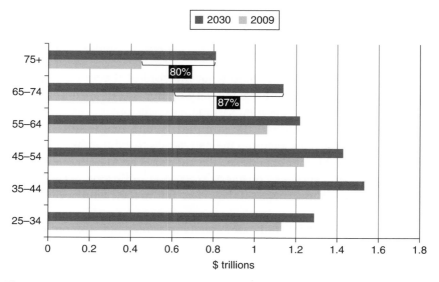

Figure 2.2   Current and potential spending by age group in the USA

Table 2.5 The level of consumer spending in Germany, Japan and the USA in 2030 and its increase during the period 2008–30 attributable to the 55-plus group

	Consumer spending in 2030 ($ trillion)		Period 2008–30 Increase in spending attributable to 55-plus
	55-plus	Under-55	
Germany	0.9	0.8	75%
Japan	1.1	0.8	66%
USA	4.0	6.1	50%

Source: Boston Consulting Group (BCG).[20]

The size of this small group of prosperous older people, often referred to as 'the Charmed Generation', varies by country. In the UK they account for less than 20 percent of their age group.[21] Increasing levels of inequality are not limited to older people; this appears to be a trend affecting all ages. The difference for older people is that they do not have the ability to materially change their financial position because they have limited time to earn and save.

This chapter demonstrates that there are significant levels of uncertainty about many of the outcomes that population ageing will have for business and society. How the forces of ageing, urbanization and global economic change combine and how policy makers respond are difficult, probably impossible, to predict.

The two certainties that should be at the core of the way companies navigate this uncertain future are the very high levels of spending power and the changing bodies and minds of the older customer.

Do businesses understand the complexity and magnitude of these changes? Are companies adapting their strategies to exploit the opportunities being created? In our experience the answer is no to both questions.

In 2011 the EIU surveyed business executives in Europe, Asia and the USA to understand how prepared they were for, in their words, *The Silver Opportunity*.[22]

The results of the EIU study are broadly in agreement with our experiences. Only 13 per cent of the sample thought they were highly effective in understanding the needs of older customers. Fewer still thought their marketing to older consumers was highly effective (10 per cent).

What is so strange about these results is that 65 per cent of the respondents expected the proportion of revenue they derive from older customers to increase during the next five years. Over a third of the research group believe that population ageing presented them with a large business opportunity. A further 46 per cent thought the opportunity to be 'middling'.

We believe this mismatch between the expected business opportunities of increasing longevity and a perceived lack of capability to exploit those opportunities results from two causes. Companies fail to understand the detail of what they are required to do to satisfy their older consumers and do not have the tools to translate these needs into the metrics that are required to implement change.

The following parts of this book will help satisfy both of these requirements.

Chapter at a glance

→ Viewed from the perspective of the individual, the past 50 years have seen prosperity and life expectancy increase. There are parts of the world that have not been so fortunate, but for most the quality and length of life have improved. But, having a population that lives longer and has fewer children creates huge challenges for the government. The corporate world is somewhere between the two extremes and is trying to decide if an ageing population is an opportunity or a threat.

→ The economic and social upheaval created by the combined trends of urbanization and ageing generate immense economic and social challenges. These would be difficult developments for governments to manage during benign economic times. The state of global economy is anything but benign. Population ageing will soon equal sustainability as a global trend that the corporate world must understand and devise policies to exploit.

→ The extent of the effect that population ageing has on governments and individuals is totally dependent on the level of economic activity of older people. If it is low and older people leave the workforce and consume state support, then the chances of an economic nightmare scenario increase. If the older population extends its economically active life it, pays more tax and reduces the period requiring state funding and sets in play a virtuous circle of rising growth.

➔ The most certain outcome of ageing is the change it creates in the minds, senses and bodies of consumers. That consumers will experience physiological ageing is a 100 per cent certainty. The other certainty, and the one that is of fundamental importance to business, is the high level of spending power of the older age group, at least for the next two decades. These two certainties should be at the core of the way companies navigate this uncertain future.

➔ There is mismatch between the expected business opportunities of increasing longevity and a perceived lack of capability that companies have to exploit the opportunities. Companies fail to understand the detail of what they are required to do to satisfy their older consumers and do not have the tools to translate these needs into the metrics that are required to implement change.

CHAPTER 3

Introduction to physiological ageing

When marketers study older consumers, which is not that often, they are normally trying to understand how ageing changes people's wants, attitudes and behaviours. What are the psychological effects of ageing that make a Baby Boomer act differently from when they were 20 years younger? Why don't they behave the way their children behave?

So much of what determines older people's behaviour depends on their nationality, gender, health, education and employment status. This makes it exceptionally difficult to isolate the emotional and behavioural changes – the psychological effects of ageing – and to use them as a foundation for marketing actions.

It is difficult to understand why there is so much interest in the psychological effects when there is another aspect of ageing that is relatively easy to understand and that has clearly defined implications for business.

Physiological ageing – the way that minds, bodies and senses change – is a wide-ranging subject but, with a few exceptions, its study applies to all types of older people, irrespective of their backgrounds. Most important, it is a factor that can be isolated, studied and applied to improving business performance.

This chapter provides an overview of the different types of physiological ageing that can be used in a conceptual model of age-friendliness that enables companies to understand their effects on the business.

Chapters 5–7 build on these ideas and explore the subject in greater detail.

Throughout this discussion, the authors have endeavoured to retain the focus on the business rather than the science of ageing. Sometimes, however, it has been necessary to explain ageing's technicalities so as to fully describe its implications.

Different types of ageing

From a business perspective, the three types of ageing that are most commonly used to determine marketing actions are:

Chronological age

This is the commonly used definition of ageing: the period in time, measured in months and years, that we have been alive.

The simplicity and universal understanding of chronological age is its greatest strength. Unfortunately, marketers often make the assumption, incorrectly, that chronological age is a good proxy for behaviour. Once they have made this assumption, this measurement becomes the driver for marketing actions.

So, for example, advertising media buying is invariably done on the basis of the audience's chronological age. The same applies to how companies segment their markets.

Chronological age is also used to group people into generational cohorts and then to attribute to them behaviours resulting from shared memories.

Why two people who have been alive for the same length of time should have a common core of beliefs that results in similar behaviours is a mystery, but this premise still determines marketing decisions.

Lifestage age

This is a variant of chronological ageing and is based on the assumption that a person's lifetime can be divided into discrete phases. For older people, the most common phases are 'empty nesters' and 'retired'.

There is a fundamental difficulty with this concept. Each of the phases has evolved into many variants. What 'retirement' means to one person could be very different from that of another. Even the regulatory basis of lifestage, the age when a person gains entitlements, such as a pension, is no longer a fixed date. Many countries make it possible to delay the age when a pension is paid.

In the USA and Europe the concept of children reaching their 20s and leaving home is fast becoming an anachronism. Rising levels of youth unemployment and the increase in the age when people buy their first home means that children can be living with their parents well into their 30s. The high incidence of divorce often means that the empty nester period is cut short when a divorced child is forced to return home.

According to the UK's Office for National Statistics the number of people aged 20 to 34 who still live with their parents increased by 20 per cent between 1997 and 2011.[1]

Finally, the divorce rates of older people are at record levels in the USA and UK. The lifestyle assumption that the family unit of older people is a constant can no longer be taken for granted.

Psychological age

There has been much speculation about the way ageing alters our values and attitudes. During a lifetime we amass experiences and knowledge and succeed or fail in achieving our hopes and aspirations. All of this experience must affect how we behave. The difficulty is translating these complex emotions into insights that can be applied to business.

In the absence of any widely accepted model of psychological ageing the insights become simplified generalizations. For example, ageing results in older people valuing experiences more than physical objects. Another example is the belief that women are better equipped to cope with retirement than men.

Anecdotal evidence suggests that these assessments are probably valid; however, what is missing is a methodology that enables business to combine these insights with other determinants of consumer behaviour such as health, wealth and education.

A person's psychological age provides a rough guide to their value system but no more than knowing where they were born or the race of their parents.

These three types of ageing vary in their usefulness for determining the behaviour of older consumers. The confidence that can be placed in the accuracy of their predictions also differs. This variation is shown in Figure 3.1.

The ideal type of ageing is one that provides companies with useful insights that can be relied on. The authors believe that physiological ageing possesses both these attributes.

What is physiological ageing?

Fifty years ago the gerontologist Bernard Strehler[2] proposed the criteria that define normal ageing. These five criteria are as appropriate now as when they were first proposed. The condition of ageing must be:

- **Cumulative** – the effects of ageing increase with time.
- **Universal** – in differing degrees it affects all members of the group.

- **Progressive** – the result of ageing is a series of gradual changes.
- **Intrinsic** – the effects are independent of external conditions.
- **Harmful** – the changes that occur compromise normal biological functions.

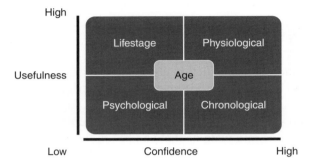

Figure 3.1   Matrix of the level of usefulness and confidence of four types of ageing

Based on Strehler's theory, the authors have created their own definition of physiological ageing.

> The systemic change to the body's ability to function caused by age-related changes to the mind, body and senses.

The timing and intensity of an individual's physical ageing can be influenced by their genetic make-up, lifestyle, ethnic origin and gender. Some 70-year-olds run marathons, read without glasses and climb mountains. Others are frail, have limited mobility and suffer the onset of dementia.

Most companies' customers are a mix of all types of older people with various combinations of physical ageing. Few companies have the luxury of dealing only with older people with 20/20 vision and perfect hearing. For this reason, companies need to plan for the median state of physiological ageing and its consequences.

It is important to distinguish the results of physical ageing from two conditions that appear to have similar outcomes.

Age-related illness

In varying degrees of severity, physiological ageing affects everybody. Age-related illness, by contrast, is more likely to occur with ageing, but affects only some of the age group, in the same way as glandular fever (infectious mononucleosis) mainly attacks younger people but the majority of the young never experience the illness. Glandular fever is not a youth illness and neither is arthritis an illness of the old.

However, when an age-related illness is so common that it affects a significant proportion of the older population and its effects result in consumers having problems interacting with business, then it has to be taken into account. For instance, a third of over-65s have sight problems caused by cataracts.[3]

Disability

At its extreme, physiological ageing, often combined with an age-related illness, results in the loss of an important physical function, such as sight, hearing or mobility. The older person with severe mobility problems has the same disability as a young person unable to walk because of an accident. Companies' responsibilities to disabled people are normally defined by national accessibility regulations. The physical conditions of most older people are not at this extreme level and therefore are not covered by these regulations.

Growing older and suffering from physiological ageing is not an option; it is our destiny. There is an established body of knowledge that explains why and when physical ageing occurs and its effects.

Before it is possible to build a conceptual model of how business can respond to the physical changes taking place in its customers, it is necessary to understand and categorize these multiple biological changes.

Types of physical ageing

To understand physiological ageing and its relevance to business, we need to divide it into its constituent parts. A doctor could probably list scores of ways bodies change with age but the authors believe there are 'only' 24 effects that have an impact on business. Figure 3.2 shows some of the physical functions and body parts that are affected.

The elements of physiological ageing can be divided into three groups:

Sensory – this describes the changes to the capabilities of our senses that affect numerous customer touchpoints (for example, reading packaging, using products and talking to sales staff).

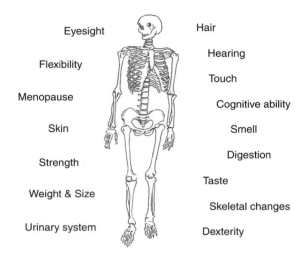

Eyesight

Flexibility

Menopause

Skin

Strength

Weight & Size

Urinary system

Hair

Hearing

Touch

Cognitive ability

Smell

Digestion

Taste

Skeletal changes

Dexterity

Figure 3.2   A summary of the bodily functions and areas affected by ageing

Cognitive – this relates to the changes in how we respond to and process information (for example, using a website and understanding promotional material).

Physical – this describes the remaining physical changes that occur during ageing (for example, the ability to open packaging and the skeletal changes that affect how we look and move).

These three groups of ageing effects are discussed in detail in Chapters 5, 6 and 7. The following are brief definitions of each ageing effect.

Sensory ageing

Eyesight

There are multiple ways that ageing affects our eyes' comfort. The two most important for business are the deterioration in the ability to focus on close-up objects and the requirement for increased levels of illumination to see.

Hearing

Age-related hearing loss affects over half of all people over 60 years old. The symptoms are difficulty hearing higher-pitched consonants in speech and understanding a voice when there is background noise. Hearing loss has implications for all of the touchpoints where customers are in a spoken dialogue with a company or its representatives.

Touch

The sense of touch includes the ability to perceive pressure, temperature, pain and vibration. The sensitivity of all of these abilities can start to decrease from the age of 50. Some of the effects are little more than a nuisance but the loss of the ability to feel pain can result in serious injury. Product design and packaging are the most obvious areas in which the loss of touch becomes an important issue.

Smell

The ability to distinguish a smell declines with age, as does the ability to differentiate between smells. The senses of taste and smell are closely interrelated. Most of the experience of a food's taste results from its odour. From the age of 70 the sense of smell declines. This form of physical ageing has obvious implications for the design of food products.

Taste

As we age, the number of our taste buds declines. This change starts around the age of 60 and begins earlier for women than men. Typically, salty and sweet are the tastes that diminish first, followed by bitter and sour tastes. These natural changes to the ability to taste are amplified for people who have smoked. As with smell, the changes to the experience of taste have implications for food design.

Oral

Ageing of the mouth can result in the creation of less saliva, which can in turn affect the quality of speech. The gums can start to recede and the tooth enamel becomes discoloured. Ageing might result in an increased incidence of tooth loss, but this is a secondary factor caused by older people taking less care of their teeth. These results of ageing, in particular the discoloration of the teeth, have created a large market for oral cosmetic products and services.

A detailed description of these six ageing effects and their implications for companies is provided in Chapter 5.

Cognitive ageing

Professor Timothy Salthouse, one of the world's experts on cognitive ageing, says in the introduction to his book *Major Issues in Cognitive Aging* that: 'it is somewhat presumptuous to use the phrase "major issues" in the title of a book because there is likely little agreement with respect to which issues are truly "major".' It is even more presumptuous of us to attempt to distil the multiple effects of cognitive ageing into just two factors. However, it is necessary to simplify this complex issue if marketers are to understand how their consumers' ageing brain affects their business.

Processing complex information

Older people appear to find it harder to retain newly acquired information that is required to undertake a task. Using an analogy from computing, it appears that ageing results in a decline in the capability of short-term memory. This can result in difficulties with following complicated written instructions or using new menu systems.

Another aspect of ageing that is associated with this factor is increased difficulty in retaining attention and not becoming distracted by salient events. This has major implications for the design of digital channels.

The effect of ageing on speed when using the web and level of errors illustrates the magnitude of the impact of the complexity factor. At the age of 55 years, the errors made using the web have increased, on average, by 20 per cent and the time taken to complete a task by 35 per cent. By the age of 65 years, these figures are 50 per cent and 60 per cent respectively.[4] This degradation of performance is by comparison with groups of younger people with similar computing skills and experience.

Comprehending new concepts

Older people appear to find it harder to understand and act on language that requires them to make new inferences. This might be a result of the degradation of short-term memory but, whatever the reason, it suggests that it is best to use familiar terms and to be explicit about the connections between concepts.

A more obvious problem of comprehension results from the difficulties older people can have in understanding the language and visual references that are used in 'youth' culture. This can result in feelings of annoyance and of being excluded or just a lack of understanding of the message.

Chapter 6 contains a detailed discussion of both these effects and their implications for marketers.

Physical ageing

Dexterity

Ageing can affect a person's dexterity in multiple ways. The most obvious is the reduced ability to grip objects. Other effects can include a reduction in the fingers' ability to react to an external stimulus and an increase in the time taken to reach and grasp.

The age-related reduction in torque strength, the movement for opening jars, starts as early as 40 and declines for women at a much steeper rate than it does for men.[5]

Like many of the effects of physical ageing, including flexibility and muscle strength, it is possible to counter these changes by taking exercise.

Understanding the challenges caused to older consumers by dexterity problems is especially important in the design of products and packaging.

Flexibility

The authors separate age-related flexibility issues into two types: body and peripheral. The first type refers to the limitations in physical movement resulting from back and hip problems.

Peripheral flexibility refers to age-related problems in the arms and the legs. In many cases, the two types of flexibility conditions are interrelated.

As muscles become shorter and lose their elasticity, they can cause the body to distort its stature to compensate. This in turn creates further joint and muscle problems that can aggravate old skeletal injuries.

In the worst cases this downward spiral continues when these changes become so painful that the person loses mobility.

An age-related disease that affects the dexterity or flexibility, or both, of the majority of older people is arthritis. Research conducted in Australia concluded that over half of the country's over-55s suffered from the disease.[6]

Body weight and amount of exercise determine the level of flexibility problems caused by ageing.

Flexibility issues might affect touchpoints that require consumers to move their body and arms in a particular way.

Muscle strength

'Sarcopenia' is the technical name for the progressive and generalized loss of muscle mass and strength that occurs with ageing. The president of the International Association of Gerontology and Geriatrics believes that: 'In the future, Sarcopenia will be known as much as osteoporosis is now.'[7] The fact that the European Union thought it necessary to create a Sarcopenia European Working Group for Older People would seem to confirm this suggestion.[8]

The loss of muscle function causes the obvious issue of being unable to cope with heavy objects but, more important, it leads to a reduction in the strength of the body's core muscles. This can lead to a vulnerability to falls and accidents.

Weight resistance exercise and good diet can reduce the effects of Sarcopenia but not halt its progression. So, for instance, the weight-lifting records for 60-year-old men are 30 per cent lower than for 30-year-olds. For women the drop-off is 50 per cent.

Companies need to understand the limitations and risks created by Sarcopenia. However, it also creates a business opportunity to supply products that can delay and reduce its effects.

Nestlé, Abbott Labs and Danone are all either selling or researching products with ingredients to counter the effects of Sarcopenia.

Weight and body size

It is believed that ageing results in a decrease in basal metabolic rate (BMR). This is a measure of the minimum amount of calories the body consumes in a resting state. Gender, height and weight also affect this rate.

A decrease in the body's requirement for calories means that unless there is a reduction in the quantity of food consumed or more calories expended through exercise, the body size and weight will increase. This is a simplistic explanation of a complex biological process that connects weight and body size to ageing.

There are other physical changes that also result in age-related weight gain. For example, the reduction in testosterone levels in men and oestrogen in postmenopausal women can result in increased body weight.

In addition to these physiological factors, the lifestyle changes resulting from retirement can be contributing factors. For some older people, stopping full-time work might result in a dramatic increase in exercise but for many it results in the opposite – a more sedentary lifestyle and increased food consumption.

Unfortunately, much of the developed world is suffering from increased levels of obesity that affects all ages. Many people enter their 50s and 60s with all of the symptoms that are associated with age-related weight gain.

Increased body size and weight affects many of the customer touch-points, especially product design and the retail channel. Products affected by body size range from cars to clothing.

Digestion

The digestive system loses its efficiency as we age. Ageing has little effect on the functioning of the gastrointestinal tract, but it does affect other parts of the digestive system. As the rate of new cell growth declines and important tissue used in the digestive process is more easily damaged.

Another of the effects of Sarcopenia is to reduce the ability of the muscles in the stomach to transport food through the digestive system. This increases the likelihood of constipation, haemorrhoids and 'heartburn'.

The stomach also decreases production of the enzymes that are necessary for the digestion process. This can result in anaemia.

The result of ageing on the digestive system doesn't directly affect any of the touchpoints but it does generate demand for a wide range of products to reduce its adverse effects.

Hair

Proctor and Gamble (P&G) conducted a long in-depth study, spanning eight years, to understand how the fibres in female hair change with age.[9] This is probably the most exhaustive study conducted on this subject. The results show that ageing results in multiple changes to the hair's structure, size and colour.

The authors simplified these changes into two categories – the hair's colour and volume. Of all the features of ageing, the changes to the hair are the most obvious and for this reason give the impression that they happen the earliest.

One factor determining the greying of the hair is a person's race. Caucasians experience grey hair earlier than Asian races. Genetic make-up is another contributing factor.

The definition of the hair's volume includes the changes to its texture that alter its appearance and how it can be styled, and hair loss. Both are important issues for both sexes.

About a quarter of men have signs of baldness by the time they are 30 years old. By the age of 60 about two-thirds of men have significant baldness.

The market for hair products and treatments is already well established and will increase with the rising numbers of older people.

Skin

The skin begins to age from the mid-20s onwards but its effect is not visible for another two to three decades. As with so many ageing factors, a person's genetic make-up is an important determinant of the timing and extent of skin ageing.

The primary reason why the appearance and texture of the skin changes is the reduced production of the protein Collagen, the principal structural protein holding the skin together. Equally important is the decline in the protein Elastin, which peaks in early adulthood and then declines. As the name suggests, this is the substance that gives skin its elasticity. Another biological cause of ageing is a slowing of the rate at which dead skin cells are replaced.

There are a number of external factors that also determine how a person's skin ages. The length of exposure to the sun is the most obvious. Other factors include smoking, nutrition and repetitive facial expressions.

The authors have grouped the effects of skin ageing into two categories – the changes to its colour and elasticity.

Ageing skin can develop fine wrinkles, lose its form and 'sag', change in colour and become thin and transparent.

The numerous 'anti-ageing' products and treatments evidence the commercial worth of this physiological effect. Mintel believed that facial skincare, at the end of 2010, was one of the strongest beauty categories in Europe's five largest countries, having a market value of €6.2 billion.[10]

Menopause

The menopause occurs when a woman's ovaries stop producing an egg every four weeks, which causes a lowering in the levels of the hormones oestrogen and progesterone.

The timing, types and intensity of a woman's menopause will vary but the effects are likely to include:

- Hot flashes – occurs when the brain decides that the woman's body is overheated and increases the blood flow to the skin. It can feel most severe in the head face or neck and can be accompanied by sweating.
- Mood changes – the reason for this symptom is not understood and could be either a biological process or a reaction to change in lifestyle, or a combination of the two.

There are many other effects of the menopause that can affect a woman's sleep, urinary function and enjoyment of sex.

Understandably, there is a large market for medication, both traditional and alternative, to try and minimize the impact of the menopause on a woman's life. There is no accurate data about the total size of the market for these products but estimates suggest it is measured in the tens of billions of dollars.[11]

Nutrition

Achieving the correct nutritional intake is important at every stage of life but especially so during childhood and the older years. The report

Nutrition – Ageing and Longevity provides a detailed analysis of how ageing changes the requirements for nutrition.[12] Like many physiological factors, the requirement for nutrition varies greatly between people. One of the results of ageing is to amplify these differences.

An older person's protein, fat, carbohydrate and water should be provided by a balanced diet. Changes to eating habits, resulting from altered lifestyles and reduced mobility, especially among the older-old, are often the reason for nutritional problems.

The body's vitamin requirements change with age, often causing a deficiency of Vitamins B6 and B12. It is thought that half of older people consume less than two-thirds of the recommended daily dose of Vitamin D.

The desire to maintain their wellness and a greater awareness of the physiology of ageing has contributed to the rapid increase in the market for 'nutraceuticals'. This is a category of products, positioned between nutrition and pharmaceutical products, that claim to provide health benefits.

The difficulty in determining which products are in this category makes estimating the market size almost impossible. One forecast sets the global market to be in excess of $240 billion by 2015.[13]

Whatever the actual size of the market, it is significant and likely to continue growing as the numbers of older people increase in parallel with their awareness of nutrition.

Urinary incontinence

Urinary incontinence (UI) is the involuntary leakage of urine. There are many types of UI, but the two thought to account for 90 per cent of incidences are:

- Stress incontinence – results from the muscles becoming too weak to prevent urine leaking when the bladder is under pressure. This typically occurs when coughing or laughing.
- Urge incontinence – occurs when the person has an urgent desire to pass urine, resulting in leaking before reaching the toilet.

It is possible to have a mixture of both stress and urge urinary incontinence.

Research in the UK found that 13 per cent of women and 5 per cent of men had some degree of UI. In general, UI affects twice as many women as men and becomes more common with increasing age.[14]

In the USA it is estimated that of the 15 million UI suffers, 85 per cent are women.[15]

There is already an established market for the drugs, diagnostic and therapeutic products that help with UI. This was forecast to reach $2.4 billion in the year 2010.[16] In Japan, the world's oldest country, the sale of incontinence pads for adults has now exceeded babies' nappies.[17]

The increasing number of consumers with UI will both drive the market for products to help with the problem and increase the quantity of toilet facilities that retailers need to provide.

Sexual

Erectile dysfunction (ED) is the inability for a man to maintain an erection of the penis during sexual intercourse. This condition increases with age. In a study of American men, it was found that 2 per cent of men reported first experiencing ED before the age of 40 years, rising to 40 per cent between 60 and 69 years.[18]

The primary reason why this happens is a drop in the levels of the hormone testosterone; however, there are many other physical and psychological factors that can also contribute to it. Some, but not all, are associated with ageing. The tendency of men to lead a less active lifestyle and to increase in weight can be contributing factors. Many of the age-related illnesses, such as diabetes, high blood pressure and prostate cancer, could also contribute.

The product that is most associated with 'treating' ED is Viagra. This was first approved for use for this condition in the USA in 1996 and achieved sales in that country of $1.9 billion in 2008. Other products have been launched to address the ED market, namely Cialis and Levitra.

There are no accurate figures for the global market for ED medication but it is thought to be in excess of $5 billion.

In Chapter 7 there is a detailed discussion of the physiological factors related to the body and their importance to business.

How to apply this knowledge

All of the ageing effects, described in the previous three sections, create the demand for existing products and new product opportunities.

Using the product categorization, discussed in Chapter 1, these will predominately be 'age silo' products, namely products designed for and sold to older consumers. Some of these products will also be sold to other age groups. For example, muscle-building supplements are also used by young people wanting to build muscle mass. Other examples of multi-age products are glasses, anti-ageing cosmetics and hair treatments.

The constituents of these products might be the same for all ages but the marketing messages and channels will differ considerably.

Examples of the new product opportunities resulting from these ageing effects are discussed in the next three chapters.

The primary reason for detailing these ageing effects is to enable them to be matched to customer touchpoints.

A central tenet of this book is that unless a company ensures it is satisfying the consumer's physiological needs it doesn't have the foundation for fulfilling their psychological needs and wants. This is illustrated in Figure 3.3.

Constructing marketing campaigns that react to the higher-level needs is worthless if the customer cannot read and hear the advertising, use the product and shop in the retail outlet.

To enable the ageing effects to be associated with each of the customer touchpoints they were divided two groups – primary and secondary.

This categorization is shown in Table 3.1.

The ageing effects in the primary group are those that alter the consumer's experience of one or more touchpoint. For instance, hearing volume is associated with eight touchpoints and cognitive flexibility affects 11 touchpoints.

There are some aspects of marketing, such as the tone and style of advertising, that are not overtly affected by biological ageing or for which the connection is too tenuous to measure. These marketing factors have been included in the discussion of customer touchpoints and, for completeness, an effect called 'sensory – independent' is included in the primary group.

Secondary effects are not involved in any customer touchpoint. This does not diminish their importance, because they could be significant opportunities for new products.

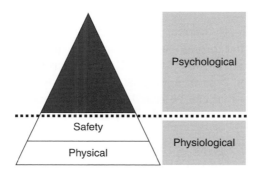

Figure 3.3 Physiological needs are the foundation for satisfying the consumer's complex psychological requirements

Table 3.1 The ageing effects divided into primary and secondary groups

	Cognitive	Sensory	Physical
Primary	Complexity Comprehension	Eyesight – clarity Eyesight – illumination Hearing – clarity Hearing – volume Touch Sensory – Independent	Dexterity Flexibility – body Flexibility – peripheral Muscle strength Weight & body size Urinary
Secondary		Smell Taste Oral	Digestion Hair – colour Hair – volume Skin – pigmentation Skin – elasticity Menopause Nutrition Sexual

Chapters 8 and 9 explain how the 13 primary effects of ageing can be combined with the touchpoints in the customer journey to create a way of measuring age-friendliness for any product or service.

Chapter at a glance

→ When using age to determine marketing actions the most common used definition is chronological age. This is the period in time, measured in months and years, that we have been alive. A variant of this is lifestage age that is based on the assumption that a person's lifetime can be divided into discrete phases. Finally, there is psychological age that assumes that throughout a person's life their values and attitudes change in a predetermined way. All three measures have their limitations. The ideal type of ageing is one that provides companies with useful insights that can be relied on. The authors believe that physiological ageing possesses both these attributes.

→ Physiological ageing – the way that minds, bodies and senses change – is a wide-ranging subject but, with a few exceptions, its study applies to all types of older people, irrespective of their backgrounds. Most important, it is a factor that can be isolated, studied and applied to improving business performance. The authors' definition of physiological ageing is: 'The systemic change to the body's ability to function caused by age-related changes to the mind, body and senses.'

→ Physiological ageing can be divided into three groups – sensory, cognitive and physical.Within these three groups there are 24 age-related physical changes that have an impact on business.

→ Unless companies ensure they are satisfying the consumer's physiological needs they lack the foundation for fulfilling their psychological requirements. Constructing marketing campaigns that target the emotional needs of the consumer are worthless if they cannot read and hear the advertising, use the product and shop in the retail outlet.

CHAPTER 4

Understanding customer touchpoints

As a result of research in the UK that highlighted the problems older people were experiencing in terms of reduced mobility and manual dexterity, the country's leading satellite TV provider Sky, developed a remote-control device specifically designed to help older customers with visual and dexterity impairments.[1]

The device was awarded special recognition for its age-friendly design, with its unique benefits of having:

- Larger and bolder graphics for easier button identification.
- Raised contoured buttons, with additional reference points for easier identification for visually impaired users.
- Increased colour contrast between buttons and the body of the remote.

Sky was rightly congratulated for this accessibility initiative but the venture was spoilt by a major oversight. The device is not visible on the company website, nor did the call centre know about the product when questioned.

No doubt the team within Sky tasked with responsibility for developing this device took its duty very seriously and achieved a great result, but the failure to think holistically about the entire acquisition cycle spoilt the initiative. Over time, Sky rectified this problem and it has now created a first-class accessible website.[2]

Sky's problems were caused by a classic case of 'silo thinking', in which a department or a team or individuals are tasked with driving an age-friendly initiative but do not synchronize the activities across all of the customer-facing departments.

A famous Chinese proverb states: 'To get through the hardest journey we need take only one step at a time, but we must keep on stepping.'

The meaning of this proverb has a relevance to understanding the journey undertaken by older people when buying products and services. Marketers need to understand the entire journey and build bridges over possible obstructions along the way.

Customer experience research

Over the past century, the types of expertise that companies require to achieve market dominance have changed. Business started with the 'Age of Manufacturing' in the first half of the twentieth century and travelled through the 'Age of Distribution' and the 'Age of Information' in the second half of last century. Many business strategists believe we are now entering the 'Age of the Customer'.[3]

Josh Bernoff, one of Forrester's leading analysts, believes that successful companies will be customer-obsessed.[4] This is a fine aspiration, although considerably harder to achieve than to say. However, it is something companies intending to capture the spending power of older consumers must achieve.

In its report on *Global Aging*,[5] the Boston Consulting Group (BCG) says: 'companies should review their channel strategies to ensure that they are compatible with the needs of the silver segment'. Not surprisingly, BCG and similar consulting and research companies have developed substantial business practices based on the concept of 'customer experience'.

Optimizing the customer's experience is also known as 'customer journeys' and 'purchase paths'. Whatever the name, the objective is to research and optimize all of the points at which customers interface with a brand using traditional market research techniques or mystery or secret shoppers.

Trying to optimize the complete customer experience is an attempt to transcend the corporate silo mentality and to give a holistic and realistic assessment of what it is like for consumers to engage with a brand.

On the surface, it is quite a simple concept. The journey undertaken by a consumer is mapped and obstacles identified that might impede or degrade the smooth access, use and fulfilment of the brand experience. Of course, the execution is not so simple and can be hugely complex and expensive; however, the results can greatly improve the net effect of the disparate initiatives being projected by a company, both intentional and unintentional, through its sales and marketing activities.

So keen are companies to obtain an independent view of the customer experience that, according to the Mystery Shopping Providers Association, in 2009 the industry was worth $1 billion and employed an estimated 1.5 million independent contractors in the USA alone.[6]

The focus of this industry is largely on the consumer retail shopping experience. However, the concept of monitoring a 'journey' can be equally useful in evaluating how employees interact with their employer, citizens with social facilities, patients with their medical providers, customers with their banking services suppliers, and so on.

Given the unique requirements of certain industries, the customer experience measurement business has spawned a host of vertical industry specialists who specialize in customer journeys in the hospitality, medical and financial services industries.

Older bodies, older minds, older senses

Useful though these techniques may be, little, if any, thinking has been applied to how the customer experience might be affected by the physical changes experienced due to ageing.

Chapter 3 discusses the details of the physiology of ageing but, as a simple illustration of the issue, imagine how your last purchase experience would have been degraded had you suffered from poor eyesight, hearing difficulties and reduced mobility and dexterity ... all at once.

The world we live in is optimized for the bodies of younger people. Little, if any, consideration or allowance is made for the impact of ageing. The relentless increase in the median age in most of the world's countries means this attitude must change. This inexorable rise in the age of consumers compels us to create 'environments where the unique physical needs of older people are satisfied in a way that is natural and beneficial for all ages'. This is the authors' definition of the concept of age-friendliness.

Much has been written about AGNES (Age Gain Now Empathy System), developed by the AgeLab at MIT. This is a 'suit' worn by students, product developers, designers, engineers, marketing planners, architects, packaging engineers and others to better understand the physical challenges associated with ageing.[7] AGNES has been calibrated to approximate the motor responses, eyesight, flexibility, dexterity and strength of a person in their mid-70s. The device has been used to simulate the way an older person reacts in retail, transportation, automobile, workplace and other environments. It is undoubtedly a clever device that enables younger people to appreciate the difficulties older people encounter as they age.

Used in isolation, AGNES has limited value, because it measures the effects of ageing for only a sub-set of the customer journey.

What companies require is a methodology to provide a complete understanding of the age-friendliness on all of the touchpoints where older consumers interface with their brands. Such an assessment system must integrate the issues of physiological ageing with a human 'journey' and provide measurable, accurate and replicable data to measure and monitor the human experience for older bodies, minds and senses.

With this as the objective, the authors created a methodology and toolset that identifies the barriers that complicate or otherwise impede a consumer's age-friendly experience.

The age-friendly customer journey

The concept of a 'journey' and the notion of an age-friendly checklist are not new ideas. Perhaps the most famous venture that combines these ideas is the Age-Friendly City initiative by the World Health Organization.[8] There are also checklists for age-friendly transportation, age-friendly hospitals, age-friendly gyms and no doubt many others. All of them offer useful insights for their specific areas.

As this is a marketing book, the focus is on the journey experienced by older consumers but the same conceptual constructs apply to older employees and older citizens.

At the overview level the customer journey divides into five stages or 'experiences'. These experiences can then be broken down further into smaller elements of the journey and ultimately to detailed 'touchpoints'. These touchpoints can become highly technical and detailed items. For example, here is a specification for accessible signage as defined in a document from the Canadian Human Rights Commission.[9]

The visual character width of a sign shall be 55 per cent minimum and 110 per cent maximum of the character height, with the width based on upper-case letter 'O' and the height letters based on the upper-case letter 'I'.

When devising the methodology, we needed to achieve a balance between providing a comprehensive view of the customer journey, with sufficient detail of each touchpoint, and avoiding a level of detailed analysis that would be impractical for companies to collect, analyse and act on.

Communications

Whether it's a product recommendation from a friend, a multimillion-dollar global advertising campaign, a discount coupon on the back of a movie ticket or a perimeter sign at the soccer World Cup final, some form of communication is usually the trigger for interest in a brand and initiates the journey to buy the product. Paid or unpaid, intended or accidental, we are exposed to thousands of messages every day enticing us to consume.

As discussed in Chapter 1, older people absorb and respond to these messages differently from younger cohorts. Older people do not behave in a homogeneous way, just as there is not a universal pattern of behaviour for teenagers or for homemakers. There is a rich tapestry of behavioural factors that determines how different types of older people respond to different types of communication message.

Although the psychological process of ageing creates behaviours that are complex and difficult to predict, the opposite is true for the effects of physiological ageing.

Table 4.1 details, at a basic level, the necessary conditions that must exist if a company's brand communications are to surmount the first hurdle to influence how older people respond. That is to say they are age-friendly.

Once a consumer's interest has been initiated by the offer contained in the brand's communication, the next part of the journey involves the

Table 4.1   Basic conditions for a company's brand communication message and offer to be age-friendly

Type of communications	Conditions for a company's communications to be age-friendly
Advertising creative	The older person must be able to:
Advertising media	• Read and see it • Hear it
Direct mail	• Feel included by the message
Public relations	• Understand the message • Perceive the benefits of the offer
Sales collateral	• Find it simple and quick to decode the brand proposition
Sponsorship	• Perceive the offer as having relevance for them • Easily understand how they can respond to the message

consumer undertaking some form of investigation to learn more about the product or service. Increasingly, for all age groups, the fact-finding phase starts online.

Online

The personal computer became mainstream in the 1980s, when the Baby Boomers generation was aged between 16 and 34. Therefore most people in this cohort, particularly those engaged in white-collar jobs, have been exposed to the personal computer and the subsequent evolution of the internet and technology, for most of their adult lives. So it is not surprising that the level of internet use among Baby Boomers worldwide averages about 70 per cent. The penetration rate drops off rapidly after 65 years, as illustrated in Table 4.2.

A person's age is only one of the factors determining the likelihood that they use the internet. Equally important are their socio-economic status and level of educational attainment.[10]

If the majority of Baby Boomers and large numbers of the better-educated and wealthier over-65s are actively engaged online, then it would seem obvious that marketers should take account of their requirements when devising online strategies. Having an age-friendly online experience would seem to be a business imperative.

A simple summary of the characteristics that improve the age-friendliness of the online experience includes the factors described in Table 4.3.

Having completed the investigation stage, the next step of the journey is likely to be to make the purchase through the retail channel.

Table 4.2   Use of the Internet in the UK, the USA, Canada and Australia by age group

Age	Use the internet			
	UK	**USA**	**Canada**	**Australia**
55–64	75%	76%	65%	71%
65–74	56%	58%	51%	37%
75+	25%	30%	27%	N/A

Source: UK: Office for National Statistics, USA: Pew Research, Australia: Australian Bureau of Statistics, Canada: Statistics Canada.

Table 4.3 Basic conditions for a company's online presence to be age-friendly

Type of online presence	Conditions for a company's online presence to be age-friendly
Search	The older person must be able to:
Website / app	• Easily search by brand or by the product's features • Read the text
Help	• Hear any associated sound • Navigate the website and app • Find the most common types of content quickly • Feel themselves included by the copy and imagery • Understand the language and jargon • Find the online brand proposition relevant • Interact with the website or app • Use the commerce functionality of the website and app easily

Retail

We are using the term 'retail' in its broadest sense to describe a place where the consumer goes to buy or to receive a service. These establishments could be the local convenience store, the mega-mall, the bank branch or the hotel or tourist office. Increasingly, the 'bricks 'n mortar' retail establishment is being replaced by the online store.

As this fictitious tale illustrates, the things that healthy younger people take for granted about the process of shopping can be frustrating, annoying and tiring for older consumers.

> A 70-year-old lady needs to buy a few items from the supermarket. After difficulty in parking her car and walking the long distance to the entrance, she looks for the first item. Craning her neck to see the signage and having difficulty reading the shelf labels, because of the poor colour contrast and glare from nearby lighting, she finds the product placed too high for her to reach. She pushes the heavy trolley through the congested aisles and approaches a store assistant to ask for help but cannot hear the response because of the loud background music. Failing to understand the answer, she gives-up having only bought a few items on her shopping list and finds the place to pay but cannot understand how to use the new self-service terminals.

Ageing has changed what once was a pleasurable experience into a debilitating challenge.

There are simple solutions to most of the difficulties described in this story. Kaiser supermarkets in Berlin, Germany, and Tesco in Newcastle, England,[11] have experimented with 'pensioner-friendly' supermarkets in which the focus is on creating an age-friendly shopping experience:

- The trolleys are lighter and easier to move.
- The signs are clear and well illuminated.
- Shelves and trolleys feature magnifying glasses.
- The aisles are extra-wide and the floors have a nonslip treatment.
- Larger signs and labels make them easier to read.
- There are emergency call buttons in case of accidents.

These changes may have had an additional cost but Kaiser reported a 30 per cent higher revenue and greater customer satisfaction as a result of its age-friendly adaptations.

The characteristics that improve the age-friendliness of the physical retail environment include the factors in Table 4.4.

Fast-moving packaged-goods marketers may argue that the retail environment is beyond their control and therefore there is little value in considering the impact of its age-friendliness on their brand or business. But because improving the customer experience is of benefit to both suppliers and retailers, marketers can use this information to encourage their retail partners to provide an environment that is more conducive to the satisfaction of older customers. Obviously, the level of influence will be proportional to the market dominance of the brand; however, imagine how retailers would respond if P&G, Unilever and PepsiCo collaborated to encourage retailers to adopt age-friendly measures.

Table 4.4 Basic conditions for a company's physical retail presence to be age-friendly

Element of the retail experience	Conditions for a company's retail experience to be age-friendly
Access	The older person must be able to:
Ambience	• Gain access to the establishment with minimum physical effort
Amenities	• Converse and not be affected by the background noise
	• Easily find and read the signage
Cleanliness	• Reach and select the most common products
Comfort	• Walk to and access the amenities
	• Sit and rest
	• Easily access assistance

The incentives for retailers to adapt their shopping experience are high because older shoppers will remain a critical part of the shopper mix for the foreseeable future, as will the competitive pressure they experience from online channels.

In Australia, for example, online shopping accounts for roughly 8 per cent of retail spending and is expected to continue to grow by between 10 and 15 per cent per year for the next three years. Given that older shoppers are less inclined to shop online than younger people, creating age-friendly shopping environments would seem basic business common sense, particularly because 37 per cent of Australia's population will be over 50 years old by 2018.

As important as the preceding stages of the customer journey are in influencing a consumer's perception of a brand, the ultimate determinant of success or failure is the perceived quality of the final product or service the brand delivers to its customers.

The product or service

In our experience, the product is usually the primary and often the only thing that companies adapt when they consider older consumers. Hopefully this chapter has demonstrated that although each stage of the journey is important, companies can achieve success only by ensuring all of the stages have been adapted to minimize the results of ageing. There is little benefit having an age-friendly product without the supporting age-friendly infrastructure.

As discussed in Chapter 1, products and services can be characterized as being either 'age-silo' (specifically designed and positioned to meet the needs of an older person) or 'age-neutral' (sold and used by people of all ages). For example:

- 'Age-silo' products include age-related insurance or banking products, age-related nutritionals, incontinence pads, assistive devices such as stairlifts and so on.
- 'Age-neutral' products include almost all other types of products, including household products, white goods, airline flights, home entertainment, sportswear, cars and so on.

There is a growing market for 'age-silo' products and services that by definition should be age-friendly. This doesn't necessarily mean that they are. But, by far the largest and most immediate opportunity for marketers lies in making age-neutral products age-friendly. After all, older consumers still consume regular products, be entertained, keep fit, keep clean, look good, improve their knowledge and so on. Often, companies believe that to appeal to older customers they must develop special products and services specifically designed for them. There is probably no worse way of alienating an older person than suggesting they should buy an older person's product.

Companies should be trying to make the experience of using their products one that is uniform irrespective of the customer's age. The way this is done is by employing one of the many sets of definitions and guides to universal design. Table 4.5 contains our simple checklist to determine whether a product or service is age-friendly.

Products should be designed in such a way that anyone can unpack and start using them intuitively or by following a few simple steps from a 'quick-start' guide. Universal design, age-friendly, call it what you will, the principles are the same. Each facet of the product needs to be accessed through the prism of somebody with failing physical, cognitive and sensory powers. When the authors appraise a product's age-friendliness, they evaluate over 30 factors.

After-sales support is the final stage of the customer journey but it is as important as all of the others. Even the best brands produce some products that fail to satisfy their customers. This might be due to faulty manufacture, unrealistic customer expectations or incorrect customer use.

If an older person is unhappy or has questions about the product they have bought, it is essential that the process to resolve their concerns

Table 4.5 Basic conditions for a company's product or service experience to be age-friendly

Product or service	Conditions for a company's product experience to be age-friendly
Assembly	The older person must be able to:
Design	• Easily read and understand the assembly and operating instructions
User interface	• Hear, see and feel the necessary controls to use the product
Packaging	• Easily remove the product from the packaging
Pricing	• Assemble and use the product even if they have age-related strength and dexterity problems
Warranty	• Understand the pricing and warranty information

does not exacerbate their situation. For this reason, the sales and support segment of the customer journey must be as effective as all of the others and that means it must be age-friendly.

Sales and support

Throughout the purchase cycle there are numerous points at which the customer will contact a company representative for sales or support. This can be face-to-face, by phone or through online channels.

A study published in the Journal of Experimental Social Psychology suggests that younger people may make more mistakes when judging the emotions of older people. Something retailers should take note of when recruiting and training young staff to serve older customers[12].

Most people dislike the multiple layers of response menus that have to be navigated before resolving a problem with a call centre.

Research conducted in the USA[13] revealed that people aged 50 and older were more annoyed than others by convoluted voice-messaging systems. Although this issue is not specifically related to older customers, the same research revealed that '71% were "tremendously annoyed" when they couldn't reach a human on the phone'.

Not only are these systems annoying, but also sometimes the voice messages are hard to hear and understand, particularly if the speaker has a foreign accent.

Table 4.6 Basic conditions for a company's sales support service experience to be age-friendly

Sales and support	Conditions for a company's sales support experience to be age-friendly
Face-to-face Phone Delivery	The older person must be able to: • Hear the sales/support person and the call-centre voice instructions • Understand the sales/support person and the call-centre voice instructions • Have the time to explain their problem or question and not feel rushed or pressured • Feel that their problem is being taken seriously • Feel confident that the delivery personnel are trusted individuals • Be able to schedule around an accurate delivery time

Table 4.6 contains our simple checklist to determine whether a company's sales support service is age-friendly.

As after-sales support is increasingly directed to the online channel, the separation between it and the fact-finding phase of the sales journey is disappearing. The way companies support sales to their customers, of all ages, is transparent to consumers deciding if they want to buy the product.

In this chapter we have introduced the idea of a customer journey that is sympathetic to the needs of ageing minds, senses and the body; the age-friendly *customer journey*. This holistic approach covering all the touch-points is important not only in terms of customer satisfaction, but it may identify barriers that can cause an older customer to simply *give up* mid-way through the course of a purchase should they find the barrier either insurmountable, or just not worth the effort.

Though presented here in the consumer context for the benefit of marketers, the same *journey* principle should be applied to other inter-actions between companies or institutions, and older people. Examples include the journeys undertaken by employees, citizens, patients and more. Of course, the fundamental 24 physiological effects of ageing remain constant.

Chapter at a glance

→ The inexorable rise in the age of consumers compels us to create 'environments where the unique physical needs of older people are satisfied in a way that is natural and beneficial for all ages'. This is the authors' definition of the concept of age-friendliness.

→ Companies require a methodology to provide a complete understanding of the age-friendliness on all of the touchpoints where older consumers interface with their brands. Such an assessment system must integrate the issues of physiological ageing with a human 'journey' and provide measurable, accurate and replicable data to measure and monitor the human experience for older bodies, minds and senses.

→ At the overview level, the customer journey divides into five stages or 'experiences' (communications, online, retail, product and support). These experiences can then be broken down further into smaller elements of the journey and ultimately to detailed 'touchpoints'.

→ The concept of an *age-friendly* customer journey is designed to overcome the diffused responsibility and departmental silos. Trying to optimize the complete customer experience is an attempt to transcend the corporate silo mentality and to give a holistic and realistic assessment of what it is like for consumers to engage with a brand.

→ Methodologies to measure age-friendliness need to achieve a balance between providing a comprehensive view of the customer journey, with sufficient detail of each touchpoint, and avoiding a level of detailed analysis that would be impractical for companies to collect, analyse and act on.

CHAPTER 5

The ageing senses

As we age, the quality of our eyesight, hearing, touch, taste and smell alters. Invariably these changes result in a loss of sensitivity and precision of how we sense and react to the world around us.

Some of these changes are very obvious. For example, when it becomes impossible to read food labels or we start complaining that store attendants speak so quietly. Sometimes, the changes are very subtle, for example, when the taste of some foods seems dulled and having difficulty opening items of packaging.

As with all aspects of physiological ageing there are two sets of implications. Nobody likes losing their ability to interface with the physical world and its contents. This means there will be new product opportunities as older consumers try to compensate for the loss of their sensory acuity.

A combination of senses is involved in successfully negotiating many of the customer touchpoints. If these touchpoints have been designed for the sensory abilities of a 30 year old's eyes, ears, hands and mouth then the customer experience of older people will progressively decline.

Business cannot ignore either of these implications of sensory ageing. For marketers to understand the results of sensory ageing it is useful to have a basic understanding of why these changes happen. The pattern and magnitude of the decline in some of the senses, such as certain aspects of eyesight, are relatively well understood. Other senses, such as hearing, have distinct gender and ethnic variations. The reasons other senses, such as taste and smell, change are only partially understood, as are the demographic differences in the extent and magnitude of the sensory decline.

To make matters more complex, the decline in the quality of the senses is often affected by the lifestyle, healthiness and genetic make-up of the individual.

This chapter systematically describes the reasons why each of the senses changes with age, when and to what extent people are affected and what companies can do in response.

Eyesight and ageing

Ageing alters the muscles, iris, retina and other components of the eye, which results in a reduction in the quality of our sight. This can create significant problems for older consumers using touchpoints in all parts of the customer journey. Of all the types of physiological ageing, failing eyesight is the most age-neutral and most accepted – both by society and by the individual. People of all ages suffer from eyesight problems and the wearing of glasses is an 'accepted' solution. What eyesight has in common with the other senses is the lack of awareness that companies have about its effect on how customers buy and use their products. The fact that over half of consumers between the ages of 60 and 70 have difficulty reading food labels, even when wearing glasses or contact lenses, demonstrates this lack of concern.[1]

The science

The deterioration of vision with age is called presbyopia – 'old eye'. It normally starts during a person's 40s and results from the degenerative changes in the lens of the eye and the muscles that enable it to focus. The first noticeable effect of presbyopia is difficulty with near vision. The instinctive correction for this problem is to hold reading material farther from the eye but then a point is reached when it is necessary to wear reading glasses.

Hypermetropia, better known as long-sightedness, is usually an inherited condition but this also becomes more noticeable at around the age of 40.

In addition to presbyopia there are other results of ageing that affect the quality of eyesight and result in:

- **Lower responsiveness to changes in ambient light.** The muscles that control the size of the pupil become less responsive. This reduces the speed at which our eyes are able to respond when we go from dark to light. Difficulty driving at night is probably the most obvious effect of this condition.
- **Requiring more light to be able to see.** Ageing affects many of the components of vision that control the levels of illumination needed to see clearly, with the result that we require more light to read. A measure of this effect is that a person in their 20s needs only a third of the ambient light that somebody in their 60s needs.
- **Increased sensitivity to glare.** In a person's 50s, the changes to the liquid within the eye, the lens and the pupil create difficulty seeing if there are high levels of reflected light. In addition to contributing to problems with night-time driving this can result in difficulty reading signs and labels

in poor light conditions, for instance, the effect when bright fluorescent lights reflect from clear plastic packaging in supermarkets.

- **Reduced peripheral vision.** A person in their 70s may have lost 20 to 30 degrees of their field of vision. This process starts from around the age of 50. For a while we are able to compensate, to an extent, by moving our heads to extend our peripheral vision.
  The importance of this problem is illustrated by research that studied a group of people aged 60–85 and found that for every 10 per cent loss in visual field, the participants were 8 per cent more likely to fall.[2]
- **Reduced perception of depth.** This is another function of the eye that deteriorates with age and results in difficulty judging distances, especially if the movement is in low lighting conditions. Accurate judgement of distance and height is a fundamental requirement for most day-to-day activities.
- **Altered perception of colour.** The sensitivity of the cells in the retina, which generate the perception of colour, declines with age. This results in a reduction in perceived brightness and contrast between colours. In particular, it becomes harder to distinguish dark blue from brown or black and pink from yellow or pale green.

Added to this long list of vision impairments, which directly result from ageing, are age-related illnesses that affect the sight, in some cases severely. The most important of these are:

- **Cataracts.** Cataracts affect nearly 22 million Americans aged 40 and older.[3] According to the Mayo Clinic, about half of all 65-year-old Americans are suffering from some degree of cataract formation. Cataracts worsen the effects of age-related problems by clouding and blurring the vision and further reducing the ability to see in dark conditions.
- **Age-related macular degeneration (ARMD).** This is the leading cause of blindness among older people. Approximately 1 per cent of people aged 65–75 and 12 per cent of people over the age of 85 years have ARMD severe enough to cause serious visual loss. About twice as many women over the age of 75 have ARMD compared with men of the same age.[4]
- **Glaucoma.** This causes the pressure within the eye to increase. If it is untreated the results, at best, are deteriorating quality of sight and in the worst cases blindness. The most common form of glaucoma affects 1 per cent of people aged over 40, rising to about 5 per cent of people over the age of 65.[5]
- **Diabetic retinopathy.** The rising level of obesity in the USA and Europe is leading to many older (and younger) people contracting

diabetes. One of the effects of this condition is to damage the retina and degrade the quality of eyesight. This condition affects approximately 40 per cent of Americans diagnosed with diabetes.[6]

Age-related eyesight conditions change the way we perceive the world in multiple dimensions. The perception of colours, the required levels of illumination, the definition and position of objects, the time needed to change between light and dark ... all of these deteriorate as we age.

For these reasons, it is essential that companies understand how their touchpoints appear when viewed through the eyes of their older customers.

Who is affected?

In 2004 it was estimated that in Europe and the USA two-thirds of the adult population wore glasses or contact lenses, a figure that reaches 90 per cent for people in their mid-60s.[7] The Vision Council of America confirms these estimates, believing the number of adults in the USA wearing prescription eyewear to be 64 per cent.[8]

Wearing glasses or contact lenses can correct many, but not all, of the problems resulting from age-related sight changes. A measure of this continuing level of visual impairment is given by data from Lighthouse International. Inability to recognize a friend across the room, or read regular newspaper print, while wearing glasses or contact lenses affects nearly 17 per cent of Americans over the age of 45. The distribution of this condition by age group is:[9]

- 15 per cent aged 45–64.
- 17 per cent aged 65–74.
- 26 per cent aged over 75.

Gender and race, in addition to genetics, determine the extent and the onset of age-related eyesight problems. Because there are so many types of vision impairment, the relationship between these variables is complex. The National Eye Institute publishes the best data in the USA on the demographics of eye conditions.[10] These are some of the insights from this research:

- Short-sightedness and cataracts affect whites more than other races until the age of 60, after which all races are equally affected, and are more prevalent in women.
- Long-sightedness is most frequent in whites and affects Hispanics more often than blacks.

- Glaucoma is initially more common in women, but by age 65 it is comparable between the sexes. In the 65–69 age group, black females are three times more likely than whites to have the disease.

These gender and race variations are of academic interest because companies need to assume that all types of consumers will progressively suffer from deteriorating eyesight as they age. Table 5.1 provides a summary of the eyesight issues that a company's older customers will be confronting. Like all generalizations there is an important caveat – some people will retain near-perfect vision into their 80s and others will start the ageing process in their 30s. At an individual level, the person's genes, lifestyle and luck will determine the extent and timing of deteriorating eyesight.

Effect on the touchpoints

Declining quality of eyesight causes customers problems with many of the touchpoints, including:

- All of the visual components of marketing communications.
- Many of the online experiences, especially involving website design and the use of mobile devices.
- Product design, assembly and packaging.
- Navigating retail channels.

Table 5.1 An approximate relationship between age and eyesight condition

Age	Conditions affecting eyesight
40s	First stages of presbyopia (difficulty reading) become noticeable. Effects of hypermetropia (long-sightedness) increase.
50s	Degree of presbyopia increases. Risks of contracting age-related illnesses increase (cataracts, ARMD and glaucoma). Become aware of needing more light to read.
60s	Diminishing ability to see in low lighting conditions. Eyesight becomes less able to react to changes between light and dark. Presbyopia becomes more intrusive. Night driving becomes more difficult.
70s	High likelihood of having cataracts. Declining colour vision and awareness of the difficulties caused by reducing field of vision and ability to judge movements in three dimensions. Many people will have stopped driving at night.

To illustrate the importance of eyesight, when the authors are working for clients, they review and measure 18 touchpoints that are related to eyesight.

Wearing glasses or contact lenses and having laser corrective surgery can help with many of the ageing eye conditions. Likewise, surgery and drug treatments can greatly improve the quality of sight for people with cataracts, glaucoma and diabetic retinopathy. As good as these treatments and aids are, however, they cannot alleviate all of the problems, especially those related to the need for increased levels of illumination.

As has been explained, ageing changes the eye's effectiveness in numerous ways. These effects can be grouped into two categories –problems related to eyesight clarity and those resulting from the levels of illumination. From a medical perspective, these two conditions are connected, but the distinction is useful when evaluating touchpoints and improving their effectiveness.

Clarity

These are some of the things that can be done to help older consumers with their difficulty seeing small and complex fonts, distinguishing colours and reading digital and physical content:

- In written material, avoid using sans serif fonts and ensure all text is at least 12-point sized, if possible 14-point. Wherever possible, avoid using italicized text, which is harder to read.
- Ensure a sufficient level of colour contrast in printed and digital content. The World Wide Web Consortium (W3C)[11] provides detailed advice for the levels of colour contrast on websites. Similar rules apply to mobile and tablet devices.
- Use high-contrast colours in printed materials and packaging and avoid shades of the same colour. For example, avoid dark green on a light-green background.
- Be aware that older people will find it progressively difficult to distinguish between certain colours and so avoid the colour combinations that are known to cause difficulty. For instance, avoid red and green, and blue and yellow. The colour blue can appear to have a greenish tint and dark blues often appear as black.
- Employ the basic rules of improving the readability of printed text by limiting the line length, providing sufficient space between the lines, avoiding extensive use of reversed-out text and avoiding over-use of capitalization.

The ability to quantify and measure the performance of many of the eyesight-related touchpoints means that it is possible to accurately evaluate their age-friendliness. There are a host of smartphone apps that enable light levels, colour contrasts, font size and line spacing to be accurately measured. All that is required is the intent to use them to measure conformance with standards.

Illumination

Below are some of the things that can be done to help older consumers alleviate their difficulty seeing in low and rapidly changing light conditions. This does not necessarily mean the universal adoption of bright fluorescent lights. So, for instance, in a restaurant the use of proximate and pinpoint lights would enable customers to read the menus in low lighting conditions. These are some of the actions that companies should undertake:

- Ensure lighting is at the level recommended by the appropriate industry authority. There are lighting standards defined for all types of environments, including the home, workplace, public space and retail outlets.[12] So, for instance, we know that the checkout area of a supermarket should have two and a half times the lighting levels of a self-service restaurant.
- The light levels in environments used by older people should be increased by at least 50 per cent over those that would be sufficient for younger people.
- Locations where you expect older people to undertake complex tasks – for example, filling in forms – require at least three times more light than other areas.
- Whenever possible, glare should be reduced by using non-reflective surfaces. Using daylight to help older people distinguish colours is a good thing but can create problems if it results in glare from the windows.
- Use high-contrast colour or different levels of lighting to highlight potentially dangerous objects, such as stair edges and doorways.
- Avoid large changes in illumination levels in spaces such as corridors and lifts. At night, transitional lighting should be used to minimize the movement between dark and light areas.
- Whenever possible, give customers control over the levels of illumination, for example, in hotel bedrooms, where variable lighting controls should be used at bedsides and in reading areas.

Business opportunities

The market for products and services to relieve the difficulties caused by problems with eyesight is large and well established. It is thought that Americans spend over $15 billion each year on eyewear products, which supports an optical industry in the USA worth more than $30 billion.[13]

The market for spectacle lenses in Europe is forecast to reach over $16 billion by the end of 2012.[14]

Spectacles, contact lenses and laser corrective treatments are used by all ages – but primarily older people. Perhaps because they are seen as age-neutral products and services, they don't carry any of the consequences that are associated with other devices used to resist the results of ageing. Needing to wear spectacles creates far fewer emotional difficulties than the admission of hearing loss and buying a hearing aid, for instance.

The spectacles industry is responsible for some very smart marketing that has changed the perception of spectacles from a utilitarian tool, bought to rectify a physical problem, to an item of fashion.

Population ageing will be a further stimulus to this already large market. In addition to the evolution of existing products and services, there are technological developments that could create totally new categories of products.

Products that improve the functionality of reading glasses

The use of liquid crystal technology provides a far more adaptable lens than the existing static product. emPower! is the first company that has created this electronic focusing technology.[15]

Technologies that make nighttime driving easier

By combining very small cameras, image-processing software and thin display screens it is possible to create intelligent car driving mirrors that improve the quality of nighttime driving.

Audi has produced a digital rear-view mirror for its motor-racing cars but, as with so many developments that start in racing and luxury cars, they can soon become standard features in low-priced cars.

Another car manufacturer, Lexus, is offering an additional option in one of its luxury cars of a night-vision system and a heads-up display to improve the driving experience. The attractiveness of such a feature should be high because private buyers of luxury cars are invariably older than younger.

New types of lighting

LED light is less expensive, longer lasting and more adaptable than traditional lighting technologies. This technology creates the potential for new types of lighting products that enable customers to customize illumination levels to their personal needs.

The same technology could create new lighting for the retail and hospitality industry to provide older people with unobtrusive sources of light in hard-to-see areas.

Improved computer interfaces

Microsoft, Apple and Google (Android) all provide discreet features in their software to help compensate for different types of eyesight problems. For example, Apple enables the user to increase text and image size, enhance the contrast of the screen and display text as white on a background.

These features are often grouped together and labelled as 'accessibility' or 'universal access'. It appears that this functionality is there to help people with disabilities but is not something that will be relevant to and used by 'normal' people. Interface designers need to rethink this assumption.

Effect on other product types

As with most new technology products, early success is usually achieved with younger people. The sales profile for tablet computers and e-readers has followed this trend but the uptake among older people has been faster than for other new technology products.[16]

Part of the reason for the success of these products is their physical size and ease of use. Other reasons are the way that the sensory controls of image size, brightness, contrast and colour and even sound translation are built into the primary interface. When consumers have the option of products that can be adapted to counter the effects of ageing, they will choose them.

Hearing and ageing

Approximately half of all people over the age of 60 will have some degree of hearing loss but only a minority of them use hearing assistance devices. Consequently, many older people will have difficulty negotiating those customer touchpoints that depend on sound but have not been adapted for their needs.

Many of the adaptations to the touchpoints that will address hearing loss are relatively simple and inexpensive. The biggest hurdle is for companies to appreciate the difficulties being faced by their customers.

Age-related hearing loss creates many new business opportunities that, to date, few companies are addressing. Before discussing the numerous business implications of this condition it is necessary to understand the fundamentals of why as we age the quality of our hearing declines.

The science

'Presbycusis' is the medical name for age-related hearing loss that is caused by the deterioration of the hair cells' nerve endings within the auditory portion of the inner ear. After high blood pressure and deterioration of the joints, it is the third-most-prevalent health problem of older adults.[17]

Exposure to noisy work environments and very loud music contribute significantly to presbycusis but gender, race and genetic make-up are the main determinants of the onset and severity of the condition.

Presbycusis reduces the quality of hearing in two ways. First, there is the loss of audibility, which means that sounds need to be louder to be heard. The second difficulty is in understanding the clarity of the noise, because the ears become less sensitive, especially at the higher frequencies. This creates problems in understanding speech.

Consumers' ability to hear clearly is an important requirement for the success of many of the touchpoints. The starting point to optimizing the touchpoints is to have a basic understanding of the process of hearing and how sound is measured.

A noise creates the movement of energy that the ears detect and translate into an electrical signal that is decoded by the brain into information we interpret as speech, the doorbell ringing, a car starting, etc.

Because of the ear's ability to detect such a wide range of energy fluctuations the most convenient way of measuring it is by calculating the ratio of a sound to near to total silence.

In this measurement system, a sound whose intensity is ten times greater than the quietest sound that we can hear is labelled as being 10 decibels (10 dB). A sound that is 100 times louder than the quietest sound is measured as 20 dB; 1000 times louder is 30 dB and so on.

The sound of a whisper is approximately 15 dB; a normal voice measures approximately 70 dB and a very loud voice 80 dB. The other factor that determines the nature of the sound is distance from the sound source. The above examples of the human voice assume the listener is a metre from the person speaking.

To improve the accuracy of measuring sound, especially speech, it is necessary for the units used to reflect the variation of the ear's sensitivity to different frequencies. Sound recording devices are normally fitted with filters that change the weightings given to frequencies to reflect how they are perceived by the ear. This more useful measure of sound is called the dB(A). Government regulations and industry standards are normally expressed in dB(A) units.

Table 5.2 shows the dB(A) levels for day-to-day activities and the acceptable level of noise in different consumer environments.

A person with normal hearing should be able to hear all of the frequencies of sound in the range 250 Hz to 8 KHz with a sound intensity of 0 to 20 dB. By the age of 65, presbycusis may have reduced a person's ability to hear the higher frequencies to around 50–60 dB. This means the higher frequencies need to have a stronger intensity to be heard.

The sounds of consonants, when compared with vowels, include higher frequencies, tend to be spoken more softly and contain more of the intelligibility of speech. This means that somebody with presbycusis has greater difficulty hearing consonants, resulting in them mishearing or failing to hear words within a conversation.

The other difficulties caused by this condition are:

- Detecting the direction from which noise is originating.
- Understanding conversations in noisy environments.
- Hearing people who are quietly spoken.

Table 5.2 dB(A) levels for day-to-day activities and acceptable sound levels in different environments[18]

dB(A) level	Sound of different noise sources	Acceptable levels of noise
20	Whisper	
35		Hotel lobby
40		Store – retail
45		Store – supermarket
40–50		Quiet office
60	Conversational speech	
80	Heavy vehicle traffic noise	

These problems are made worse if, in addition to presbycusis, a person also suffers from one of the other conditions that often occur in older adults, such as tinnitus. This is when people have a ringing, buzzing or roaring noise in their ears that is not caused by an external sound source.

Who is affected?

Some people experience a significant loss of hearing when they are in their 50s; others only have a negligible loss at the age of 80. As already discussed, the propensity for age-related hearing loss depends on the person's gender, race, genetics, exposure to loud noises and good luck.

Researchers from Johns Hopkins School of Medicine used a modified version of the World Health Organization's (WHO) hearing impairment standards[19] to measure the levels of hearing loss in a sample of 70-year-old Americans.[20]

Figure 5.1 shows the results of the study. In addition to showing the extent of hearing loss, the research also demonstrated that black people had less hearing loss than whites. Why this happens is not fully understood

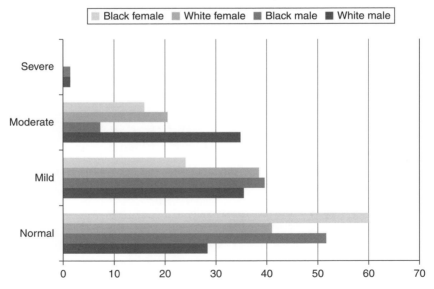

Figure 5.1 Severity of hearing loss by sex and race for US adults aged 70 years and older

Source: National Health and Nutritional Examination Survey 2005–6.

but part of the reason is likely to be the differences in the skin pigmentation of the inner part of the ear.

The research also showed that women are less likely to suffer hearing loss than men of their own race.

Another research study came to similar conclusions about the connection of hearing loss and gender and race.[21]

The Johns Hopkins School of Medicine researchers also studied the frequency with which older people, with different levels of hearing loss, used hearing aids. Only 3 per cent of people with mild hearing loss used hearing aids. This number increased to over 40 per cent for those with moderate or worse hearing loss.

The use of hearing assistance devices in the UK, where they are free, is very nearly the same as in the USA, where many patients pay the costs. This suggests that the reason for not using the aids is not solely dependent on cost.

This unwillingness of older people, especially men, to use a technical aid to help alleviate the problems has a number of implications for business, which are discussed later in the chapter.

Because there are many definitions of 'hearing loss' and the different ways that research has been conducted, it is difficult to make international comparisons about the frequency and severity of presbycusis. For instance, a small sample size of research from Korea suggests that the difference in hearing between men and women may be less than that in the USA.

What is undisputed is that age-related hearing loss is widespread, is more often than not untreated and results in considerable difficulty in verbal communication for many people over the age of 60.

Effect on the touchpoints

If customers have difficulty in hearing, it can affect many of their interactions with a company, including:

- The audio components of product assembly and design.
- All of the audio elements of the marketing communications.
- All face-to-face and phone dialogues.
- The retail shopping environment.

It is a fundamental requirement that customers can understand what sales and support staff say – without that, the best-crafted customer engagement techniques are useless.

When companies outsourced their telephone support operations they often received complaints from their older customers who had difficulty understanding what the operator was saying. The clarity and accent of the operator's voice made them difficult to hear. Not surprisingly, companies are increasingly reversing the outsourcing policy and staffing their contact centres with mother-tongue speakers.

The retail environment must account for those with hearing loss. High levels of background noise might be enjoyable for those with good hearing but they can make it difficult, stressful and at worst impossible to talk and listen for those with presbycusis. Radio and television stations including the BBC sometimes play loud background music which makes it difficult for some people to hear the spoken words.[22]

Products that rely on sound need to ensure that their volume and clarity can be heard by those with the first three levels of hearing loss as defined by the WHO.

Even though hearing loss is widespread among the older population, companies rarely adapt their touchpoints to compensate for its effects. Unlike presbyopia, which results in large numbers of people wearing glasses, the results of Presbycusis are invisible. As already mentioned, only 3 per cent of older people with hearing problems use a hearing aid – and those who do use them, make them as inconspicuous as possible. Perhaps the condition's lack of visibility may account for why it is ignored.

By making a few changes to their procedures and training, companies can easily improve the customer journey for older people. These are a selection of the actions they can take:

- In the design of all product and communications with audible content, ensure it is optimized for those with difficulty hearing high frequencies.
- When a product uses sounds as a warning signal then the sound should be below 2,000 Hz and with an intensity of at least 60 dB.
- When there is an audible signal, both the tone and the volume should be adjustable by the user.
- Remove compression and speeding of speech on auto-response devices, such as the menu systems used in telephone support centres.
- Add assistive functionality in products that process speech. For example, 'cleaning' the sound of recorded voices and providing the listener with controls to slow the rate at which words are spoken.
- Ensure that background noise is kept to a minimum in areas where customers need to talk. In very noisy environments, use sound-absorbing materials.

- Train staff with the techniques to improve how they talk to older people. For example, always face the person; use good diction; do not talk quietly. This is especially important for female staff, who have higher-frequency voices than men. Such training needs to be done with care because the worst outcome is that staff start shouting at older customers.
- When appropriate, use assistive technologies, such as induction loops, to make it easier for people with hearing aids.

Business opportunities

If older people were to use hearing aids with the same readiness as they do glasses it would radically change the dynamics of what is already a fast-growing market. There are some good reasons that this might occur:

- New technology and better design are improving the appearance of hearing devices.
- More discussion about the extent and effect of hearing loss will encourage people to rectify the problem.
- Different attitudes of the Boomer generation, who want (and need), to remain engaged with work will encourage them to solve their hearing problems. On the other hand, they feel that wearing a hearing device labels them as 'old'.
- More and better distribution channels that remove the mystique and fear of hearing tests and most of the costs.

There is a sizeable financial prize for the brands that 'make it OK' for customers to be seen wearing a hearing device. In an era when people spend much of their lives wearing earphones, earbuds and devices connected to their mobile phones it cannot be long before the stigma of hearing aids ends.

There are other business opportunities created by the need to help older people to retain the quality of their hearing. These include:

- Adapting audio devices, especially telephones and smartphones, to directly communicate with hearing assistance devices that are discreetly integrated into spectacles.
- Products and services that can test the voices of customer contact staff for the quality of their audibility.
- Noise-reducing technology that can be applied in retail spaces.
- Low-cost noise-measurement devices that make it easier to know when older people will have difficulty hearing.

Touch and ageing

It is easy to think that touch is associated only with the skin but it also controls our sensitivity to internal organs, joints and muscles.

The somatosensory systems enable us to experience the external environment through the sensitivity of the skin, the 'sense' of the position and movement of the body, the stimulation of muscles and joints and the sensitivity to temperature, pain, itching and pressure.

The biological systems that detect, communicate and translate these physical effects are extremely complex and involve the sensory pathways, the nervous system and cognitive processing. For a host of reasons, some of which are not fully understood, the efficiency of these systems deteriorates with age.

The science

The reason why the sensitivity of the skin declines with age is partly explained by the progressive loss of the nerve endings in the skin called Meissner's corpuscles. These are the nerves that are responsive to very light touch. The number of these corpuscles drops by a factor of four between the ages of 12 and 50 and this is a significant contributor to the skin's loss of sensitivity.[23] In some older people, normally over the age of 70, the skin's sensitivity can increase as the skin of the hand thins.

There is another type of nerve ending in the skin called the Pacinian corpuscles, which are responsible for sensitivity to vibration and pressure. The number of these corpuscles appears to decrease with age.

Table 5.3 shows that effect of age on reducing the sensitivity of various parts of the hand. The score is a ratio of the sensitivity of younger people (aged 20–30) and an older group (aged 60–80). The larger the ratio, the greater the decline in the sensitivity of the older person.

Table 5.3 The sensitivity ratio comparing younger (aged 20–30) and older (aged 60–80) people for various parts of the hand[24]

Part of the hand	Older/younger
Hand palm	1.2
Thumb pad	1.7
Little finger pad	3
Index finger pad	1.2

Ageing affects the sensitivity of all parts of the hand but especially the little finger.

As the sensitivity on the fingers deteriorates, they become less sensitive to vibrations, tactile feedback and pressure. One of the leading academic papers about the effects of ageing estimates that between the ages of 20 and 80 touch sensitivity reduces at 1 per cent per annum.[25]

The most pronounced changes in skin sensitivity are in the feet, which is a contributing factor to the higher incidence of falls among older people. The loss of sensitivity in the hands results in a higher incidence of dropping objects.

As with all of the other changes to the senses the loss in sensitivity will be affected by lifestyle, especially the person's diet and if they smoked.

Effect on the touchpoints

The somatosensory systems affect all of those touchpoints that are reliant, for their successful operation, on the body's sensitivity to threshold levels of vibration, pressure or temperature. If these threshold levels are designed and tested with younger people they may not work at all, or may perform badly, for older people.

The touchpoints that are most affected are those involved with the design, assembly and packing of products. There are numerous examples of companies that ignore the changing sensitivity of touch – mainly in the electronic products and fast-moving consumer goods industries.

Product and package designers need to be particularly conscious of the following:

- Because of a loss of sensitivity to temperature, hot water taps need to be limited in the temperature of the water they dispense, for example, the hot water facilities in hotels and the toilets in retail outlets.
- The tactile feedback buttons that control products need to be set at levels where they can be accessed by older fingers.
- The size, spacing and profile of buttons on electronic products must account for the tactile acuity of all ages.
- When the tactile feel of a product is part of its appeal, it is a dimension that older consumer are less able to appreciate, for example, the casing of electronic devices, clothing and decorations.
- Older people will have problems with packaging if the combination of touch, flexibility and strength is critical to how it is opened. This is often the case with 'safe' packaging that is intentionally designed to require a series of twist, pressure and lateral movements.

- They will also have problems if the smooth surface of a product is part of its controls. The most obvious examples are tablet computers, smart-phones and touchpads. The sensitivity of the touch controls should be set at levels that work for all ages.

The success of the iPhone and iPad has resulted in a surge in the use of touchscreen devices. Currently the mechanism that controls the interaction between touching the screen and the software is very simple. The next generation of touchscreens will be far more sophisticated, by enabling the screen's texture to be changed by the software application. This innovation will make it much easier for devices to be designed to account for varying levels of tactile sensitivity.

The senses in the nose and mouth

The effects of ageing on the senses of smell and taste do not directly affect any of the touchpoints. However, they do create new product opportunities. For this reason it is useful to understand the reasons why these sensory changes occur and their effects. Likewise, it is necessary to understand why the ageing of the teeth, gums and the process that produces saliva leads to new business opportunities.

The changes to the perception of taste and smell are, unlike the changes to eyesight and hearing, subtle and unobtrusive. Most people are unaware, and probably unconcerned, that the quality of these senses is declining. When, however, older people are prompted to comment about the taste and smell of 'food today' they invariably respond that it is tasteless and doesn't smell the same as in their childhood.

The enjoyment of food results from a combination of smell and taste. Suffering from a cold or hayfever, which affects the sense of smell, can render food tasteless or distort its appreciation.

Despite these senses being integrally linked, it is easier to consider their workings and commercial opportunities if they are discussed separately. There are instances where new product opportunities will depend solely on smell or taste and not the combination of the two.

For many people, getting older leads them to change their eating habits for dietary reasons. The message from doctors and the media is to reduce consumption of foods high in sugar, salt and saturated fats and increase consumption of fish oils, fibre, fresh vegetables and fruit. The challenge for food designers is to create appealing products that both satisfy these healthiness requirements and taste and smell good to the older person. To make their task harder, the older person is likely to be taking a combination of medications that will also affect their senses of taste and smell.

Smell

There are many explanations, some conflicting, of why the acuity and memory of smell change and deteriorate with age. They all involve the changes that occur to the:

- Number and sensitivity of the olfactory receptors, the mechanism that detects the different molecules that constitute a smell.
- Processes in the olfactory bulb, the part of the brain that processes the output from the receptors.
- Nervous system, the conduit that links the different components of the olfactory function.

In addition to the changes directly resulting from physiological ageing, there are those occurring because of the accumulation of years of exposure to illnesses, smoking, poor diet and environmental pollution.

The largest ever survey of the effects of age on the quality of smell was the 1986 *National Geographic* Smell Survey.[26] Over a million readers of the magazine responded to a request and completed a questionnaire recounting their appreciation of smell.

The main conclusion was that: 'Odour perception, on average, tends to decline with age. This decline, however, is by no means uniform, either across subjects, odorants, or measures of response. Heterogeneity appears to be the hallmark of age-related change in the olfactory function.'

The survey showed that on average the ability of men to distinguish different intensities of odours declined by approximately 20 per cent; however, this was over the age range 20–100 years. There was an increased deterioration in smell past the age of 70. The intensity and rate of decline was not the same for all types of smells.

More recent studies have measured differences of between two and 15 times in the ability of younger and older people to distinguish between different types of smell. The ability to remember odours also appears to decline with age. Other research reports suggest that over 75 per cent of people over the age of 80 have lost a considerable proportion of their olfactory function.

For most people, this loss of smell is a nuisance but in extreme cases the implications can be unpleasant and dangerous when it becomes impossible to recognize noxious fumes and decaying food.

Business opportunities

The largest and most obvious business opportunity is adapting products whose smell is the primary feature so that they continue to satisfy and appeal to older people for example, perfumery, household aerosols and cosmetics.

Another significant group of products are those where smell is of dual or secondary importance to their appeal – products such as soap and detergents.

In the same way as designers need to view products through the failing eyes of their older consumers they need to consider how their products smell.

There are some stand-alone business opportunities that result from the changes to the sense of smell:

- Devices that generate artificial smell types that can be blended to the requirements and likes of the individual. The rationale for these products could for pleasure, create feelings of nostalgia or to help stimulate appetite. So, for instance, a house could be made to smell of coffee and wood smoke with a hint of lavender. These types of devices are already being tested. In the UK, a company is prototyping a product that can generate combinations of smells, at set times of the day, to help people with dementia to remember to eat.
- Products, especially 'natural' ones, such as scented candles, that generate intense smells.
- Products that compensate for the loss of ability to detect when food is no longer suitable to be eaten. The rapid growth in the over-80s age group, whose sense of smell rapidly deteriorates, should stimulate demand for these types of products.
- More advanced smoke and gas detectors that use electronic sniffers to warn of danger. These products would have visual and audible warning mechanisms that take account of the other types of sensory ageing. Like the previous example, the demand for these products will be stimulated by the rapid growth in the numbers of the older-old.

Taste

'Gustatory dysfunction' is a grand-sounding term given to the increase in the taste threshold and difficulty in discriminating between the intensity of salty, sweet, sour and bitter substances.

The reason why the sense of taste declines is not fully understood but is caused by a combination of the declining:

- Number of taste buds.
- Density of taste buds.
- Sensitivity of taste buds.
- Efficiency of neural processing and retrieval mechanisms.

As a measure of the change in the condition of the taste buds, between the ages of 30 and 70 the overall density of taste buds falls by a factor of three; however, this doesn't necessarily mean that the acuity of taste falls at the same rate.

In common with all of the senses, lifestyle, medical condition and genes affect the timing and degree of loss of taste.

When taste sensation is lost, it is usually salty and sweet tastes that are lost first, with bitter and sour tastes lasting slightly longer. There have been many research studies to quantify the extent and the rate of loss of sensitivity to different food types and food additives. One measured the difference in the detection thresholds, for a range of substances, for people aged 19–33 and those aged 60–75. The results concluded that older men were less sensitive than young men and women for detecting acetic acid, sucrose, citric acid, sodium and potassium chloride and the food additive IMP.[27]

Younger people were able to detect the different substances at lower levels of concentration. For instance, the older age group needed a 1.3 higher concentration to detect aspartame, which is an artificial sugar substitute. IMP required 5.7 times more concentration.

Food design is a complex and specialized subject and an activity on which companies spend astronomical sums of money. The purpose of this short section of the book is not to make the reader a food designer but to stress the magnitude of change that results from ageing in the way older people perceive smells and taste.

The age-related changes that take place in the mouth do not just affect the sense of taste. Ageing changes the condition of the teeth, muscles of the face, creation of saliva, condition of the gums and movement of the tongue. These all influence how we:

- Appear.
- Speak.
- Eat.

A common assumption is that tooth loss is a physiological effect of ageing. This is incorrect. Ageing increases the likelihood of suffering from oral diseases and cumulative 'wear and tear' of the teeth. In the older-old the problems are compounded by difficulty in receiving dental services and physically being able to care for the teeth.

A person's education, social class, race and ethnicity are as good a predictor for the state of their teeth as their age.[28] The secondary effect of these social variables is the likelihood of a person smoking, a factor that greatly influences oral healthiness.

One of the most noticeable conditions of the teeth, which do change with age, is a darkening of their appearance. This occurs because of changes to the constituents and type of dentine in the teeth. The light transmission through the teeth is also affected by changes in the enamel.

The other oral functions affected by age are the:

- Condition and mass of the gums.
- Volume and constituents of the saliva.
- Strength and functioning of the tongue.
- Ability to swallow.

Many of these physical changes are unperceivable and have little impact on wellbeing. When the conditions are at their extreme and extenuated by other medical conditions, they can create product opportunities.

Business opportunities

The most important business opportunity, by far, is adapting the existing constituents of food and creating new food types that take into account the consumer's sensory changes.

This can be done as a stand-alone activity or as part of a redesign of food to allow for changing dietary requirements, especially low salt and sugar, and the availability of food additives to provide medical benefits. For example, ingredients that increase muscle mass could be combined with additives that reduce cholesterol and help with digestion problems.

If the constituents of the food are not changed, then designers will need to place greater emphasis on food appearance because this will become more important in the consumer's decision-making.

Cosmetic dentistry and cosmetic surgery are other areas of business that should benefit from the ageing of the mouth. The already buoyant market for teeth-whitening products and services would seem likely to prosper.

Most older consumers are unaware about the changes taking place in their mouth, the consequences and the possible treatments. As awareness increases it is likely to create new demand for products that:

- Protect mouth hygiene.
- Supplement saliva creation.
- Assist in chewing and swallowing.

These products will be either stand-alone or constituents of other food-stuffs.

Existing toothpaste ingredients that claim to protect against heat sensitivity are likely be joined by those that counter other ageing effects.

The electric toothbrush was a significant change to oral hygiene but there are other products whose design has remained the same for decades. For instance, the products for flossing the teeth make considerable demands on dexterity and flexibility. It is likely that there will be product opportunities that make the process of all types of oral hygiene easier for older people.

The business implications of sensory ageing

The medical reasons why ageing causes the quality of the senses to change and decline are only partially understood. However, there is little doubt about the effects these changes have on the way older people perceive and relate to their environment.

How consumers' sight, hearing, touch, taste and smell change throughout their lifetime has profound effects on their requirements and appreciation of products. At their most basic, products and services that are optimized for a 30 year old might not work for somebody aged 70. Even if they still work their quality may be greatly compromised.

The commercial opportunities of sensory ageing vary greatly by type of industry. As this chapter illustrates, manufacturers of food and some categories of household goods would be well advised to consider adapting their products. For other industries, such as financial services, things will not change, because the senses are not integrally involved in the product's experience or quality.

For companies already serving the market for sensory ageing, such as eyesight, hearing and dental products, the ageing population should provide considerable organic growth to their business.

Irrespective of the type of products that a company sells, sensory ageing affects many of the ways in which it interrelates with its customers. The matrix in Table 5.4 illustrates the span of marketing and operational activity that depends on the efficient working of the customer's senses for their success.

All types of marketing communications, both physical and digital, start with the fundamental assumption that the prospective customer can see, hear and touch the message or proposition. Only when this is achieved, does the sophistication of that message become important.

There are multiple business functions within a company that must adapt their practices to ensure that sensory ageing doesn't diminish the customer experience. These include:

- Marketing communications.
- Digital design.
- Product design.
- Packing design.
- Retail channel operations.
- Training of customer contact staff.

Table 5.4   Marketing and operational activity that depends on the efficient working of customer senses for success

		Eyesight	Hearing	Touch	Taste and smell
Marketing communications	Advertising creative Direct mail Sales collateral	▓	▓		
Online	Website Mobile site App	▓	▓	▓	
Product	Assembly Design Packaging	▓		▓	▓
Retail	Signage Ambience	▓	▓		▓
Sales	Face-to-face Phone		▓		
Support	Face-to-face Phone		▓		

The first step to ensuring that companies adapt to the challenges created by sensory ageing is to ensure all the affected parts of the business understand why change is necessary. The extent of change to each of the touchpoints is likely to be small. The combination of these multiple small changes is what results in older customers getting a materially better buying experience.

To help readers impart the knowledge covered in this chapter a PowerPoint presentation can be downloaded that summarizes the reasons why sensory ageing is so important and the scope of the actions that companies need to undertake. (www.age-friendly.com/downloads/Chapter5.pdf).

Chapter at a glance

→ As we age the quality of our eyesight, hearing, touch, taste and smell alters. Invariably these changes result in a loss of sensitivity and precision of how we sense and react to the world around us. This chapter systematically describes the reasons why each of the senses changes with age, when and to what extent people are affected and what companies can do in response.

→ All types of marketing communications, both physical and digital, start with the fundamental assumption that the prospective customer can see, hear and touch the message or proposition. Only when this is achieved, does the sophistication of that message become important.

→ A combination of senses are involved in successfully negotiating many of the customer touchpoints. If these touchpoints have been designed for the sensory abilities of a 30 year old's eyes, ears, hands and mouth, then the customer experience of older people will progressively decline. The medical reasons why ageing causes the quality of the senses to change and decline are only partially understood. To make matters more complex, the decline in the quality of the senses is often affected by the lifestyle, healthiness and genetic make-up of the individual.

→ Approximately half of all people over the age of 60 will have some degree of hearing loss and half of consumers between the ages of 60 and 70 have difficulty reading food labels, even when wearing glasses or contact lenses. The majority of older consumers will suffer from one or more type of sensory ageing.

➜ How consumers' sight, hearing, touch, taste and smell change throughout their lifetime has profound effects on their requirements and appreciation of products. At their most basic, products and services that are optimized for a 30 year old might not work for somebody aged 70. Even if they still work their quality may be greatly compromised.

TO BUY

- [ ] Bananas
- [ ] Milk
- [ ] Ham & Cheese
- [ ]
- [ ]
- [ ]
- [ ]
- [ ]
- [ ]
- [ ]
- [ ]
- [ ]
- [ ]
- [ ]
- [ ]
- [ ]
- [ ]
- [ ]
- [ ]
- [ ]
- [ ]
- [ ]
- [ ]
- [ ]
- [ ]
- [ ]
- [ ]
- [ ]
- [ ]
- [ ]

- [ ] GOT IT

CHAPTER 6

The ageing mind

Cognitive ageing affects the quality of our memory, recall, attention, reasoning, insights, perception and knowledge. It is also involved in the process of sensory ageing and the way that behaviours and values change over a lifetime.

Unlike the ageing of the body and senses, the changes to the mind are largely invisible. Difficulty remembering names and faces is a small irritant compared with the need to wear glasses, the constant pain of arthritis or difficulty hearing.

What most consumers and marketers don't realize is that the changing performance of the mind is a pervasive force affecting most aspects of a consumer's life and, consequently, many of the customer touchpoints.

Unlike all of the other physiological effects, some results of cognitive ageing are positive, leading to an improvement in mental performance. Unfortunately, these are greatly outnumbered by those having the opposite result.

There is no shortage of research and opinion about the reasons for and results of cognitive ageing. Much of this research is based on small sample sizes, which makes it impossible to exclude the influence of other factors, such as education and social background.

Professor Timothy Salthouse, one of the world's experts on cognitive ageing, says: 'Although there is no shortage of opinions about cognitive aging, it sometimes seems that relatively few of the claims are based on well-established empirical evidence ... assertions about cognitive aging may be influenced as much by the authors' preconceptions and attitudes as by systematic evaluations of empirical research.'

Despite this difficulty, there is enough soundly based research to enable the main factors of cognitive ageing to be identified and quantified. Even if there is uncertainty about why these changes happen it is possible to predict their likely effects on business.

'Normal' cognitive ageing

The reason for highlighting 'normal' in the title of this section is make the distinction between the range of lifetime cognitive changes that might affect anybody and dementia. This is the term for the illnesses of the mind, the best-known and most-feared being Alzheimer's disease. The symptoms of these illnesses, during their initial phase of development, can appear similar to age-related cognitive decline.

The term 'normal' cognitive ageing is a little misleading because there is no normal profile of how fast and how much mental capacity diminishes with age. In the same way as there is a wide variation in the cognitive powers of young people there is a large variation in how these abilities change with age. A 90 year old may have lost little mental capacity but a 60 year old's memory and reasoning skills can have appreciably declined.

The science

An advisory report produced for the UK government concluded that: 'On average, aspects of memory, reasoning, speed of information processing, and executive functioning decline in a fashion that is similar to the age-related changes in physical functioning.'[1]

These changes can be observed but only partially explained.

High blood pressure and diabetes appear to affect the rate of cognitive decline, as do certain genetically inherited conditions. The scientific evidence increasingly suggests that a person's lifestyle, during the early and mid-period of life, is a determining factor.

The traditional view of brain ageing was that it resulted from the loss of neurons, the nerve cells in the brain, and their synapses, the points of communication between the neurons.

Contemporary opinion suggests another explanation, whereby the number of neurons remains stable, with the deterioration resulting from the reduced capacity of the synaptic connections to adapt and reconfigure.

Whatever the physical processes involved, the result is that certain aspects of memory and the speed and way information is processed change with age. With terms such as 'memory', 'processing' and 'information', it is natural to perceive the brain as some sort of biological computer. This conceptual model has its benefits, in that it provides a common language to discuss the elements of the brain's functioning, but also its dangers, if the analogy is taken too far, leading to generalizations and false assumptions. For example, ideas such as 'rebooting the brain' and 'bandwidth overload' are not helpful or accurate.

Using the computer conceptual model, it appears the following changes happen with age:

- A decline in the efficiency of retaining newly acquired information in 'working memory' (short-term memory).
- A decline in the speed of processing information and performing multiple tasks simultaneously.
- A decline in the efficiency of 'prospective memory', the ability to recall actions that must be done in the future.
- A decline in the ability to manipulate visual objects.
- A decline in the capability to focus on a task and not be distracted and to switch attention between tasks.
- A decline in the efficient balancing, when undertaking tasks, between speed and accuracy.
- But the efficiency of 'semantic memory', the ability to recall concepts, vocabulary, language and facts, remains stable.

Another useful way of categorizing the age-related changes in cognitive abilities is to use the concepts of fluid and crystallized intelligence that are used in the study of psychology.[2]

Fluid intelligence involves the cognitive abilities to think abstractly and solve problems in new situations that are independent of prior knowledge or experience. This form of intelligence, which requires the formation of new associations, reasoning and the ability to solve new types of problems, decreases with age.

Crystallized intelligence involves knowledge acquired from past experience and learning. Intelligence of this type, which requires access to accumulated vocabulary and general information, remains stable and probably increases with age.

Research into these types of intelligence is discussed later in the chapter.

The final explanation for the results of cognitive ageing, which is particularly useful for improving the design of customer touchpoints, involves the concept of 'inhibitory deficit'.

Getting older appears to be accompanied by an increasing difficulty in stopping superfluous visual information from distracting the concentration when focusing on a task. As I am writing these words I am using the focus view in Microsoft Word because it minimizes the distraction of unnecessary icons and other applications. Perhaps Microsoft implemented this feature to help counter the effects of inhibitory deficit. Irrespective of the reason for the feature, that is the result it has.

In 2008 an important research paper was published that linked together the model of the brain behaving like a computer, in which the processing speed declines with age, and the inhibitory deficit hypothesis.[3] The research found that older adults had difficulty suppressing irrelevant information during the early stages of processing visual information.

The mechanism that suppresses visual noise is not generally affected by ageing but rather its effectiveness, during the first moments of processing new visual images, is impaired by a decline in the brain's processing speed. This results in an initial period of visual distraction.

Subsequent studies have shown that people who are the most affected by this initial visual interference also seem to have the most trouble staying focused.

Most of the research into ageing and cognitive abilities has been concentrated on people over the age of 60. However, there is a suspicion that the decline in mental powers starts at a much earlier age.

It is not all bad news

As has already been explained, crystallized intelligence, the cognitive skill that involves knowledge acquired from past experience, remains stable and probably increases with age.

In general, living longer leads to more life-experience and this can result in the improvement of certain cognitive skills. However, some of these improvements are accompanied by negative consequences.

Older people have a greater capacity for empathy because empathy is learned and refined as we age. Younger people may have brilliant innovative ideas but they are likely to be limited only to things of which they have direct experience. It is very difficult for a son and daughter to think like their parents and grandparents but, although difficult, it is not impossible for the older person to understand the younger person's emotions.

Steve Jobs, the founder of Apple, expressed this point well when he was explaining why there are so few well-designed products: 'A lot of people in our industry haven't had very diverse experiences. So they don't have enough dots to connect, and they end up with very linear solutions without a broad perspective of the problem. The broader one's understanding of the human experience, the better design we will have.'[4]

There is a counter to this argument that values the energy, drive and commitment of young people – also mentioned by Steve Jobs: 'You can't connect the dots looking forward; you can only connect them looking backwards. So you have to trust that the dots will somehow connect in your future. You have to trust in something – your gut, destiny, life, karma, whatever. This approach has never let me down, and it has made all the difference in my life.'[5]

It appears that the skills required for complex reasoning continue to improve with age. The process of problem-solving improves with the greater number of past experiences that can be used to inform the decision. Older people have more experience in the bank. The counterpoint to this argument is that young people are forced to solve problems, unconstrained by past experience, and in doing so can achieve radically new solutions.

Another effect of accumulated life-experiences is the ability not to allow emotions to affect cognitive performance. Researchers in the USA exposed young and older people to distressing imagery and found that the cognitive performance of the young declined more than that of the old.[6] Work done by Nielsen Neuroscience suggests that older people filter our negative messages, unless they are immediately relevant to the decision being made.[7]

More concerning is the potential 'deficit in scepticism' that might result from ageing. Research conducted at the University of Iowa[8] has shown that in people with certain types of brain damage experience an increased likelihood of being duped by misleading information.

Even though the stereotypes of older people are often associated with grumpiness, it appears that this is not an accurate representation. There are a number of research papers demonstrating that the sense of wellbeing increases with age – not the opposite. The most recent research that confirmed this conclusion was a longitudinal study conducted at Stanford University in 2010. Another result of this research was that: 'Individuals who experience relatively more positive than negative emotions in everyday life were more likely to have survived over the period of the research.'

It is depressing, reading the long list of cognitive skills that decline and the effect that this has on fluid intelligence. However, as explained by Professor Salthouse, the outcome on how most people function in their daily lives might not be as bad as it appears.[9] The reasons for this are:

- The day-to-day tasks that most people perform do not require the maximum exertion of their cognitive powers. So, even though these might be declining they do not curtail people living a normal life.
- Most of the daily tasks we undertake are familiar. Only rarely do we need to solve problems in which our past experiences are not of value.
- Laboratory tests are by definition artificial and intentionally isolate the aspects of cognitive reasoning or memory that are being studied. The tasks we undertake in real life employ multiple cognitive and sensory skills. Those cognitive abilities that have declined can be compensated for by those that have not.

- The ability to remember, reason, solve problems and concentrate, although important, are only part of what is required to function successfully in daily life. Also, just because younger people have some better cognitive abilities does not mean that they apply them.
- One of the greatest skills of humans is the ability to adapt. Older people seem to be able to navigate around those aspects of their cognitive powers that have declined by using different problem-solving strategies and using external aids. Perhaps this explains the tendency for older people to increasingly use paper or electronic 'to do' lists.

Just because the loss of cognitive powers is partially compensated for by those abilities that improve and the adaptability to find new solutions, this is not an excuse for ignoring their effect on business.

The practical results of declining fluid intelligence and the distractionary effects caused by inhibitory deficiency can be annoying, frustrating, constraining and, at their worst, dangerous.

Who is affected?

In a research paper published in 2010, it was claimed that fluid intelligence decreases at approximately 1 percentile a year after the age of 20.[10] Using a series of tests that measured working memory, reasoning, spatial visualization and cognitive processing speed, a distribution of results similar to those shown in Figure 6.1 was obtained.[11]

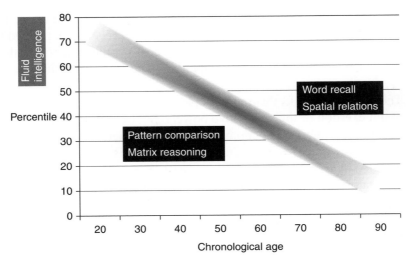

Figure 6.1   Age-related changes in fluid intelligence

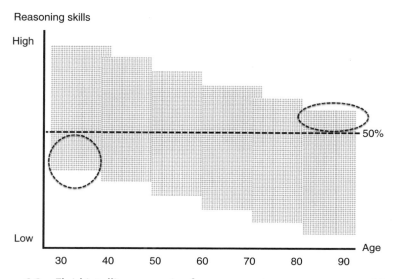

Reasoning skills

Figure 6.2 Fluid intelligence varies from person to person, so some 90 year olds have better reasoning skills than some 30 year olds

The distribution of these results shows a clear pattern of age-related decline in cognitive powers. However, as has been stated throughout this chapter, studying a large sample of individuals will reveal a link between age and cognitive powers, but the actual loss varies greatly by the individual. Figure 6.2 is a conceptual chart that illustrates this point.

By the age of 90 there are far more older people than younger ones with lower levels of reasoning skills, but there will be some with cognitive abilities better than those of some 30 year olds.

Only in rare instances will this wide range of results occur in other aspects of physiological ageing. The simple, but very important, point is that we know the trend of cognitive change but there will be many individuals who don't follow the predicted pattern.

The UK's civil service conducted one of the largest longitudinal studies of how ageing affects mental powers. This measured the ten-year change in the cognitive abilities of a group of 5,200 men and 2,200 women, who were aged 45–70 at the start of the test, between 1997–9 and 2007–9.[12]

Figure 6.3 shows the results for the men, who were grouped into five age bands.

As can be seen, the reasoning skill showed the largest rate and absolute level of decline. Memory and verbal fluency declined but not as much and some elements of vocabulary increased.

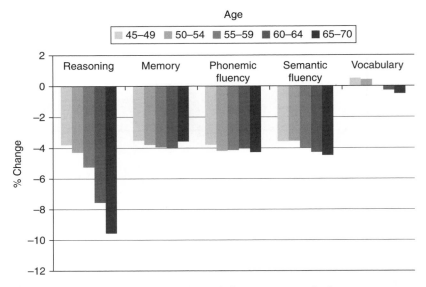

Figure 6.3   Change in male cognitive skills over a period of ten years

So what are the implications of all of these research findings for companies and, in particular, marketers?

Effects on the touchpoints

Ageing degrades many older people's ability to process new complex information and to comprehend new concepts, especially when they cannot use their past experiences or employ alternative coping strategies. In addition, the ability to focus on a task and not be distracted by superfluous visual stimuli declines with age. These effects of ageing on the mind have important implications for many touchpoints along the customer journey.

Many older people will retain cognitive skills that are more acute than younger people's. Unfortunately, companies cannot cater only to this select group. Customer touchpoints have to be designed to function for people with all levels of age-related cognitive decline.

The areas of marketing most affected by customer problems with memory, reasoning and attention capacity are:

- Market research.
- Marketing communications.

- Digital design.
- Product design.
- Packaging design.
- Design of support collateral.
- Retail channel operations.
- Training of customer contact staff.

Often the results of cognitive decline are compounded by the difficulties caused by poor hearing and eyesight. A small decline in mental powers can be amplified by difficulty reading and listening to instructions.

Companies should not view the need to adapt their touchpoints to compensate for these ageing problems as a constraint. Rather, it should be seen as an opportunity, because touchpoints that work well for older people will also improve the customer journey for younger customers.

The implications of cognitive ageing

A detailed analysis of all of the implications of cognitive ageing is outside the scope of this book. As a measure of the complexity, the author's AF Audit tool uses over 30 measures to evaluate the resilience of a company's touchpoints to cognitive ageing.

The following illustrate the types of marketing activities that can be affected.

Market research
Older respondents react to market research measurement tools differently from the young. A research paper studied the effects of ageing on brand attitude measurement and showed that age materially changed the responses to different types of measurement scale.[13]

Language comprehension
Ageing has little effect on the comprehension of familiar language. Older people often have better vocabularies than the young. Where problems arise is when the language is unfamiliar or words are used in a different context, with a different meaning. For instance, many older people were confused and found it difficult to remember why pressing the 'start' button in Microsoft Windows turned the computer 'off'.

Product design
When learning new procedures, older people can be slower and less successful than the young. Problems are exacerbated when designers assume,

in most cases unconsciously, that a new user will have prior knowledge of a procedure that is critical to using a product.

For instance, before the invention of the smartphone, there was an implicit assumption that users of mobile phones understood the principles of the hierarchical menu structure. Similar menu structures were used in other types of electronic products. Many older people found these devices difficult to use because they had no prior experience of these procedures, which were not adequately explained.

Speed of response

Older people's movements and reactions are often slower, less precise and more variable than those made by the young. It becomes increasingly difficult to listen and remember quickly spoken speech, or to understand fast-moving scrolling text and menu systems that display for only short periods of time.

Younger people are better at balancing speed and accuracy of their responses to achieve a task goal. Older people instinctively attempt to minimize errors at the expense of speed.

When products are designed with the assumption that all users will have the speed of movement and the same type of problem-solving approach as those of the young, they create difficulties for older people.

Interface design

The effects of poorly designed interfaces cannot be overstated. As was mentioned in Chapter 3, ageing has a significant impact on the speed and number of mistakes when using the web. By the age of 65, the rate of errors and time taken to use a website will, on average, have increased by 50 per cent and 60 per cent respectively.[14] This degradation of performance is by comparison with groups of younger people with similar computing skills and experience.

The decline in attention capacity may create problems when driving and using a global positioning system (GPS) device. Most of these products assume the user has good eyesight and the ability to focus quickly on the required information on what is invariably a very busy screen. It is clear that little consideration has been given to the problems this creates for older drivers.

The solutions

There is no single list of solutions that will optimize a company's touch-points for the effects of cognitive ageing. Evaluating and adapting touchpoints requires a bespoke approach, rather than applying general rules and guidelines. However, the following suggestions can be applied to most touchpoints and in most companies.

Use familiar language

Whenever possible, employ language that is widely used and is unlikely to be misunderstood. Designers should enable users to make use of learned and familiar experiences. Be explicit about the connections between concepts rather than expecting the person to make their own inferences.

Generally, people perceive and respond rapidly to things that they expect on the basis of their experience.

These ideas run against most marketers' instincts of maximizing originality, newness and the idea that customers respond well to continual change. A good example of an organization that changed a familiar and highly regarded service is the BBC. Its original website had become an example of clean simple design and many millions of people had learnt how to use its navigation structure. The site was changed to have a radically different navigation model. A year after the new site was launched, the authors regularly encounter complaints by older users that they find it impossible to use.

Another example is supermarkets' habit of changing the locations of products for no apparent reason. This might be a small issue for the supermarket but it means thousands of customers have to learn new procedures.

Products, websites, advertising and retail designs do have to change but if the change is too extreme, for no good reason and inadequately explained, it risks disproportionally affecting older consumers.

Provide good instructions

Very few companies provide adequate paper, video, embedded or online instructions for their products. Designers seem to think that people don't read instructions or that the way their products work is so intuitive that instructions are unnecessary. Both these points may have some element of truth but the availability of easy-to-read and easy-to-use instructions is vital for older customers.

This situation is made more important by the increasingly common requirement for the customer to assemble the product.

There is no shortcut to creating workable instructions – they have to be tested with the target customers.

Because instructions tend to be so bad, there is a competitive advantage to be gained for the company that excels at making it easy for its customers to use its products. This includes providing high-quality written instructions but also access to phone and online help.

Provide easy access to instructions

If it is feasible, make available to the user the information required to perform a task rather than relying on them to know the procedure intuitively. Minimize the number of actions that users have to remember to complete a task.

The need to provide easy access to instructions is particularly important for those tasks that are infrequently undertaken. For instance, the computer company HP always provides simple visual instructions attached to its print cartridges to remind the user how they should be used. Apple has a simple and consistent way of accessing the rarely used functions in its applications, which are always accompanied by simple instructions.

Provide enough time

Be conscious that some older people will have difficulty understanding and remembering instructions and messages that are presented too quickly. This applies to the speed at which telephone menu options are presented, the speed of recording voice messages and the speed at which sales and support staff speak. If the person also has poor hearing it will compound their difficulty understanding the information.

The same problem also applies to the speed at which visual information is presented. Web and app designers must ensure that the speed of moving imagery is at a rate that is suitable for older people.

The need to provide enough time does not just apply to the rate at which information is presented but also to the time it might take an older person to fully understand instructions.

When mobile phones were first sold via retail outlets, the sales staff were renowned for their inability to communicate with older people. They spoke too fast and expected the customer to understand the product after a few minutes of explanation. This problem was compounded by their use of jargon and their assumptions about a level of procedural experience that most customers did not have. It is not surprising that these retail outlets became 'no-go areas' for older consumers. Fortunately, this situation has greatly improved.

Keep menu structures simple and logical

When designing written instructions, websites, TV channel controls and the menus that control household electronics products it is essential to keep them as simple and logical as possible.

The hierarchy of the menus must be clear and only the information that is necessary for the user to make a decision should be presented. These are common sense and simple requirements but they are regularly ignored.

Give prominence and ease of access to the most important options and those that are most frequently used. The grouping of information and options should be done from the user's perspective, not that of the system's designers.

Older people are more likely to get lost when navigating complicated menus. It is necessary to provide visual clues to enable them to continually orientate themselves.

The name of the book about usability, written by Steve Krug, expresses the key goal for designers of products, instructions and signage – *Don't make me think*. This is particularly important for older users.

Reduce visual clutter

Suppressing visual distractions becomes increasingly difficult with age. We know that this applies to computer screens and control panels but it is also likely to happen with written marketing collateral. The result is that it takes an older person longer to process a task but, in our experience, it can also create frustration and annoyance – two things best avoided with customers.

The simple solution is to use moving or highly coloured imagery only when it is absolutely necessary and not just as eye candy, particularly in areas where the user needs to concentrate.

This is another of those issues that contradicts the normal reactions of marketers and designers, who often feel impelled to fill white space with imagery or animations.

Put the user in control

One of the reasons the iPad has been so successful with older people is that it puts the user in control.[15] If a user wants only to use email and the internet they are not forced to see or learn other applications. If they want only applications that enable them to read newspapers and books, then that is all they will see.

This principle applies to all types of user experience, which should be dictated by the user, not the designer or brand manager.

Give feedback on positive and negative outcomes

Whenever appropriate, provide clear feedback to the user about the status of the task they are undertaking. This requirement applies to all ages but especially to older people.

Completing a transaction online is the most obvious example of where this is necessary but it also applies to spoken and written communications.

Business opportunities

As people age, they become aware that their cognitive skills are changing, but have no easy way of measuring how fast or by how much. The decline in eyesight and hearing can be tested in minutes in most retail centres. Muscle strength, bone density, fat levels, grip strength and most of the other age-related physiological changes can be quantified by a short visit to the hospital. Cognitive ageing is different.

The most noticeable change in mental skill is the speed and accuracy of memory. Table 6.1 shows the types of day-to-day memory problems suffered by older people.[16]

These memory lapses are annoying and embarrassing and most people accept them as a natural part of ageing. What is far more significant is the worry that they are not just the symptoms of normal ageing but may be the precursor of the nightmare of dementia, a subject that is discussed later in this chapter.

Many people in their 50s and 60s have first-hand experience of older relatives or friends' relatives with dementia. Because of the horrible implications of contracting this disease the over-50s fear it even more than cancer.

Older people realize that their mental powers are changing and hope this is just a normal part of ageing, but have no easy way of knowing. However, they are fearful of what the future could hold if the decline were to accelerate and they have dementia. This leads to a large business opportunity to provide products and services that might act to prevent or slow down the rate of cognitive decline.

Table 6.1   Analysis of everyday memory problems among older people

Everyday memory problems	Percentage agreeing
A word is 'on the tip of the tongue' but cannot find it.	61
Forgetting what the sentence you last read was about and having to reread it.	55
Forgetting where you have put something and losing things around the house.	46
Forgetting something you were told yesterday or a few days ago.	40
Forgetting how to spell words.	39
Forgetting the meaning of unusual words.	37
Forgetting what you just said – 'what was I talking about?'	29

Is it possible to prevent or slow cognitive decline? In his book about the major issues in cognitive ageing, Professor Salthouse is clear about the answer.

Although there has been considerable interest in interventions that might prevent or reverse age-related cognitive decline, the current available research findings are more intriguing than they are definitive.

But, Salthouse does have an opinion about the most likely thing that will influence cogitative ageing.

The causal linkages between physical exercise and rate of cognitive ageing have not yet been definitively established, but at least some of the relations are highly plausible, and encouraging results have been reported from a few scientifically rigorous studies.

In the absence of rigorous scientific research, there are daily examples of academic and commercial research that claim to have found remedies for the problem:

- 'Obesity is associated with reduced memory and thinking skills in adults aged 60 to 70.'[17]
- 'Coffee reported to ward off dementia.'[18]
- 'Tai Chi does good things for aging brains.'[19]

The great majority of consumers don't understand the science or the research findings about cognitive decline and dementia. In the absence of knowledge, they have looked for 'common sense' ways to try and protect themselves.

Professor Salthouse's views about the connection between the wellness of the body and mind are being echoed in the professional and general media. Not surprisingly, the food and wellness industry is likely to be the main beneficiary as older consumers realize that time spent exercising helps maintain both their bodies and their brains.

All the business opportunities identified in Chapter 7, associated with the maintenance of healthy muscles and body mass, are relevant to cognitive ageing. Companies have a great opportunity to construct propositions for products and services that give consumers benefits that help with most of the physiological issues of ageing – including cognitive.

Large numbers of consumers have already been convinced about another solution to their cognitive decline that is best described as 'use it or lose it'. If using the body provides protection against ageing then maybe the same logic applies to the mind.

Nintendo was one of the first companies to realize the opportunity of 'brain training'. Many other companies have entered this sector of the games market with varying degrees of success. Not only do these types of products claim to improve mental processes, they also provide customers with mechanisms to measure if their use has been successful. Cynics might say that these measures only indicate how well customers have learnt the rules of using the game.

The paper equivalents of mental puzzles, crosswords and Sudoku, have been another way that older people have tried to protect their minds and to give an objective measure of their mental decline.

How successful these products are in providing protection against cognitive ageing is hotly debated but in the absence of any proven solution they will remain extremely popular.

The consumer emotions driving the business opportunities related to cognitive ageing are fear, uncertainty and the desire to control the changes taking place in the mind. There are substantial opportunities for companies that understand these emotions and can provide credible solutions.

One of the reasons why cognitive ageing doesn't affect people's lives as much as the laboratory tests would suggest is that they find ways of coping, especially with the problem of failing memory.

There are over 100 apps on iTunes that provide 'to do' lists, alerts, prompts and other ways that people can ensure they don't forget to do important tasks.

The perennial problem of forgetting the location of keys, wallets and other items can now be solved using Bluetooth technology linked to a mobile phone.[20]

The business opportunities for 'coping' tools are limited by the fact that there are many excellent products provided for free. Most computers, tablets and mobile phones come equipped with alerts and diary software.

Google is probably the most-used tool to resolve memory problems. There is even concern that our reliance on Googling has an adverse effect on our memory abilities because we no longer bother to remember facts.[21]

Undoubtedly technological innovations will create new products that can be sold to help older people cope with memory loss, but the market will remain tiny compared with that for products and services that claim to prevent cognitive decline.

Age-related cognitive illness

Each era has illnesses that people most fear contracting – tuberculosis, polio, cancer, HIV and now dementia.

As has already been discussed, most people don't understand the technicalities of where age-related cognitive decline finishes and dementia starts. Some of the symptoms are the same but they are very different conditions, as are the business opportunities they create.

The science

According to the UK's Alzheimer's Society the term 'dementia': 'Describes a set of symptoms which include loss of memory, mood changes, and problems with communication and reasoning.' The symptoms result from an illness, not ageing.

In some cases, people with dementia suffer major changes to their personality, becoming angry and delusional and acting in ways totally different from their normal behaviour.

There are no cures for dementia, only drugs that slow the rate of decline.

Alzheimer's disease is the cause of nearly two-thirds of dementia cases. It is thought that the changes to the brain's structure, responsible for the condition, start decades before the first symptoms become evident. The onset of the disease is slow and the symptoms are often assumed to be associated with ageing.

The second most common cause of dementia, representing nearly 20 per cent of cases, is vascular dementia. This condition results from brain damage caused by constraints to the oxygen supply. The symptoms of this illness are either a sudden loss in mental functions, following a stroke, or over time through a series of small strokes.

There are a dozen other illnesses that account for the remaining 20 per cent of dementia sufferers.

The prevalence rates for dementia in the UK, by age, are shown in Table 6.2.[22]

The rates of dementia vary only a little by gender. In the UK, at the age of 65–69, men are a little more likely to have the condition; by the age of 75–79 the situation is reversed.[23] A person's race and genetic history do not appear to influence their chances of developing the condition. However, there are a very small number of instances in which genetics have been identified as a major cause.

Table 6.2   Prevalence of dementia in the UK

Age	Frequency in the population
40–64 years	1 in 1400
65–69 years	1 in 100
70–79 years	1 in 25
80+ years	1 in 6

What makes it so difficult to obtain accurate data about the subsidiary causes of dementia is that nearly half the people with the condition are unaware they have it.[24]

The one thing that we do know about dementia is that its prevalence rapidly increases with age. This is what makes it such a concern for individuals and governments and such a business opportunity for companies.

Business opportunities

These few facts help us to appreciate the magnitude of the effect of dementia on carers, hospitals, care providers and government finances.

At any given time, approximately 25 per cent of all hospital patients aged over 65 have dementia.

In the USA in 2008, 8.5 billion hours of unpaid care were provided by friends and family to people with dementia, an average of 16.6 hours per week.[25]

In 2008 in Europe, the cost of Alzheimer's disease and other dementias was €177 billion.[26] The cost in the USA is estimated at $200 billion.[27]

There will be a substantial financial prize for companies that find ways of curing, delaying or ameliorating the effects of the disease. It can only be hoped that the pharmaceutical industry is close to creating such treatments. Unfortunately, most reports suggest that a cure for the disease is unlikely for another decade.

Until these treatments become available, the business opportunities will lie in ways of making life more tolerable for people with the disease and their carers.

There are three types of business that will benefit from the rising number of dementia suffers. Each of these is already an established market but the changes in the levels of funding available, the magnitude of demand and the opportunity to apply innovative thinking to service delivery means there are few barriers for new entrants to the market.

Care homes

Few countries have the public finances to adequately fund the care of the rapidly rising numbers of dementia suffers. The most expensive form of care is in specialist care homes that can provide the 24-hour attention that is required.

Already there are signs that the lack of funds is causing patients to remain longer in hospitals while they wait to be moved to a specialist unit.

Those with private funds will be able to buy their own dementia care services. As the levels of state-funded care deteriorate, more people will be encouraged to go private. There will be opportunities for new financial services products to help people pay for these services.

Over the past decade there have been few innovations in the care of dementia sufferers. The village of Hogewey in the Netherlands illustrates how new thinking can radically change the concept of dementia care. The facility was opened at the end of 2009 and its residents live in a protected environment where the visual references are from the past. Within this living space the residents can live as normal a life as possible. There is a high ratio of carers to patients and the costs are around $7,000 a month.

Companies have an opportunity to offer hope to older people and their families that the end-of-life years with dementia can at least be tolerable.

There are business opportunities to improve the care of dementia sufferers who are reliant on state funding. At the moment the current dementia care providers are continually reducing the costs of running their existing facilities while trying to maintain the quality of service. This can only be accomplished for a short time.

An opportunity exists for companies to provide a radically different type of mass dementia care provision.

Day-care centres

These centres are likely to grow in popularity as they provide the dementia patient with access to specialist advice and the carer with the opportunity to be free from the responsibility of looking after their loved one. Often these centres are staffed and funded by volunteers.

There is an opportunity to commercialize the day-care service and offer it on a similar basis to children's crèches. This would involve providing the facility, staff and safe transport to collect and return the patient.

Care at home

There are strong financial and emotional benefits to enabling people to live in their own homes for as long as possible. The same arguments apply to older people with other physical conditions needing care.

The market for private domiciliary care services has been steadily growing. There is scope for providing variants of these services that specifically cater for dementia suffers.

Applying new technologies to enhance and reduce the cost of care at home has been a goal pursued for the past decade by many companies, large and small. Intel and GE independently tried to create solutions for this market without very much success. Recently they combined their efforts in a joint venture company. Numerous small start-ups have been attracted by the prospect of a large guaranteed base of customers and the functionality that combining the internet and low-cost computer processing creates to monitor and assist patients.

The reason why these services have not succeeded is not an absence of technology but the inability to deliver them as fully functioning services that integrate with other care services. The companies that solve this problem should do very well.

The business implications of cognitive ageing

Unlike the other types of physiological ageing, the primary business opportunities result from an age-related illness and not from the normal effects of cognitive decline.

Even though there is no definitive proof that any of the remedies to prevent mental decline work, they have already developed well-established markets.

The benefits of exercise and healthy eating are a constant factor in all types of physiological ageing. Even though this advice is often ignored, the constant repetition of the message ensures that older consumers will increasingly be attracted to products delivering wellness benefits. Being able to demonstrate that the investment of money and time provides both physical and mental resilience creates a compelling sales proposition.

Westminster City Council
Charing Cross Library

Borrowed Items 06/02/2014 17:22
XXXXXXXXX1387

Item Title	Due Date
Long road to Baghdad 30117800852952	27/02/2014
Marketing to the ageing consumer : the se 30117800185577	27/02/2014
How to write reports and proposals 30117800365377	27/02/2014
101 ways to pay less tax : Tax saving adv 30117800883684	27/02/2014

Thank you
Westminster Libraries
www.westminster.gov.uk
020 7641 1300

Table 6.3 Marketing and operational activities that may be affected by cognitive decline

		Cognitive
Marketing communications	Advertising creative Direct mail Sales collateral	
Online	Website Mobile site App	
Product	Assembly Design Packaging	
Retail	Signage Ambience	
Sales	Face-to-face Phone	
Support	Face-to-face Phone	

The other major business opportunity results from the care of people with dementia. In common with other markets, dementia care will fragment into the provision of high-end luxury services and low-cost, high-volume care homes and day centres. The latter will be slower to become established as existing care providers and funders attempt to keep the current uneconomic model working.

Large numbers of older people will suffer only minor problems because of mental ageing and will find ways of coping. An equally large group of older people will encounter a significant degradation in their powers of memory and reasoning.

Companies need to adapt their touchpoints around the worst-case group, not the best. Most of the required adaptations to the touchpoints involve doing things differently, not spending more money.

Table 6.3 shows the touchpoints that are affected and that need to be evaluated. If the necessary changes are implemented as part of routine upgrades, then the cost to companies will be minimal.

To help readers share the knowledge covered in this chapter, a PowerPoint presentation summarizes why cognitive ageing is so important and the scope of the actions that companies need to undertake (www. age-friendly.com/downloads/Chapter6.pdf).

Chapter at a glance

→ Cognitive ageing affects the quality of our memory, recall, attention, reasoning, insights, perception and knowledge. It is also involved in the process of sensory ageing and the way that behaviours and values change over a lifetime. Some results of cognitive ageing are positive, leading to an improvement in mental performance. Unfortunately, these are greatly outnumbered by those having the opposite result. There is a link between age and cognitive powers, but the actual loss varies greatly according to the individual.

→ Ageing degrades many older people's ability to process new complex information and to comprehend new concepts, especially when they cannot use their past experiences or employ alternative coping strategies. In addition, the ability to focus on a task and not be distracted by superfluous visual stimuli declines with age. The areas of marketing most affected by customer problems with memory, reasoning and attention capacity are:

- Market research.
- Marketing communications.
- Digital design.
- Product design.
- Packaging design.
- Design of support collateral.
- Retail channel operations.
- Training of customer contact staff.

→ Evaluating and adapting touchpoints requires a bespoke approach, rather than applying general rules and guidelines. However, the following suggestions can be applied to most touchpoints and in most companies.

- Use familiar language.
- Provide good instructions.
- Provide easy access to instructions.
- Provide enough time.
- Keep menu structures simple and logical.
- Reduce visual clutter.
- Put the user in control.
- Give feedback on positive and negative outcomes.

➔ The consumer emotions driving the business opportunities related to cognitive ageing are fear, uncertainty and the desire to control the changes taking place in the mind. There are substantial opportunities for companies that understand these emotions and can provide credible solutions. The great majority of consumers don't understand the science or the research findings about cognitive decline and dementia. In the absence of knowledge, they have looked for 'common sense' ways to try and protect themselves.

- The food and wellness industry is likely to be the main beneficiary as older consumers realize that time spent exercising helps maintain both their bodies and their brains.
- The 'use it or lose it' concept is another solution that consumers adopt. If exercising the body provides protection against ageing, then maybe the same logic applies to the mind?

➔ At any given time, approximately 25 per cent of all hospital patients aged over 65 have dementia.

Until treatments for the condition become available, the business opportunities will be in ways of making life more tolerable for people with the disease and their carers. There are three types of business that will benefit from the rising number of dementia suffers.

- Care homes.
- Day-care centres.
- Care at home.

Each of these is already an established market but there are few barriers for new entrants to the market.

CHAPTER 7

The ageing body

The preceding chapters explained how the ageing of the senses and the mind profoundly impacts the relationship between companies and their older customers. The effects of ageing on the 11 organ systems and an estimated 100 trillion cells of the human body are equally important, bringing about a transformation in the way people look, feel and behave.

As the body ages the results are immediately visible – greying hair, wrinkled skin and changing body shape. These physical changes have spawned massive businesses in the cosmetics, skin care and dietary industries. Driven largely by the ageing Baby Boomer segment, the US market for just one of these industries, anti-ageing products, is expected to grow from about $80 billion now to more than $114 billion by 2015.

Body ageing conjures up a spectrum of stereotyped images ranging from bent posture, stiff movements and arthritic hands to urinary incontinence. The resulting therapeutic product requirements have not been lost on the pharmaceutical industry.

However, in addition to the business opportunities, it is important to consider how all these aspects of body ageing affect the way people go about the normal process of buying and consuming.

The science explaining why body ageing occurs and its results is wide-ranging and complex. In this chapter, the authors' challenge is to simplify the subject, enabling readers to appreciate why these multiple changes happen to the body, the business opportunities they create and the customer touchpoints they affect.

Knowing that these physical changes can be unpleasant and are relentless and universal can make for depressing reading. However, it is not all bad news. A worldwide study of marathon participants over 50 revealed little difference in the post event effects from runners between 18 and 40 years of age[1]. Other studies suggest that getting older can result in decreased tooth sensitivity, lower sensitivity to allergies, fewer colds and viruses and, according to some, heightened sexuality.[2] Furthermore, many of the effects of physical ageing can be delayed through the right nutritional mix, regular exercise and a positive attitude.

First thing in the morning, the public spaces in China are filled with older people practising exercises such as tai chi, qigong and ballroom dancing. In India, older people have a tradition of practising yoga.

What are the drivers that make them do it? There is no research that definitively answers this question but there seem to be three reasons – a desire to remain healthy; wanting to maintain their appearance; and because it is fun and makes them feel better. These motivations help our understanding of the challenges and the huge business opportunities created by the ageing of the body.

The Curves fitness franchise targets women over 50 and has successfully tapped into the similar needs of western women. Launched 20 years ago in the USA, the franchise operates 10,000 clubs in over 85 countries serving 4 million members. Customers pay to 'enjoy' a 30-minute fitness circuit, a very different form of exercise from the slow-moving tai chi but done to achieve the same goals.

The first part of this chapter discusses the types of body ageing that both affect customer touchpoints and result in new business opportunities:

- Flexibility.
- Dexterity.
- Strength.
- Body mass.
- Urinary issues.

Effects of body ageing that do not affect touchpoints but do result in new business opportunities are discussed in the second part of the chapter:

- Digestion.
- Hair.
- Skin.
- Menopause.
- Sexual changes.

Flexibility and ageing

Flexibility is defined as the absolute range of movement in a joint or series of joints that is attainable in a momentary effort with the help of a partner or a piece of equipment.[3]

The customer touchpoints affected by reaching or other movement of the arms or legs are different from those involved with moving the central core of the body and bending at the waist. For this reason, the authors divide the physical effects of flexibility into two types – peripheral and body:

- Peripheral flexibility is required when raising the arms to reach a product on a high shelf or to bend the arms when assembling a product.
- Body flexibility is required when bending down to a low shelf in a supermarket or in the physical effort of trying on a pair of shoes.

The reasons why ageing affects both types of flexibility are similar and are summarized in the next few paragraphs.

The science of flexibility

Reduced flexibility results from physiological changes in the muscles, bones and joints.

As muscles age, they begin to shrink and lose mass. The number and size of muscle fibres decreases, explaining why older muscles take longer to respond. There is a further loss of suppleness because the muscle fibres are replaced with fatty, collagenous fibres. The changes to the muscles are explained in more detail in the 'Strength and ageing' section of this chapter.

Ageing reduces the range of movement afforded by the joints. Within a joint the bones are protected by cartilage, which acts like a shock absorber. There is also a fluid in the membranes around the joint that acts as lubrication. As the joint ages, the amount of lubricating fluid decreases and the cartilage becomes thinner. Ligaments, the connective tissues between bones, tend to shorten and lose flexibility.

The result of these physical changes is that people alter the way they walk and how they hold their bodies. Common signs of 'stiff joints' are shortening of the step, decreased extension of the ankle and a reduced range of twisting movements, caused by limited ability to rotate the pelvis.[4]

Many of these age-related changes to joints are aggravated by lack of exercise and the physical stress caused by obesity. As the body ages, it is common for old injuries to the joints to become apparent. Maintaining the body at its correct weight and taking regular exercise can help alleviate these conditions and maintain flexibility.[5]

As people age, there is a change in the balance between bone resorption, the process by which bones release calcium to the blood, and new bone formation. The result is that they become fragile as the mineral content of the bones decreases.

The most important consequence of the loss of bone mass is the condition osteoporosis. Affecting women more often than men, osteoporosis can lead to bone fractures, often of the vertebrae and hip. For older people in their late 70s and 80s, osteoporosis is one of the main conditions resulting in loss of mobility.

There are a host of other conditions that result in joint pain and reduced mobility. The most common is arthritis. Rheumatoid arthritis affects the immune system and can afflict people of all ages. Osteoarthritis is a consequence of wear and tear and though not a condition of ageing, the chance of developing the disease increases with age. The severity of this disease can range from the occasional inconvenience of a stiff joint through to constant pain in all of the joints that greatly constrains movement.

Who is affected?

The relationship between declining flexibility and age has been proven through numerous studies but is most obvious when observing the movements of older people. Activities such as bending, twisting and reaching that young people naturally undertake can become difficult and painful for people over the age of 60.

Osteoarthritis and other rheumatic conditions affecting flexibility are the most common causes of disability among US adults and have been for the past 15 years.[6] As Table 7.1 illustrates, the incidence of arthritis is closely related to age. By the age of 65 the disease affects 50 per cent of the age group. This analysis also reveals that women are more likely to suffer from the disease.

The impact of reduced flexibility on the customer experience is emphasized by the data in Table 7.2. This shows the number of arthritis sufferers in the USA who report significant limitations performing day-to-day activities.[8]

Table 7.1 USA rates of doctor-diagnosed arthritis by age group[7]

Age range	Incidence
18–44	7.6%
45–64	29.8%
65+	50%
Males	18.3%
Females	25.9%

Table 7.2   Limitations in day-to-day activities caused by arthritis

Activity	Number of cases in USA
Walking 1/4 mile	6 million
Stooping/bending/kneeling	8 million
Climbing stairs	5 million
Social activities such as church and family gatherings	2 million

Reduced flexibility of the joints affects the majority of older people and is a condition that becomes progressively worse with age. The extent of the disability is partly due to lifestyle, a lifetime's wear and tear on the body and genetic make-up. What is certain is that reduced flexibility will change most older people's range of movements.

Effects on the touchpoints

Companies need to consider the effects of reduced flexibility on touch-points related to the use and assembly of their products:

- **Getting the product home.** Does the product packaging allow it to be carried or moved easily?
- **Preparing the product for use.** Can the product be assembled regard-less of the user's posture and mobility?
- **Using the product.** Will lack of flexibility restrict a customer's ability to use the product?

The design of hotel rooms offers a good example of how consideration of the customers' flexibility can greatly improve their experience:

- Are the drawers and wardrobe racks positioned at the best height?
- Can the safety deposit box be accessed without excessive bending?
- Can the shower be used without large pelvis movements and without bending the legs?
- Is seating at a height that ensures it is easy for an older person to use?
- Is the bed too high or too low?

Impaired flexibility can also create problems within the retail channel. For example, in clothing stores the simple act of dressing and undress-ing requires a degree of flexibility, yet not all clothing outlets provide big enough changing rooms with seating.

The positioning of products on shelves, within easy reach for people with flexibility issues, is rarely considered. The ideal height should be level with the customer's shoulder so that products can be seen and reached without needing to bend the neck or the body or to reach with the arms. Some retailers in Germany and Japan are now positioning the products most frequently bought by older customers within easy reach.

Supermarkets should consider how a combination of staff assistance and specially adapted shopping baskets could improve the buying experience of customers with severe flexibility problems. As explained in Chapter 3, this is a different level of support that stores will already be providing for disabled people – for instance, wheelchair ramps and basket attachments.

A possible result of declining flexibility is a restricted walking gait. This can result in older customers having difficulty using stairs and steps and when moving from one surface to another that requires a change in the length of stride. These circumstances occur in both hotels and retail channels. The subject of falls is covered in more detail later in the 'Strength and ageing' section of this chapter. The frightening fact is that almost half of all older people's falls happen in the bathroom and on the stairs.[9]

All companies that expect their customer to negotiate stairs and steps need to try and minimize the chances of falls. Chapter 10 discusses the reasons why companies need to start incorporating age-friendliness principles into their design of buildings now. Minimizing the causes of falls by older customers is best done when facilities are built, not retrospectively.

Business opportunities

There is already a large market for drugs to treat arthritis, osteoporosis and other ailments that affect the joints. The increasing numbers of older people mean that this market will grow organically, as will the demand for surgical treatments to replace hips and knees. It is not surprising that over a quarter of the capital in the JP Morgan fund that invests in companies that will benefit from the ageing population is in the healthcare industry.[10]

In addition to drugs and medical treatments, the loss of flexibility creates requirements for products and services to help with exercise and mobility.

Exercise

Physical exercise is one of the most effective ways of delaying the onset and extent of disability caused by age-related flexibility problems.

This presents opportunities to the sports, fitness and wellness industries. The meteoric rise of companies such as Curves, targeted at 50-plus women, and the growing popularity of gym classes for yoga, tai chi, pilates, body-pump and the multitude of different types of dancing is evidence of this.

'Fitness programs for older adults' is one of the major business opportunities identified by a 2010 worldwide survey of fitness trends.[11] Not only is the market increasing, because of demographic change, but it is also benefiting from the growing awareness by large sections of society that maintaining fitness is one of the few ways of protecting the mind and body from the effects of ageing.

Health and fitness professionals can take advantage of this growing population of older and retired people by providing age-appropriate exercise programmes.

Some of the ways fitness companies might respond to this demand is with exercise-related initiatives, including:

- Differential rates for membership that enable older people to use fitness centres during off-peak periods.
- Modified versions of yoga, tai chi, pilates and water exercises designed specifically for age, condition and body types.
- New sports, or the resurrection of old ones, that encourage stretching and joint movements.
- Sports apparel for participants in these activities.
- Shape-memory materials designed into apparel that supports stretching and flexing.
- Exercise machines or apparatus that enable safe stretching and flexing even when alone.
- Tablet apps that help people measure and monitor their flexibility.
- Food and food supplements that include additives to help with muscle growth and lowering blood pressure and cholesterol.

Already there are signs that fitness companies are responding to this opportunity, which can be combined with the desire of many older people to lose weight.

Mobility

There will always be a large number, perhaps the majority, of older people for whom inflexibility becomes chronic and affects their mobility. This may be due to their sedentary lifestyles or the misfortune of contracting an aggressive and untreatable type of arthritis.

There is already an array of mobility assistance aids and adapted products that are normally sold via specialist stores, by catalogue and online. These include walking trolleys that help with stability, powered chairs to help people reach an upright position and a panoply of walking sticks and aids. For the reasons already discussed, the demand for these types of products will steadily increase.

In future, the challenge for suppliers of mobility assistance products is to design and sell them so that they are not immediately associated with frailty and disability – even though these are the reasons they are being bought.

Tomorrow's older consumer will try and reconcile what seem like two mutually exclusive situations – wanting to maintain their youthful lifestyle and level of mobility in a body with ageing joints.

Already there are signs that companies are responding to this opportunity. Operators of some ski slopes that are popular with Baby Boomers are flattening out the moguls so as to reduce the impact on the skiers joints.

Walkers of all ages are now using sticks to distribute the weight when descending. It is common to see large groups of older people using the same type of sticks for their power-walking exercise on the beaches of Florida.

Sports shops have suddenly starting selling a large array of knee, elbow and ankle supports alongside the latest Nike and Adidas training outfits.

Older people will be prepared to pay for the luxury of retaining mobility without the stigma of being seen as old.

Dexterity and ageing

Manual dexterity, the skill and ease of using the hands, affects so many of the touchpoints that we discuss it as a separate category from flexibility.

The hands play a critical role at almost every stage of a consumer's involvement with a company. Dialling a helpline, opening a direct mail package, using the mouse and keyboard and the host of touchpoints involved in shopping, unpacking and using a product.

Touchpoints that were easily navigated when we were young can become frustrating barriers for people with impaired dexterity.

Through an appreciation of the extent of the challenge facing older customers with declining manual dexterity, marketers can make the necessary adjustments and contribute to a more pleasant and productive experience.

The science of dexterity

Ageing affects the strength of the fingers, the ability to pinch, grasp and rotate objects and the overall sensitivity of the hand.

What appears to be a simple task, such as holding a glass jar and twisting the metal seal, employs a combination of physical systems including the muscles, bones, joints, tendons, skin, sensory and nervous systems. All of these physical systems decline in effectiveness as people age.

As will be covered in the 'Strength and ageing' section of this chapter, older adults experience considerable loss in muscle mass as they age, but this is less visible in the hands compared with other muscle groups.

After the age of 60, older adults can experience as much as 20 to 25 per cent decline in hand-grip strength. In general, a 15 per cent loss in strength per decade is observed for older adults aged 50 to 70.[12]

One of the most important elements of dexterity, which is involved in using most products, is the ability to precisely grip an object between the thumb and finger. This capability declines with age.

To lift an object using the thumb and finger, requires sufficient grip force to stabilize the object against the effects of gravity. If the grip force is too low, then the object will slip from grasp.

Researchers consistently report that ageing diminishes the ability to make fast and accurate movements and the ability to successfully regulate the motor skills needed to grip.[13]

There are other physiological reasons why manual dexterity declines with age:

- Older adults experience impaired hand muscle control due to changes in both the central and the peripheral nervous systems. This is discussed in Chapter 6.
- The skin on older hands becomes drier and more slippery. This exacerbates the problem with gripping objects.
- Changes to the texture and sensitivity of the fingernails can affect tactile sensitivity.

There is a common belief that ageing results in hands suffering from tremor, although there is no conclusive research that substantiates this conclusion. However, there are age-related illnesses that result in anything from minor tremors to uncontrolled shaking, Parkinson's Disease being the most common of these ailments that normally affect people after the age of 60.

In addition to the reasons already listed, the impairment of manual dexterity is an indirect result of declining eyesight and cognitive ability, which affects the coordination of the hands.

Who is affected?

To measure the strength of hands at different ages, researchers at Sheffield Hallam University tested a sample of 3000 people, asking them to open a jar that was similar to one found in a supermarket.[14]

Figure 7.1 illustrates the results of this research, plotting the torque strength of men and women by their age. Clearly men are stronger than women. Hand strength declines with age for both sexes.

Another result of ageing is the slowing of the speed with which people grip and release objects. This can cause an instinctive increase in the force of grip, which makes handling delicate objects difficult.

Ageing musicians are living proof that not all people lose their fine hand motor skills with age. So it is believed that the onset of these effects can be delayed through regular practice and exercise.

In addition to the natural effects of ageing, arthritis in the hands is one of the most common problems that adversely affect the fine motor skills of older people. It can cause inflammation in the joints of the hand, leading to weakened grip strength and swelling of the fingers.

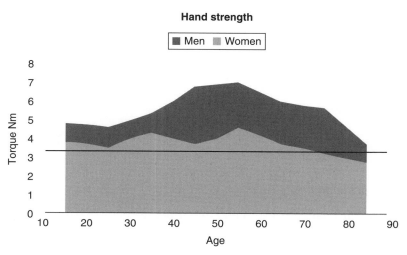

Figure 7.1   Average torque strength for males and females

Women are far more likely to suffer from arthritis in the hands than are men. One study in the USA found that older women had a higher likelihood of arthritis in nearly every joint in the hand by a factor of three to one.[15]

Effects on the touchpoints

To experience the invasive way that reduced dexterity affects the lives of people, consider the simple act of driving a car. Painful or stiff fingers can make simple tasks more difficult, such as buckling a seat belt, turning a key, adjusting seats and mirrors or even simply steering.

The American Automobile Association suggests adaptations to the car's controls and interior that would benefit older drivers. They include features such as:

- Thicker steering wheels that would be easier to grip.
- Keyless entry and ignition systems that eliminate twisting and turning motions.
- Power mirrors and seats that require less strength and range of motion to adjust.[16]

It is very difficult for young, and many older, designers to fully appreciate the limitations created by loss of manual dexterity. One way of simulating its effects is to wear the Arthritis Simulation Gloves, produced by Georgia Tech Research Institute.[17] Wires are woven into the fingers of the gloves to stiffen and reduce their range of motion; neoprene is used to reduce tactile sensitivity and a slick fabric reduces grip.

These gloves are ideal for experiencing the effects of reduced dexterity in three important areas of business:

- Product packaging.
- Product design.
- Retail.

Product packaging

In 2004, the readers of a magazine aimed at people over the age of 50 were asked for their views about product packaging. Of the 2,000 respondents, 99 per cent thought that packaging had become harder to open in the past ten years. The results of the survey are shown in Figure 7.2.

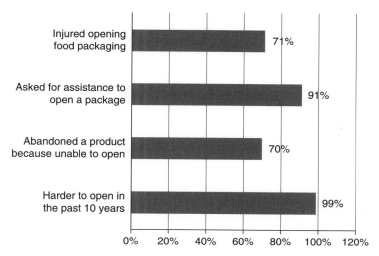

Figure 7.2 Attitudes to packaging among older people

It is an indictment of packaging designers that 70 per cent of the sample had to abandon a product they were unable to open, and 91 per cent needed to ask for help.[18]

It is not products that are rarely bought that create the greatest difficulty, but rather commonly used items such as bleach bottles, jars, shrink-wrapped cheese, ring-pull cans, meat and fish tins, milk and juice cartons and child-proof tops on medicine bottles. The same research revealed that 71 per cent of respondents claimed they had been injured as they struggled to open food packaging.

A UK Department of Trade and Industry report estimated that 67,000 people visited hospital casualty departments every year due to an accident involving food or drink packaging.[19] This number is a conservative estimate, given that a minority of packaging accidents are reported to hospitals.

Other research from the UK revealed that nearly half of people over 65 struggle to remove lids or caps from products such as plastic milk bottles and jars. Difficulty opening packaging is not limited to older people, however, with 15 per cent of people under 40 reporting similar problems.[20]

Understandably, companies are always seeking ways of reducing the cost of their packaging; they should also consider the potential impact on their revenue. When questioned, one in three older respondents stated that hard-to-open packaging and poor design are the features most likely to put them off buying a product.[21]

However, there are encouraging signs that business is responding to the failing dexterity of older hands. Crown, a metal packaging technology company, has introduced the Orbit closure, designed to be universally easy to open for consumers of all ages.[22] Tests by the authors have validated this claim.

Another example is Diamond Foods of the USA, which re-engineered the packaging of its Emerald snack nut line to accommodate the reduced dexterity of older hands. Indented sides make the canister comfortable to hold, grooves make the lid easier to grip and a reduced rotation of the lid makes it easier to remove. Just seven years after its launch, the brand achieved record sales and a market share of nearly 12 per cent of the shelled snack nuts category in the USA grocery channel.

Other companies have introduced 'easy-open' pack designs and used the feature to imply superior quality of the products they contain.

Perhaps the highest-profile attempt to improve the quality of packaging is Amazon's attempt to promote 'frustration-free packaging' that describes itself as an: 'initiative designed to alleviate "wrap rage" – the frustration of trying to free a product from a nearly impenetrable package'.[23] The majority of older people would hope all companies would help Amazon achieve this objective.

Product design

Observing an older person grappling with the in-flight entertainment controls on modern aircraft provides a vivid lesson in the difficulties created by age-related dexterity problems.

It is obvious that age-friendliness was not the primary, or even the secondary, criterion when these systems were designed. The same criticism can be made about the remote control devices for audio-visual appliances in the home.

Such devices should be of a size, shape and material that make them easy to grip and difficult to drop. Buttons should be larger and elevated, allowing tactile feedback when the button is properly activated.

The OXO brand of kitchen utensils was founded in 1989 when its founder responded to the reduced dexterity of his wife's arthritic hands. The company designers developed a handle design that does not rotate and is large enough not to strain the hand by distributing the pressure across the hand when in use.

Each product has a tapered hole to make it easy for people with poor vision or reduced coordination to hang the utensil. The range is now heralded as a classic example of universal design and the company has grown 50 per cent each year since 1991.

Ironically, the ubiquitous teacup is not at all age-friendly. It requires the entire weight of its contents to be leveraged on the middle finger

Figure 7.3   Villeroy and Boch Wave coffee mug

and pinched between the second finger and the thumb. By contrast, the coffee mug manufactured by Villeroy and Boch, illustrated in Figure 7.3, employs all the aspects of age-friendly design. The wide elliptical handle allows more of the hand to grasp the cup and spreads the pressure over a wider area atop the first finger.[24]

Unfortunately, few companies are following the example set by OXO and the Wave mug by Villeroy and Boch by combining style with age-friendly design in their products.

Retail

These are some of the most obvious difficulties encountered by older consumers with impaired dexterity as they negotiate a retail store:

- Checkout staff who place the coins on top of notes when they hand them to customers. Worse still is when the change is placed on the counter surface. Staff should be trained to hand the notes first, then place the coins directly into the hand, allowing the customer to grasp them more easily.
- Poorly designed point-of-sale credit and debit card devices that are not only difficult to hold and use but also difficult to see in low light conditions.
- Placing heavy products on high shelves, which requires the customer to reach and grip. The tendency for manufacturers to combine multiple products into single packs, often using shrink-wrapped packing, exacerbates the difficulty.

- Stacking small items too closely together, which makes them difficult to grip. This often happens with products such as spice jars.
- Using spherical handles, which are difficult for older hands to grasp.

Business opportunities

Clearly, there is a growing need for products and services that accommodate the reduced manual dexterity of older customers. There is even a financial incentive to provide these products, in the knowledge that poor packaging can adversely affect sales.

The examples of OXO and Villeroy and Boch show that style and age-friendly design are not mutually exclusive.

These are some general considerations that should be incorporated in any products aiming to appeal to older consumers suffering from dexterity problems:

- Design clothing fasteners that employ larger buttons, buttonholes and zips, which are easier to grip.
- Make sure that dials, knobs and switches are large enough, far enough apart and provide reassuring tactile feedback. Wherever possible, provide additional sensory responses: audio (beep sound) and visual (light).
- Pay special attention to delicate objects that require careful dexterity.
- Consider the unpacking of products and the finger strength required to remove items from the box.
- Make shapes and surfaces easy to grip and avoid smooth straight surfaces that rely solely on grip-force.

The first priority for companies is to ensure that the design of their current products takes account of the physical limitations caused by impaired dexterity. There will, however, be business opportunities to directly help the sufferers of these physical problems, such as those mentioned below.

Therapy

Hand exercise devices, such as a therapeutic electric hand massager, that help to exercise and stretch the hand could be widely welcomed. So could treatments and food additives that relieve and protect the hands from failing dexterity. Food stores are already selling tablets and gel that contain Glucosamine, a naturally occurring compound in the body that is thought to help repair damaged joint cartilage.

Assistive devices

Sufferers of extreme forms of arthritis often wear protective wrist braces to protect the hand from further damage. However, there are few examples of innovative thinking applied to create devices that help the person keep functioning normally rather than just stopping their deterioration.

For instance, a shoulder harness, like a simple sling, could be designed that would share the weight of objects otherwise dependent entirely on the grip of the hand. This could be used for carrying shopping bags or other goods. A similar type of device could help in the domestic environment by making it easier to handle a vacuum cleaner or a leaf blower. There are new materials that have super-grip surfaces that could be used to produce gloves.

Technology

The Japanese believe that the adaptation of manufacturing robotic technology, used to create products that help older people in their home, will be a solution to many of their physiological ageing issues – loss of dexterity being one of them. So far, there are few examples of success.

Two technologies that have made a rapid jump from research projects into commercial products are gesture controls and voice-recognition software. Microsoft Kinect gesture-control technology was originally developed as an integral part of the company's gaming products. It was soon evident that controlling computers by gesturing, rather than touching, had applications far outside the gaming domain. Microsoft is now actively encouraging companies to incorporate the technology into their products.[25]

An important part of Apple's iPhone 4S is Siri, a software component that enables the users to control many of the phone's functions by voice rather than with their fingers. This development holds out the prospect for older people of never again having to fumble with their mobile phone.

Strength and ageing

Movements that require a customer to walk, lift, push, pull, step, kick, rise or sit all involve muscle strength. When this strength declines, it affects all areas of a person's life. For example, weakness in the lower extremities can lead to falls and hip fractures. Weakening in the strength of the upper body increases the risk of accidents from movements such as removing a new television from its packaging, assembling furniture and so on. Weakness of the lower-back muscles can contribute to problems such as a herniated disk and chronic low-back pain.

The loss of muscle size and strength with age can lead to fatigue, weakness and reduced tolerance for exercise.

Understanding the reasons and consequences of muscle strength loss helps us formulate the best way of adapting customer touchpoints.

The science of strength

Ageing results in a decrease in the size and number of muscle fibres. The muscle tissue is replaced more slowly and its replacement is tougher and more fibrous. Also, changes in the nervous system cause muscles to have reduced tone and less ability to contract.

There are four reasons why muscle weakening occurs as people age:

- Sarcopenia – age-related muscle loss. The term is derived from Greek, meaning 'poverty of flesh'.
- Disuse – although muscle deterioration is a natural process, it is accelerated by a sedentary lifestyle.
- Medication-related – certain medications, such as systemic corticosteroids (often prescribed for people with asthma or inflammatory conditions such as rheumatoid arthritis or lupus), can result in muscle weakness.
- Disease-related – this can be more difficult to overcome, especially when it involves nerve damage or disease of the muscle itself.

The reasons for muscle shrinkage in sarcopenia are only partially understood. They are likely to include a reduction in the nerve cells that initiate movement, decreasing concentrations of some hormones and a reduction of the body's ability to synthesize protein. Changes in diet that reduce the calorie intake may also be a contributing factor.

Muscle loss begins at around the age of 40, with a 15 per cent loss in muscle strength per decade between the ages of 50 and 70.[26] The consensus view of researchers is that approximately 30 per cent of those over 60 years of age and half of those over 80 experience muscle loss because of sarcopenia.

Muscular strength is rarely used without physical movement. A more important factor is muscle power, which is the combination of strength and speed of action that is required in dynamic activities such as climbing stairs, rising from a chair, getting on to a bus and getting out of a bath. Muscle power tends to decline faster than muscle strength.[27]

There are three dimensions of muscle power that provide insights into how it declines with age and the differences between men and women:[28]

- **Explosive power/weight ratio.** When this falls below a critical level some people will not manage a 30cm step and fewer than one in three will manage a 50cm step.
- **Knee extension strength/weight ratio.** The critical level of strength needed to extend the knee to be confident of rising out of a low chair without using the arms is equivalent to 35 per cent of body weight.
- **Aerobic power/weight ratio.** When this is below a critical level, it becomes uncomfortable to walk on the level at 3 mph.

Table 7.3 shows the percentage of people aged between 50 and 70 who do not have the critical levels of muscle power to execute each of the three tests. As would be expected, the percentage of people failing to achieve these critical levels increases with age, but it increases much faster in women than men.

In addition to the loss of muscle power, the ageing consumer also suffers from diminishing endurance – the ability to sustain prolonged periods of physical activity. If the muscles do not receive enough oxygen, the result is fatigue and breathlessness. In these circumstances, individuals slow down or stop to rest, allowing the oxygen supply to the muscles to recover. One obvious implication, for industries that require their customers to walk and stand, is the need to supply adequate seating.

Who is affected?

As shown in Table 7.3, muscle power declines with age and affects women more than men. Another dimension of muscle strength is that in the upper body and how it affects pushing, pulling, twisting and left and right gripping. Research has found that no significant loss of upper-body strength occurs between 22 and 55. After 55, however, the upper-body strength decreases steadily with age.

Table 7.3 Thresholds of muscle power in ageing adults

Test	50–74 years below critical level	
	Men	**Women**
Explosive power/weight ratio	7%	28%
Knee extension strength/weight ratio	2%	14%
Aerobic power/weight ratio	9%	38%

Table 7.4　Upper-body strength loss by comparison with adults aged 20–30

Age	Strength loss
50–59	9%
60–69	18%
70–79	30%
80+	40%

Table 7.4 shows the loss for four age groups by comparison with strength at age 20–30.[29]

Sarcopenia affects races in different ways. Research conducted by the American Geriatrics Society showed that among people over 60 years of age, the prevalence of sarcopenia is higher for white than black people.[30]

There are many studies linking the benefits of exercise to better health, longevity and muscular strength. It is difficult to know the validity of many of these claims because often the research is not peer-reviewed and comes from small research samples. However, time and time again, academic literature stresses the benefits of physical exercise as summarized by this statement.[31]

> *A growing number of studies support the idea that physical exercise is a lifestyle factor that might lead to increased physical and mental health throughout life.*

Lack of exercise, on the other hand, is thought to be a significant risk factor leading to sarcopenia, particularly a lack of exercise that involves putting the muscles under strain. Physically inactive people experience a faster and greater loss of muscle mass than those who are physically active. This is a worrying conclusion in light of the decline in physical exercise that occurs because of obesity, a subject that is discussed in the 'Body mass and ageing' section of this chapter.

Effects on the touchpoints

The loss of strength that results from ageing is important to four sets of touchpoints:

- Access.
- Rest areas.

- Location.
- Delivery.

Access

Although this book's focus is on the opportunities to be realized through the adoption of age-friendly business practices, companies must also consider their liability arising from the risks created by ageing.

The most likely accident is for older customers to fall – sarcopenia being one of the contributing reasons.

A cursory study of USA lawyers' websites provides details of the causes of accidents that enabled them to successfully prosecute for personal injury. Many of the reasons related to clients falling because of:

- Wet slippery floors.
- Uneven floors.
- Unlit stairways.
- Defective sidewalks.
- Unmarked holes.
- Items blocking walkways.

Of course, people of all ages can fall, but both the likelihood and the consequences of the resulting injury increase with the age.

A measure of the problem is shown by data from Australia, where in 2008 there were nearly 80,000 hospitalized injury cases due to falls among people aged 65 and over, the majority occurring to women.[32]

Rest areas

Children's play areas and minding facilities are common in many retail stores yet there is an increasing likelihood that people will shop with their older parents, rather than with their children.

Retail companies need to start considering how they should respond to their customers' changing strength capabilities, especially in those geographic areas with high densities of older people.

An obvious facility to consider is the provision of rest areas. Large supermarkets and department stores are probably already satisfying this requirement with their cafeterias.

Irrespective of whether it is a dedicated rest area or using an existing space, an important factor to consider is the seat design. Backless seats may be aesthetically pleasing but they are not age-friendly. Seating should be selected because it takes account of the strength limitations of older customers.

For instance, the seat height in speciality chairs for older people can be twice the height of normal chairs. Above all, chairs should have arms that provide leverage support to help people lower into the seat and rise from it.

Location

A store's location and its accessibility, from public transport and car parking, will become increasingly important factors for older shoppers.

The total walking distance involved in accessing a store is one of the factors the authors use when determining the age-friendliness of a retail outlet.

Within the store there are things that can be done to minimize the difficulties caused by declining muscle strength such as ensuring that shopping trolleys are manoeuvrable and locating items most needed by older customers towards the front of the store.

Delivery

Older people often report that the act of shopping is as much an opportunity to leave the home and meet people as it is a necessary task to buy goods. Retailers should seek to minimize those shopping tasks that require physical strength, enabling older customers to retain the positive experiences of shopping without the physical challenges.

One of the most obvious ways is to separate the buying from the physical act of carrying the goods. There are many ways of tackling this issue.

Supermarkets in Japan often feature smaller, lighter shopping trolleys that look and function more like assistive walkers. Most large supermarkets provide assistance for packing and carrying to the car; however, it is normally on demand rather than a service that is freely offered to the customer.

As more products require home assembly, it is likely that older people will be willing to pay for a service that delivers, carries, assembles and ensures the goods are properly installed and in working order. This also addresses the product assembly issues caused by cognitive ageing discussed in Chapter 6.

During an interview with the BBC, in 2012, the chief executive of Coca-Cola stated that his company had to respond to the mega-trends that are shaping all markets. One of these is the ageing of the company's customers and as a result he expected to see home delivery become increasingly important.[33]

Business opportunities

In addition to adapting existing products and retail channels, the loss of muscle power creates new business opportunities in:

- Exercise.
- Therapies.
- Accessories.

Exercise

Previous sections of the chapter have discussed the importance and value of exercise in helping to delay and alleviate the results of ageing. Maintaining muscle strength requires an exercise regime to have a high component of resistance training. As falls are often attributed to weakened leg muscles, resistance-training machines that develop these muscles should see increasing demand. As retirees have fewer restrictions on their time schedule, gyms could use their off-peak hours to offer tailored exercise classes providing a mix of cardiovascular and resistance training.

Therapies

Products designed to stimulate muscle protein synthesis to improve muscle strength are now the subject of considerable research and development among leading consumer and pharmaceutical companies.

Nestlé, Abbott and Danone are all either selling or researching products with ingredients to counter the effects of sarcopenia.

Increasing consumer awareness of the condition is likely to boost demand for these products.

Much of the effort and marketing of sarcopenia treatments to date has focused on the older-old. However, as the effects of the condition are better understood the focus for treatment will move to younger adults.

It is likely that the sales proposition for products that counter sarcopenia will expand from being purely about maintaining body muscle strength to include the cosmetic benefits of reducing the loss of texture and appearance of facial, neck and arm muscles.

Accessories

It is not uncommon to see older people using hikers' trekking poles as a walking stick. These products are well-suited for the task but the choice is also likely to result from trying to avoid the stereotypes associated with the original walking stick.

By any name, a walking stick provides stability and relieves stress on the joints caused by weakening muscles. There are already signs that manufacturers of hi-tech walking sticks are capitalizing on the increasing number of older consumers.

It is now possible to buy walking sticks that incorporate an LED torch and a foot-fall floodlight to ensure safe footing at night. There are sticks that monitor vital signs, such as blood pressure and heart rate. It is even possible to buy sticks that incorporate seats and umbrellas.

For those older consumers intent on maintaining their active lifestyle, sarcopenia will be seen as a challenge to be overcome by exercise and the acquisition of whatever new products enable them to keep functioning as in their youth.

Body mass and ageing

There is a tendency for body weight to increase with age. This was highlighted in a 2009 report titled *Obesity Among Older Americans* presented to the American Congress. The report referred to 'the obesity epidemic that the United States is facing'.[34]

> *Not only is this an immediate issue but the future also looks over-weight. In developing countries the world over, the maximum rates of obesity tend to be reached at around 40 years old. It is reasonable to assume that these overweight 40-somethings will face significant difficulty trying to lose weight as they move into their 50s and beyond, due to the slowing metabolism that accompanies age.*

When combined with other age-related factors of the body's changing shape, size and height, the implications for businesses are vast. What to eat, how much to eat, the style and size of apparel and so on, will present challenges as well as opportunities.

The science of weight

The title of this section is 'Body mass and ageing'. This refers to the changes in body bulk and weight. It is the latter that is the primary factor that determines the changes that need to be made to the customer touchpoints. Understanding the science that causes body weight to increase with age is important to determining how customer touchpoints need to be adapted.

Basal metabolic rate (BMR) is a measurement of the body's use of energy and is usually interpreted as the minimum level of calories the body needs in its resting state each day, including sleeping time. The factors affecting BMR are gender, age, height and weight.

Ageing results in a fall in the BMR.

There are many factors that contribute to this decline; however, the interaction and importance of these factors is not fully understood. What is known is that as people age, the amount and distribution of fat, lean tissue (muscles and organs), bones, water and other substances change.

An important reason for the decline in BMR is the high energy requirements of muscle tissue. As discussed in the previous section, muscle mass declines with age, as does the demand for energy.

Summarizing what is a complex set of physiological interactions, unless older people either reduce their calorie intake or increase their energy consumption, preferably both, their body fat increases, as does their weight.

The globally recognized standard for measuring and comparing body fat is the body mass index (BMI). The World Health Organization (WHO) defines BMI as a person's weight in kilograms divided by the square of their height in metres (kilograms/metres^2). For example, an adult who weighs 70kg and whose height is 1.75m will have a BMI of 22.9.

In recent years, there has been a growing debate, particularly among Asia Pacific nations, on the need for different recommended BMIs for different ethnic groups. For example, Singapore revised its BMI recommendation in 2005, following studies showing that many Asian populations, including Singaporeans, have a higher proportion of body fat and increased risk of cardiovascular diseases and diabetes, compared with Caucasians at the same BMI. Japan has its own BMI recommended levels.

Table 7.5 shows the BMI levels at which the WHO defines adults as underweight, overweight and obese.

Table 7.5 WHO international classification of adult underweight, overweight and obesity according to BMI

Classification	BMI (kg/m^2)
Underweight	<18.50
Normal range	18.50–24.99
Overweight	≥25.00
Obese	≥30.00

There is much debate about the accuracy of the BMI measurement as a useful way of determining optimum weight levels. It may underestimate body fat in older persons and people who have lost muscle for reasons other than ageing. On the contrary, it may overestimate body fat in fit young people. However, because most studies of ageing and older people use BMI as their measure, it is necessary to understand its meaning and limitations.

Another factor that determines body mass is the person's height and this is something else that changes with age. There is a tendency for all races and both sexes to decline in height.

This happens because the discs between vertebrae lose fluid over the years and flatten. Muscles lose mass and weaken, especially in the abdomen, which causes the posture to change and results in stooping. Even the arches of the foot flatten out slightly, reducing height by a few millimetres.

People typically lose about 1cm every ten years after the age of 40. Height loss is even greater after 70. Some reports suggest that, in total, people may lose 2–8cm in height over their adult lifetime.

Who is affected?

Table 7.6 shows the magnitude of the numbers of people who are overweight and obese.[35]

In Europe, the Eastern Mediterranean and the Americas, over 50 per cent of women are overweight. In all three regions, approximately half of these overweight women are obese.[36]

There is a simple conclusion from this data – all parts of the developed world are too fat.

Unless there is a radical change in dietary and exercise habits, it is estimated that by the year 2025 levels of obesity could be as high as 45–50 per cent in the USA and 30–40 per cent in Australia and the UK.[37]

A 2008 study, across 27 European countries, showed that the highest incidence of overweight or obesity among adults, as measured by their BMI, was among people 45–59 years of age.[38]

Table 7.6   Prevalence of overweight and obese individuals

	Males and females	
	Overweight	Obese
Americas	62%	26%
South-East Asia	14%	3%

Extreme values of BMI (either high or low), in older people, are a predictor of their likelihood of suffering general health and movement problems as they age.

There is also a behavioural factor that contributes to rising obesity in older people. The more overweight a person becomes, the harder it is to achieve levels of exercise that reduce their BMI. This creates a dangerous negative feedback loop of weight increase, making it harder to exercise, leading to even further increases in body weight.

Most studies show that in developed countries the levels of obesity are higher in the lower socio-economic groups. In developing countries, this relationship is reversed. The transition from a rural to an urban lifestyle is associated with increased levels of obesity resulting from the dramatic change in lifestyle.

Obesity not only affects the health of older people, but also affects their day-to-day lives. Older people who are obese report more activity limitations and more feelings of sadness and hopelessness than those who are not obese.[39]

It is easy for the eyes to glaze over the facts and figures about obesity and its effects on older people. The possible tragic consequences of the increasing weight and inflexibility of older people were thrust into the news spotlight in 2005 when on Lake George, New York State, a sightseeing vessel carrying 47 senior citizens capsized, killing 20 passengers. The accident reports cited the weight of the older passengers as a contributing factor in the disaster, because many were unable to locate and fit their life jackets and evacuate the boat.

Since the accident, the coastguard has raised its average weight assumptions per passenger by 33 per cent.

Effects on the touchpoints

Changes in weight, shape and height as people age will influence what and how they buy.

The ageing consumer who is overweight will have to contend with a perfect storm of issues. The decline in flexibility and strength will be exacerbated if the customer is overweight. The requirements for adapting the touchpoints that were detailed in the sections about flexibility and strength become even more important for overweight consumers.

The dimensions of supermarket aisles, hotel bathrooms, car interiors and airline seats will need to be adapted to accommodate the changing shape of customers.

Airbus appears to have anticipated this requirement, because it is now offering US airlines buying its A320 aircraft extra-wide seats for overweight passengers. The seat layout provides two 50cm seats, either side of the single aisle, instead of three 45cm seats. The interesting question is whether airlines will charge for this facility or whether they will have to accept that as their customers change in size so does the product they provide.

Business opportunities

There are three areas of business that should benefit from the results of obesity among older people and their desire to maintain a healthy weight:

- Apparel.
- Footwear.
- Weight control.

Apparel

There is already a market for XX and XXX-fitting clothes for overweight people. Where clothing designers have been slow to respond is creating clothes that take account of the naturally occurring changes in body shape of older consumers who are not overweight.

Whenever the authors conduct focus groups with older women, a persistent complaint is the limited selection of garments appropriate to their age and shape.

Marks & Spencer has adopted 62-year-old former model Twiggy as part of its age-neutral advertising campaigns. This is the exception not the rule.

The mismatch between the body shape of customers and clothes affects men as well as women. There is a fashion-conscious male segment among the Baby Boomers that is far larger than in the previous generations. However much exercise and dieting this group undertakes, they will not have the same body shape as their sons.

Footwear

By altering sensory feedback to the foot and ankle and modifying frictional conditions where the shoe meets the floor, footwear influences balance and can reduce the risk of slips, trips and falls.

The design of the shoe – such as heel collar height, sole hardness, tread and heel geometry – influences balance and gait. There is a tendency for older feet to broaden and for the support of the arches to weaken.

Wearing shoes that account for all of these ageing effects not only improves comfort but helps reduce the incidence of knee and hip problems that result from incorrect foot placement.

Older people often wear training shoes because of the thick cushioning they offer but no doubt the connotation of youthful sportiness is also a driver.

So far, none of the major sports and fashion shoe suppliers appears to be responding to what seems like an obvious customer need.

Weight control

Helping older people control their weight is both a socially responsible thing to do and one that has considerable revenue opportunities. The USA weight loss market is already estimated to be $60 billion.[40]

There are three types of business opportunities resulting from the desire to control weight. Although many of the following products are already available, there is plenty of opportunity for them to be improved and extended by new innovations.

Foods
- Lower-calorie, high-protein dishes and entire restaurants specializing in these foods.
- Controlled (smaller) portion sizes.
- Clear nutritional (caloric) indications on menus and labels. These can be combined with data about sugar and salt content.
- More attractive low-calorie snacks. These could be combined with food additives to combat sarcopenia.

Exercise
- Lower-cost, household calorie-burning exercise machines.
- Exercise machine suppliers and gyms that use the competitive instincts of older people, especially men, to improve their fitness levels. Concept2, a rowing machine manufacturer, runs competitions in which the oldest age category is 90-plus.
- Sponsorship by brands of competitions to increase the fitness of older people, the aim being for the brand to be seen uniting with its older customers to combat weight gain.
- Retailers providing details of the total calorific value of food bought and the implications for levels of exercise.

Devices
- BMI-measuring weighing scales.
- Calorie, BMI, age-adjusted app for mobile devices.

- Using QR codes to make it easier to see the calorific and sugar and salt content of foods.

The success of any of these product ideas requires older consumers to be aware of the health issues related to weight gain and to have the motivation to want to keep it under control.

The authors' experience of working with older consumers suggests that approximately a quarter of them are aware and have the motivation to change to a healthier lifestyle. Another quarter are both unaware and have no intention of changing their exercise and eating habits. The remainder are persuadable.

Urinary issues and ageing

In 2011, Japan's largest nappy maker reported that, for the first time, sales of its products to older Japanese exceeded those for babies. Apart from highlighting the super-ageing of Japanese society, this also highlighted the prevalence of incontinence among older people.

Urinary incontinence (UI) is an under-diagnosed and under-reported condition with major economic and psychosocial implications.

As people grow older, bladder and bowel problems become more common. Urinary systems become less efficient and medications increase the frequency of urination and disturb the digestion functions. Mobility problems make it difficult for the seriously infirm to reach a toilet in time.

Among all the effects of ageing, incontinence remains a social taboo. Even in relatively open societies such difficulties are rarely discussed.

As with the other effects of ageing, UI has two sets of business consequences: first, the changes it requires to a small number of the customer touchpoints and, second, the business opportunities it creates.

The science of urinary issues

Some argue that UI is not a natural result of ageing but is one of those conditions that happen to be more common in older people. Whichever view is correct, the condition occurs because of a combination of physical changes:

- Weakening of the muscles that regulate the bladder.
- Bladder muscles becoming overactive and tightening and relaxing without warning.

- Nerves that control the bladder becoming damaged, either through ageing or disease.
- Enlargement of the prostate gland in men.
- Diabetes.
- The side-effect of medication taken for other conditions.

There are many types of UI, but the two thought to account for 90 per cent of incidences are:

- Stress incontinence – when the pressure in the bladder as it fills with urine becomes greater than the urethra's strength to keep it closed. In men, removal of the prostate gland can lead to stress incontinence. Stress incontinence is thought to account for about half of all global cases of incontinence.[41]
- Urge incontinence – can be accompanied by overactive bladder syndrome, a condition that causes an urgent need to pass urine, often during the night.

Who is affected?

Although UI is not limited to older adults, the incidence of the condition definitely increases with age.

Data from Australia, shown in Figure 7.4, gives an insight into the way the incidence of UI varies with age and by gender.[42]

Even though the removal of the prostate gland may increase a man's risk of UI in later life, the chance of severe incontinence in men in their 70s is still only about half that of women.

In every age group, women are more likely to suffer UI. The significant difference in the incidence of UI in the younger age groups is largely explained by the connection between UI and childbirth and the menopause.

Effects on the touchpoints

The most obvious effect is to increase demand for toilets and the quality of signage to make them easy to find.

Although it is a natural body function, asking another person for the location of a toilet still causes embarrassment, regardless of age. This can be even harder for older people with heightened self-consciousness of their incontinence.

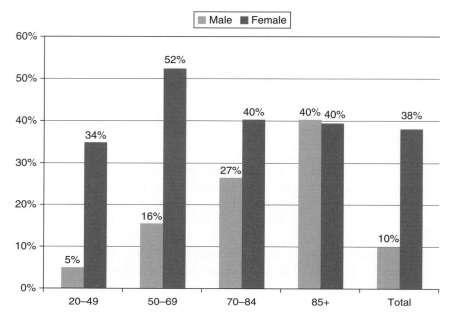

Figure 7.4   People reporting UI in Australia by age group and gender

The normal frequency of urinating is about six to seven times in a 24-hour period,[43] and more frequent for older people, particularly those with UI. So, during a normal shopping journey of a few hours, it is very likely that an older person will need to visit a toilet.

Retailers and other industries that expect customers to spend prolonged periods of time on their premises need to evaluate whether they provide enough toilets and how easy they are to find.

Research conducted in the UK, among older people, looked at the issues that most concern them about public toilets. Their responses provide useful insights for companies providing toilet facilities.[44]

The things of most concern were:

- Journey – how far to reach them? This becomes an issue for older people with reduced mobility.
- Location – are they easy to find? This involves the visibility of the signage and the icons used to represent men and women.
- Provision – are there enough toilets for men and women? The International Building Code requires a 2:1 female–male ratio of toilets. Women very often complain about the lack of toilet facilities.

- Hygiene – are the toilets clean? The condition of the toilets is a direct reflection on the company.

The similarities between the physical conditions of older people and the disabled have been discussed throughout this book. The issue of disabled toilets, which must be provided by law in most countries, raises an interesting question – is an older person with UI designated as disabled? Currently, a healthy older person who has UI may not feel entitled to use toilets marked for the disabled, and perhaps may feel intimidated about doing so. There may be scope to redesignate the disabled facilities to make them available to disabled and older people.

Business opportunities

The most obvious business opportunity resulting from the increasing incidence of UI is the invention of new drugs and treatments that alleviate the condition.

However, until medical science can treat UI, there will be a buoyant market for products that minimize its effects, namely incontinence pads.

Global companies such as Kimberly-Clarke, with its Depend range of products, and Svenska Cellulosa Aktiebolaget, with its TENA products, have employed sophisticated marketing techniques in an effort to remove the stigma from UI. The thrust of their marketing has been to demonstrate that UI affects a large percentage of the population and all types of people, both young and old.

In an attempt to make the product more acceptable, the packaging for Depend products looks more like a pack of standard underwear. TENA's Canadian subsidiary staged a 'Laugh Away with TENA' contest to inform and engage its target market about the condition.

As the numbers of older people increase so will the demand for these products. Eliminating the stigma of using them will liberate a tranche of older people who have suffered with the condition but have not used incontinence pads.

It would seem that the market is large enough for new entrants that bring even more innovation to product naming, design and marketing.

The secondary issues of ageing bodies

All of the physical changes to the body that have been described create new business opportunities and have consequences for a company's customer touchpoints.

There are other age-related changes to the body that have no effect on customer touchpoints but that result in new product and service opportunities. These include changes to the digestive system, hair and skin and the effects of the menopause and sexual changes.

The rest of this chapter will briefly describe these physical changes and highlight the new product opportunities that might result.

It is important to note that there is another layer of physical changes that affect the body's primary organs – the kidneys, liver, heart and so on. These give rise to the massive market in geriatric pharmaceutical products, which is outside the scope of this book.

Digestion

In its mildest form, weakening of the muscle that regulates the flow of food into the stomach can cause indigestion or 'heart burn'. It can also lead to far more serious issues. Poor digestion leads to constipation as well as haemorrhoids and even contributes to cases of malnutrition.

Like other parts of the body, within the digestive system the rate of new cell growth declines and tissues become more susceptible to damage.

However, the loss of muscle strength is likely to slow the movement of food through the digestive system and reduced elasticity in the wall of the stomach will affect the volume of food the stomach can hold. Finally, the lining of the stomach becomes more susceptible to damage from the gastric juices that digest food.

The combination of these changes can cause multiple physical problems. It is more likely that older people will suffer from bloating and stomach pain. As the digestive system's ability to absorb nutrients declines, people may have insufficient levels of calcium, folic acid and iron. Finally, the weakening of the muscles in the digestive tract can lead to constipation and haemorrhoids.

Suffering from these unpleasant medical conditions is not inevitable. For many the normal process of digestion and nutrient absorption can continue through to extreme old age.

Business opportunities

- Food manufacturers could create new products designed to provide older people with the best nutritional mix. These could be created to satisfy the special demands by gender and age. There is no shortage of research that defines the food types and nutrition that older people should include in their diet.[45]

- Restaurants and supplement manufacturers could use the same nutritional data to influence the food and products they produce.
- Supermarkets and food manufacturers could extend the range of smaller or single-serve portions. Older people who live alone or who have reduced appetites often complain that it is difficult to buy pack sizes that are not intended for two people or a family. There is the opportunity to create meals that meet the nutritional requirements of older people and to package them so they can be used for several days or in smaller portions.
- Pharmaceutical and health food manufacturers have long been producing products for sufferers of gastrointestinal complaints such as heart burn, constipation, haemorrhoids and stomach pain. There is an opportunity to create derivatives of those products specifically designed for the older digestive system in a tablet, liquid or spray form, or some other age-friendly delivery mechanism.

Hair

The cosmetic appearance of the hair is considered one of the most powerful and earliest clues of the ageing process, both to ourselves and to others. The first grey hair or signs of baldness, along with the first signs of wrinkles, marks, for a lot of people, the point where ageing begins. This can trigger a lifelong demand for anti-ageing products.

Procter & Gamble conducted one of the largest known longitudinal studies to understand how hair changes with age.[46] The hair properties of over 200 women ranging in age from infants to 88 years were tracked over four to eight years. P&G's researchers proved that as women age, their hair changes in:

- Fibre diameter.
- Tensile properties.
- Surface texture.
- Hair greying.

A single hair may live for about four or five years and in that time can be subjected to enormous wear and tear, leaving it more prone to breakage and rougher appearance. Given that hair grows, on average, a little less than 1cm per month, hair that is 30cm in length has experienced almost three years'-worth of ultraviolet light, friction from brushing, heat from dryers and possible chemical exposure through colouring, perming or straightening.

Why hair turns grey is not well understood. Greying typically begins in Caucasians in the early 30s, and often ten years later in people with darker skin. Its onset is largely determined by genetics. It is often said that by 50 years of age, 50 per cent of people have 50 per cent grey hair.

Greying of the hair and its loss of texture can be distressing, but not to the same extent as hair loss, which has the scientific name 'alopecia'.

The androgenetic form of alopecia is a genetic condition that affects both men and women. As many as 70 per cent of males suffer from what is often called 'male-pattern baldness'.[47] It is believed that the hair follicles of these men produce smaller and less-visible hairs as a result of hormonal changes.

Women may also experience thinning hair as they age due to hormonal changes, vitamin deficiencies or genetic make-up.

Multi-billion-dollar businesses have been built around the conditions of ageing hair. These include products that change the hair's colour, texture and appearance, and products and services that claim to delay and reverse the loss of hair, that 'replant' the hair and use synthetic materials that look like hair.

Business opportunities

The market for products and services that delay and reverse the effects of ageing hair is arguably the most mature of all those associated with physiological ageing. Possibly, it shares this position with the market for anti-ageing skin products.

With companies the size of Unilever, L'Oreal and P&G involved in the market, it is unlikely that there are any radically new product opportunities that have not already been identified, if not yet converted into products.

The biggest opportunity for ageing-hair products does not come from new products with radically new formulations but in the way the product 'offerings' are presented to older people.

A cursory look at the websites of the major hair-treatment brands shows that they are attempting to present the products as age-neutral. In most instances, this is to be applauded, but there might be opportunities also to create age-silo products – products that are especially formulated for a 60 or 70 year old rather than being suitable for all ages.

Of course there are untold profits available for the company that can create a product that stops or reduces the balding process.

Skin

As with the hair, the skin's appearance is a visible indicator of a person's age, which explains why it receives so much attention from consumers who buy, and companies that supply, numerous types of anti-ageing skin products.

As the largest human organ, skin accounts for between 15 and 20 per cent of total body weight and is the barrier protecting the organs, skeleton, muscles and soft tissue from harmful agents in the environment. Its other role is to insulate and regulate the body's temperature and rate of water loss.

There are multiple ways that ageing changes the skin and the underlying tissues. A very simplified statement of these effects is that it becomes:

- Transparent.
- Fragile and easily bruised.
- Less firm and 'saggy'.
- Dry and irritable.
- Wrinkled.

Many of the changes to the skin are uncontrollable, but there are two major contributors to skin, texture and appearance, that we can influence.

Smokers tend to have more wrinkles than non-smokers of the same age and complexion.

The sun's ultraviolet light damages the skin, causing it to sag, stretch and lose its elasticity. Unprotected exposure to the sun is thought to contribute up to 90 per cent of the visible changes that are commonly attributed to ageing.[48]

Other than the cosmetic damage of sun exposure, it is thought that approximately 40 per cent of Americans who live to age 65 will have skin cancer at least once – often as a result of sun exposure.[49]

The rate and extent of skin ageing is very dependent on a person's race.

Business opportunities

Industry analysts project that the global market for anti-ageing products will grow to more than $300 billion by 2015, fuelled largely by older consumers.[50]

This includes all types of 'anti-ageing' products and services but a sizeable amount of this spend will be on products to maintain the appearance of the skin.

There are a host of potions, creams, remedies and treatments that purport to return the skin's appearance to a more youthful look. There are treatments that lighten the skin's colour that older people use to remove darker patches damaged by sunlight. There are also treatments to darken the skin that older people use to counter the naturally occurring greying of the skin.

Perhaps the most popular of the anti-ageing treatments is the wrinkle-smoothing injection of drugs such as Botox and Dysport, which inhibit the facial muscles from contracting so that the wrinkles relax and soften. This provides the temporary appearance of smoother skin.

Older peoples' desire to retain a youthful-looking facial appearance and complexion has already encouraged companies to produce a vast array of products and treatments ranging from simple lotions to invasive cosmetic surgery.

There should be scope for many more innovations in products that reduce the damage caused by excessive exposure to sunshine because it is such a contributor to the skin's ageing and is largely avoidable. For instance, products providing protection from UV rays such as light, multi-purpose UV shields, hats and visors, as well as clothing.

Like the products for ageing hair, most of the skincare products are intentionally positioned to appeal to all age groups. Shiseido, the Japanese supplier of the Elixir Prior range of skincare, has adopted a different approach and is targeting women over 60. According to Nikkei Net, in 2007 the Japanese beauty market for women over-60 was 19 per cent of the total and showed a remarkable 104 per cent growth over the previous year. Many older women, and some older men, would be better targeted using this age-silo approach.

Whatever marketing strategy is adopted, the demand for products and services that help older people delay the effects of ageing to their skin looks set to thrive.

Menopause

Menopause is a normal condition that all women experience as they age. The term 'menopause' refers to the woman's final menstrual period, marking the end of her reproductive period.

According to the USA National Institute on Aging, the average age when women have their last period is 51.[51] This can vary considerably and can happen during a woman's 30s or even her 60s. The symptoms of menopause can last for months or years.

The menopause occurs when levels of the female hormones oestrogen and progesterone fall and the body stops producing eggs. A result of these changing hormone levels is that women can experience vaginal and urinary problems, disturbed sleep patterns and changes to the sex drive – both positive and negative.

Perhaps the condition most commonly associated with menopause is the hot flash, also known as hot flushes, when the brain decides that the body is overheated and can feel most severe in the face and neck. These 'hot flashes' can also happen during sleep and become 'night sweats'. Menopause can also be accompanied by memory problems, mood swings and stiff and aching joints and muscles.

Business opportunities

Of particular importance to marketers are changes to a woman's temperature and body shape. These will influence the choice of clothing style, size and fabric. In addition to the sudden feelings of heat, the reduced production of oestrogen has a tendency to redistribute fat from the buttocks, hips and thighs to the waist or abdomen.

The daytime and nocturnal 'hot flashes' create the need for lightweight and absorbent clothing. This demand is being addressed by a few companies, such as Cool Jams and Dry Dreams. It doesn't appear that any of the very large clothing suppliers have attempted to target this product need.

Women are often in a difficult position when selecting treatments to alleviate the effects of the menopause.

In the USA it is thought that most gynaecologists still recommend that women use hormone replacement treatments (HRT), even though these have possible health risks.

Another option for women is to take a prescription or over-the-counter bio-identical hormone treatment, sometimes called 'natural hormone therapy'. There is mounting evidence that these drugs have the same safety concerns as hormone replacement therapy but may not have the same benefits. The only other option is the use of alternative therapies, such as black cohosh or red clover, even though there is little evidence that they are effective. In short, there is no effective, risk-free treatment.

Kimberly-Clarke has a line of products under its Poise brand of pads and liners, designed to help women manage the symptoms of menopause. The product initiative is supported by a communications campaign; 'The 2nd Talk' created to remove stigma associated with menopause by stimulating conversation among women. Other companies that create a safe and effective treatment for menopausal symptoms will have a massive market opportunity.

Sexual changes

Declining levels of testosterone are considered the main cause of erectile dysfunction (ED) in men as they age. The question of whether this decline is a natural result of ageing or something that happens more often with older men is actively debated.[52] It is known that heart disease, high blood pressure and diabetes are other causes of ED.

Whatever the reason, ED affects a lot of men. A study of men over 50 in the USA found that a third of the men reported ED in the past three months.[53]

Some age-related diseases, such as joint pain caused by arthritis, or other bone and muscle conditions, can make the physical act of sex uncomfortable for older people.

In addition to the physiological factors related to sex there is the much broader issue of how older peoples' relationships change and how this affects their sex life. These changes might be connected to the physical aspects of sex or be triggered by their children leaving home or the change in living pattern following retirement. It may simply be the realization that 'the clock is ticking' and if a relationship has been tolerable, but unsatisfactory, the time is running out to start a new one.

For whatever reason, the divorce rate among older people is rising. A study in the USA showed the divorce rate for adults aged 50 and older doubled between 1990 and 2009. Roughly a quarter of divorces in 2009 involved people aged 50 and older, compared with about one in ten in 1990.[54] This tendency for older people to divorce is the same in the UK, Japan and Australia.

Business opportunities

The increasing numbers of older people divorcing has resulted in a surge in demand for online dating services.

The over-55s is the fastest-growing age group using online dating websites in the USA, where they already account for approximately 25 per cent of customers.[55] The situation is similar in the UK, Australia and Canada.

The increasing number of technology-savvy older people looking to meet people will further expand the senior dating industry. It will also create a demand for physical rather than online places to meet, such as themed music bars, and other venues to socialize and have fun in familiar surroundings, for example, bars featuring classic 1970s and 1980s rock music – these have already started appearing in the USA.

Another implication of increasing numbers of single older people, looking for friendship and sex, is the demand it creates for products to counter the effects of ED. This demand is not just limited to the newly single, however, but also includes men who have been in long-term relationships.

Already the global annual sales of testosterone therapies are approximately US$1.2 billion. The USA alone accounts for $1 billion of sales and the market is growing at 20 per cent per year.[56]

Annual global sales of treatments for men with ED were over US$4.2 billion in 2010, including brands such as Viagra, Cialis and Levitra.[57]

Both these markets seem set to continue growing, fuelled by the increasing numbers of older men.

A worrying effect of the rising numbers of newly single older people is the rise in sexually transmitted diseases among the over-50s. It has recently been shown that this age group, in the USA, the UK and Canada, accounts for the greatest increase in people receiving treatment for these diseases.[58]

Older people may be in more danger of contracting sexually transmitted diseases than the young. Reasons include the lack of regular screening, postmenopausal vaginal changes and having less-effective immune systems. But the most likely reason is the lack of the habit of using condoms, during long periods when they were with a regular partner. The increasing demand and the need for 'education' of the older user would seem to offer many marketing opportunities for contraceptive suppliers.

The business implications of the ageing body

The natural process of ageing of the human body has already created significant markets, which have been discussed in this chapter. Pharmaceutical companies have begun to focus their attention on creating therapies to delay the onset and to treat the effects of the various forms of body ageing. The market for these products is evolving but its future looks guaranteed.

The effects of body ageing on other industries are less defined, but, through a better understanding of the physiology of older bodies, companies can create brands or transform existing ones to profit from this inevitable change in their customers.

The fitness industry looks poised to prosper from the increasing desire of older people to manage the natural declines in their flexibility and strength and to manage their weight and overall aerobic health. Food companies are equally well positioned to satisfy older people's need to eat the right types and quantities of food.

Regardless of the industry, companies that successfully exploit the physical changes to the bodies of millions of older people have an opportunity to generate new revenue and gain customer loyalty.

As important as the new business opportunities arising from body-ageing is the need to ensure that the customer touchpoints are adapted to account for these physical changes.

As has been discussed, marketing communications must allow for the reduced dexterity of the hands in manipulating sales collateral and the demands of using computers, tablets and mobile phones. All aspects of product design must be adapted to the difficulties older people have in bending, walking, holding, gripping and so on.

The example of the Depend brand of incontinence pads vividly demonstrates the need for companies to understand the emotional as well as the practical needs of adults who are coming to terms with the realities of growing old.

To create retail environments where older people want to, and can, shop will require a reappraisal of their design and the attitudes and skills of the staff. Throughout this chapter, the retail touchpoint has been a common thread where the ageing body will be challenged performing ordinary shopping tasks.

The matrix in Table 7.7 illustrates the span of marketing and operational activity that will be affected by the ageing of the body.

To help readers share the knowledge covered in this chapter a PowerPoint presentation summarizes why body ageing is so important and the scope of the actions that companies need to undertake (www.age-friendly.com/downloads/Chapter7.pdf).

Table 7.7 Marketing and operational activity that depends on the efficient working of the customer's body for success

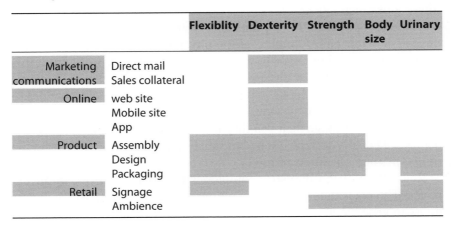

		Flexiblity	Dexterity	Strength	Body size	Urinary
Marketing communications	Direct mail Sales collateral		▓			
Online	web site Mobile site App		▓			
Product	Assembly Design Packaging	▓	▓	▓	▓	▓
Retail	Signage Ambience	▓		▓		▓

Chapter at a glance

→ The effects of ageing on the 11 organ systems and an estimated 100 trillion cells of the human body are as important as cognitive and sensory ageing, bringing about a transformation in the way people look, feel and behave. There are types of body ageing that both affect customer touchpoints and result in new business opportunities:

- Flexibility.
- Dexterity.
- Strength.
- Body mass.
- Urinary issues.

Some effects of body ageing do not affect touchpoints but do result in new business opportunities:

- Digestion.
- Hair.
- Skin.
- Menopause.
- Sexual changes.

→ Most older people suffer from one or more effects of body ageing. Osteoarthritis and other rheumatic conditions affecting flexibility are the most common causes of disability among US adults and have been for the past 15 years. Muscle loss begins at around the age of 40, with a 15 per cent loss in muscle strength per decade between the ages of 50 and 70. There are small gender and race differences in the extent and onset of body ageing but it is a universal condition that steadily increases with age.

→ Body ageing affects the touchpoints involved in marketing communications and the online channel. The most affected are products. The ageing consumer who is overweight will have to contend with a perfect storm of issues. The decline in flexibility and strength will be exacerbated if the customer is overweight.

→ Regardless of the industry, companies that successfully exploit the physical changes to the bodies of millions of older people have an opportunity to generate new revenue and gain customer loyalty. The natural process of ageing of the human body has already created significant markets. For example, pharmaceutical companies have begun to focus their attention on creating therapies to delay the onset and to treat the effects of the various forms of body ageing.

CHAPTER 8

The meaning of 'age-friendly'

We live in a world designed by younger people, for younger people. That's not a criticism; it's a fact. Our cities, our businesses, our pastimes have been shaped at a time when the median age was younger and life expectancy shorter.

The demographic changes that motivated the writing of this book have been predictable for decades, yet society and business have been slow to act. Perhaps the reason for this apathy is that there are no historical precedents on which to shape our response.

> *Population ageing is unprecedented, a process without parallel in the history of humanity.* *United Nations*[1]

Chapter 2 described the magnitude of change and breadth of effects that the rise in the older and fall in younger populations will have on our daily lives. Awareness and understanding the facts of ageing are relatively easy – what to do about it is much more difficult.

In response to this phenomenon and the social challenges it invokes, the World Health Organization (WHO) in 2006 assembled representatives from 33 cities in 22 countries to help determine the key elements of the urban environment that support active and healthy ageing. They did so because they recognized that the combination of increased longevity and decreased fertility meant that older people must extend their active role in society.

Urban environments must be made inclusive, accessible and encouraging of active ageing. The WHO's 'Age-Friendly Cities' programme now includes some of the world's leading cities, which are striving to create age-friendly urban environments. For example, British Columbia has been implementing its age-friendly initiative since 2007.[2]

Just as we need age-friendly cities for citizens, we need age-friendly medical services for patients, age-friendly workplaces for employees and, most relevant to the focus of this book, age-friendly businesses and brand interactions for consumers.

Consider a recent study in which 54 per cent of people in their 60s complained they could not read product labels even with their reading glasses[3] and a separate study that revealed nearly half of people over 65 struggle to remove lids or caps off products such as plastic milk bottles or jars because of the packaging.[4] More seriously, a UK government report estimated 67,000 people in the UK visit hospital casualty departments every year due to an accident involving food or drink packaging. It is reasonable to assume that a disproportionate number of victims were over 50.[5]

The business world needs to re-think its practices in the face of this ageing phenomenon so that people can continue to consume and enjoy products and services as they age. To achieve this, we need to recognize that the ageing of senses, bodies and minds of consumers may begin to restrict the use, enjoyment or relevance of products and services they have been accustomed to using all their adult lives – and, if they can, will probably continue to use until a very old age. In addition, we need to consider the requirements for products and services specifically designed to ameliorate the effects of ageing.

If companies are to adapt to the 'new normal' they have to change their marketing mindset – but where to begin?

In this chapter we will discuss the importance of universal design and the associated dangers if it is perceived as being the only component of age-friendliness. Using the example of Apple Inc., we will illustrate how age-friendly principles can be applied without compromising a sense of 'cool' and the profitable consequences of unintentionally appealing to older consumers by adopting age-neutral practices. We conclude by defining the criteria of an ideal process of age-friendly assessment and the challenges for companies wanting to apply the principles to their operations.

Universal design

The discipline of universal design gave birth to a maxim for our times.

> *Design for the young and you'll exclude the old. Design for the old and you'll include the young.*

With its roots dating back to the 1950s, universal design is not a new concept. It has evolved from the design considerations for people with disabilities to the broader concept of creating products with the minimum restrictions on their accessibility. Despite this history and increasing government legislation mandating accessibility standards, examples of universal design are rare.

However, there are some well-documented cases demonstrating that products can be designed to accommodate the changing physiology of consumers of all ages without diminishing their appeal. The fact that these examples are continually quoted indicates they are the exception rather than the rule.

It makes no business sense for companies to adversely affect their customer's experience of using their products because they are not prepared, or aware of the need, to adapt their design procedures.

Universal design tends to focus on the human factors of product design, only one of many elements in the consumer purchase cycle. To ensure they deliver a truly age-friendly experience, companies must view the entire customer journey through a prism of ageing, covering all the touchpoints and removing all the possible barriers. This was further discussed in Chapter 4.

Older people do not want to be constantly reminded of their ageing state, particularly when engaging in the pleasurable process of buying new products. Rather than appealing to customers on the basis of their age, companies need to minimize the barriers and inconveniences it causes and weave this seamlessly and naturally into the customer journey.

With the above thoughts in mind, the authors have defined the concept of age-friendliness as: 'an environment in which the unique physical needs of older people are satisfied in a way that is natural and beneficial for all ages'.

An age-friendly Apple?

The concern companies have about alienating their young customers if they create products that also appeal to older consumers is shown to be nonsense by the example of Apple Inc.

Anyone who has recently bought an Apple product will have experienced the benefits of an age-friendly customer journey. Whether the Apple brand is age-friendly by intention, or results from the company's legendary obsession with detail and design elegance, is uncertain. But, a quick inspection of the customer journey highlights some of the reasons for Apple's age-neutral status.

- Communications – the journey begins with advertising messages and images that often focus on the product and sometimes feature inter-generational imagery. No one is excluded. Classic age-neutral marketing. All communications are clear and simple, both visually and linguistically.

- Online – the website is easy to navigate and avoids the flaws evident in the websites of many technology companies, which are confused with technical jargon, animated menus and other functionality that distracts older eyes and minds.

- Retail – the Apple stores feature bright, spacious layouts with easy waist-height product access, labels clearly visible, minimal ambient noise levels and, in some stores, provision for seating.

- Product – at the product level, Apple's intuitive software interface is legendary for its simplicity and ease of use. The iPad and the accompanying host of apps have made the user interface even easier. So much so that during the American House of Representatives primary elections in November 2011, nursing home residents used the iPad to vote.[6]

- Sales support – as mentioned in Chapter 4 on touchpoints, older people are impatient with automated phone answering systems and much prefer to speak to real people. Despite some inevitable waiting time, Apple's call centre works well with knowledgeable, helpful humans who are patient and understanding.

Is there a commercial reward for Apple's age-friendliness?

Research conducted on the USA market declared that 46 per cent of Apple's customer-base was aged 55 and older – nearly double the share of average home PC users (25 per cent).[7] Apple responded that the share of its 55+ users was not as high as stated, but cleverly added 'We are thrilled that our products appeal to people of ages 1 to 100.'[8] Furthermore, Apple recently became the world's most valuable company.[9]

Apple's financial success cannot be solely attributed to its adoption of age-friendly principles. However, what cannot be disputed is that the company's inclusive approach and its obsession with simplicity and detail are critical ingredients of delivering age-friendliness. Apple has built a phenomenally successful business that appeals to children, young people, their parents and their grandparents. A truly age-neutral company.

Apple is not the only company that has achieved commercial success as a result of its ability to appeal to multiple generations of customers.

Table 8.1 details other examples of successful age-neutral products. In most cases, the success was an unintentional benefit rather than a planned outcome.

These examples provide convincing evidence that using age segmentation should no longer be the default marketing strategy.

Table 8.1 Companies and product types that have achieved success because of their age-neutral appeal

Initiative	Consequence
Facebook was designed for college students	Currently experiencing fastest growth among the over-55s
OXO Good Grips were designed for (older) people with arthritic hands	Universal design makes them popular with all ages. Sales have grown by 50% each year[10]
The **adventure holiday** category is assumed to be the exclusive domain of younger thrill-seekers	Older adventure-seekers have the money and time to spend, which has resulted in a proliferation of speciality travel services
iPad. Early adopters of new technology are assumed to be younger	22% of tablet users and 31% of e-readers in the USA are over 50[11]
Luxury cars Assumed to be purchased by business people	The average age of owners of leading luxury car marques in the USA is 55 years[12]

Age-neutral positioning with age-friendly customer experiences is the marketing approach best suited to the future demographic profile of customers.

Criteria for success

Where is the best place to start building a successful model to guide age-friendly thinking? Understand the strengths and limitations of existing techniques already being employed in different industries.

Mentioned earlier in this book, the WHO's Age-Friendly Cities programme is probably the most famous. However, its criteria for measurement cover just 84 items.[13] These are actually 'issues' to be assessed, rather than objective tests to be applied.

Other industries have established codes of age-friendliness and/or accessibility but these are very technical and too industry-specific for general application.

MIT's age-suit (see Chapter 4) is an excellent, although difficult to access, simulator that gives young designers a way of experiencing what it is like to be old.[14] The hope is that by improving the designers' empathy with the needs of older users, it improves the products they create. But this is a qualitative experiential process that does not provide any data that enables its success to be evaluated.

Mystery shoppers, in-depth interviews and usability testing all play an important but specific role in understanding how (older) consumers might respond to products, services and environments both online and offline. However, one of the great challenges when facing these techniques was expertly captured by Steve Jobs, who said, 'The job of a great company is to make a product that its customers would never have thought of, but which immediately makes them salivate.'

Because many older consumers are in a state of denial about their physiological ageing, they are uncomfortable commenting beyond the most obvious complaints linked to visibility and dexterity. Furthermore, they may simply be unaware of the creative possibilities that might improve their user experience. For example, in a client project to assess the most age-friendly remote TV control device, our AF Audit Tool revealed the need for auditory feedback on the control buttons, as is already common on mobile phone keypads. Yet in none of the 12 in-depth interviews with older users was this mentioned as a requirement because it was not a feature they had experienced.

Lord Kelvin was a UK physicist who at the turn of the twentieth century commented, 'If you cannot measure it, you cannot improve it.' So it follows that if we want to improve the state of age-friendliness, we need the tools to measure it. But we are dealing with a phenomenon that is 'unprecedented in the history of mankind' so not surprisingly we had to invent a solution.

The authors decided that to advance the concept of age-friendliness, a process must be created that satisfied seven key criteria.

1. Comprehensive

The process must encompass all of the major physiological effects of ageing and all the common touchpoints that might influence consumer behaviour. Even though some effects or touchpoints may not apply in certain cases, the concept must accommodate them. For example, the physiological effects of taste and smell would not be relevant for apparel or financial services but would be critical for food and cosmetics.

2. Flexible

As mentioned earlier in this chapter, there are a number of highly specialized systems for measuring age-friendliness and accessibility for particular industries and environments. It would be unrealistic to attempt to create a platform that would be relevant to all businesses to the same level of specific detail. However, to become a generally accepted measurement model the process must be flexible enough to apply to all types of products and services, regardless of the industry.

Furthermore, each business or brand might have unique characteristics that require measurement of specific physiological effects and touchpoints along their particular customer journey. The process must be flexible enough to incorporate these into different forms of communication channels, retail environments and so on.

3. Holistic

In Chapter 4 we discussed why it is crucial to investigate the entire customer journey when researching potential barriers to engaging and servicing older customers. Our experience suggests that the instinctive response is for companies to make superficial changes to individual elements of their marketing process. This is bound to lead to failure.

Regardless of which department leads an age-friendly initiative, unless all these elements are interrogated and measured then the age-friendliness of the organization will be only as good as the weakest link.

To help overcome this hazard of organizational silos, the tool must be capable of, indeed it must encourage, a holistic evaluation of all the touchpoints along the entire customer journey.

4. Consistent

Is the lighting insufficient? Is the ambient noise too loud? Are the shelves too high? These are just a few of the kinds of issues that need to be considered along the journey. But to ensure consistent and accurate evaluation over time and across locations, subjectivity has to be minimized in favour of objective measures. For example, lumens levels used to measure lighting, decibel levels to measure ambient noise and distance to measure shelf height and distance traversed.

Using absolute rather than subjective measures will reduce the chance of human error and lead to more consistent results regardless of where the tests are being undertaken or by whom.

5. Comparable

However the tests are conducted, they must produce a dataset that enables the changes in age-friendliness to be compared over time, and between customer journeys in different geographies. The changes in age-friendliness also need to be compared with the relative age-friendliness of the organization's competitors.

6. Affordable

If age-friendliness is to become a universally adopted management metric then the process of its measurement must be accessible on a large scale. This applies both to the cost of conducting the tests and to the prerequisite skills to perform them competently and accurately.

In some cases it may be preferable or even critical to conduct laboratory or controlled tests on certain aspects of the journey, such as retail store layouts, and to measure the force required to open and close packaging. Such tests could be expensive and require specialist skills.

The core methodology must provide an affordable foundation that will highlight the need for these specialist tests and studies.

7. Actionable

Medical science has provided numerous insights into the effect of ageing on human physiology but few ways of translating this knowledge into information that enables business decisions to be made.

The critical requirement for any evaluation system, then, is to distil the research and science into a process that creates outputs that can be understood and acted on by business leaders, without the need for a doctorate in gerontology.

In summary, there is a need for a tool that enables individuals with limited training to conduct assessments of age-friendliness that result in an accurate, clear, actionable roadmap to improve the appeal of a brand or business to its older customers.

Using these criteria, how do the current methods of assessment rate?

The matrix in Table 8.2 assesses the current techniques that could be used to measure age-friendliness against the above criteria.

There are a number of useful tools that can help businesses understand the possible barriers between them and their older customers, but none satisfies all of the criteria for success.

Ideally, while fulfilling its principal task of measuring age-friendliness the evaluation process could also serve to elevate general awareness of the age-friendly imperative. This would be similar to how 'green audits' have both improved the impact that companies have on the environment and raised awareness of the sustainability issue.

Over time and through its ubiquitous application, through various segments of business and government, the concept of age-friendliness could make the world a better place for our ageing populations as well as creating business opportunities.

Table 8.2   The suitability of the current techniques that could be used to measure age-friendliness, assessed against the above criteria

	Comprehensive	Relevant	Holistic	Consistent	Comparable	Affordable
WHO Age-Friendly Cities			✓			✓
Industry standards	✓		✓			✓
MIT age-suit		✓				
Mystery shoppers		✓		✓	✓	
Usabilty tests		✓			✓	

Why are companies slow to embrace age-friendliness?

If the business opportunities associated with population ageing are so obvious and vast, why then are companies slow to respond?

As already mentioned, the lack of precedent is an excellent excuse for inaction. Many companies simply don't know where to begin. There doesn't appear to be any penalty to adopting a 'wait and see' approach to see how their industry as a whole and their direct competitors respond.

In the meantime, there is no shortage of other issues demanding management attention. If the company is based in Europe or the USA then how to survive the recession is at the top of the list. Companies in Asia Pacific have the opposite set of 'problems': how to cope with rapid growth.

There are many other reasons why companies have been slow to react. These are the five most common excuses.

1.   The attraction of youth
The natural tendency for us all is to be attracted by things youthful.

Ask a 30-something brand manager or advertising executive whether they would prefer to work on a campaign targeted at the young or one needing to be inclusive of the older consumer. Young will invariably beat old.

It is much easier for a younger person to conceptualize the motivations and emotions of their peer group than to 'think old' like their parents and grandparents. Everybody has experienced the younger phases in life but no one has experience of what it is like to be older. We have to deduce, often inaccurately, based on observations of our parents and relatives.

Regrettably, there have been many advertising campaigns based on the creative director's observations of their mum and dad.

From an organizational point of view, the corporate imperative must be to overcome institutionalized ageist prejudices – notions that are embedded in many corporate cultures.

2.   A perception that the customers are 'not that old'

Remarkably, many companies don't actually know the overall demographic composition of their customer base. Sometimes, their decisions are based on instincts that may be hopelessly wrong. Our experience is that companies often believe their customers are younger than is the case.

Even if the median customer age is not old, on careful examination there may be high-density areas of older people. As was discussed in Chapter 2, the population in urban areas is normally younger than in smaller towns and rural districts.

Often the variation in population age is greater within a country than it is between countries.

3.   Higher priorities

Just as the hole in the ozone layer took decades and global government pressure to coax companies into action, an ageing customer base is rarely one of the most pressing priorities. Particularly in a world of short-tenure executives it is easy to sideline the issue for their successor to action. Consequently, customer ageing often gets displaced by sexier projects and ones that are thought more likely to generate immediate results.

Demographic change is not stopping or slowing; it is accelerating. Companies deciding to grasp the opportunities it creates will achieve first-mover advantage and the significant cost and competitive benefits that accrue.

Among the clients the authors have worked with, most prefer to keep their age-friendly initiatives confidential because they know the power of being first to act. Transforming an organization's customer journey takes time and companies don't want to reveal their strategy until they have tangible proof of its success.

4.   A lack of ownership

As mentioned repeatedly throughout this book, transforming a business to be age-friendly is a company-wide challenge. If it is initiated by an individual department, it may be difficult to enlist the active co-operation of all the necessary parties. Without top management support and encouragement, endeavours to anticipate the opportunities result-ing from customer ageing may remain limited to a single department.

Just like the corporate challenges of process re-engineering, environmental sustainability and social responsibility, the initiative must be companywide and therefore must be driven by top management with a senior-level champion empowered to ensure inter-department compliance.

5. A lack of resident, requisite skills

Few companies believe they have the staff with the requisite skill-set to understand and act on the implications of population change. This might be true but it is something that could, and most certainly should, be rectified considering it is one of the greatest challenges the developed economies face.

Companies could do a lot worse than look within their swelling ranks of ageing executives and assemble a competent team with the requisite skills to lead this challenge.

Adopting inclusive, age-friendly strategies is simple common sense in a world that is ageing, not only for companies to retain their growing age-ing customer base by removing possible barriers throughout the customer experience but as a strategic weapon to attract customers from competi-tors slow to make the inevitable changes.

The changes may be grand, involving product or retail store design, or subtle, but changes must almost certainly be made. The questions are where and how to begin.

We need a standard process of assessment that provides clear guidance on what needs to be done. In the next chapter, we will propose a solution.

Process aside, to ensure the successful transformation of a business to become truly age-friendly, the corporate mindset will need changing and must become aligned across all departments.

Chapter at a glance

→ The demographic changes the world is now witnessing have been predictable for decades, yet society and business have been slow to act. We continue to live in a world designed by younger people, for younger people. That's not a criticism; it's a fact.

→ Just as we need age-friendly cities, we need age-friendly medical serv-ices for patients, age-friendly workplaces for employees and age-friendly businesses and brand interactions for consumers. The business world needs to re-think its practices in the face of the ageing phenomenon so that people can continue to consume and enjoy products and services as they age.

→ Companies need to recognize that the ageing of senses, bodies and minds of consumers may begin to restrict the use, enjoyment or relevance of products and services they have been accustomed to using all their adult lives – and, if they can, will probably continue to use until a very old age. In addition, we need to consider the requirements for products and services specifically designed to ameliorate the effects of ageing.

→ The concern companies have about alienating their young customers if they create products that also appeal to older consumers is shown to be nonsense by the example of Apple Inc. Age-friendly principles can be applied without compromising a sense of 'cool'. Companies that segment customer on the basis of age risk excluding the large and lucrative market of ageing consumers.

→ To advance the concept of age-friendliness, an evaluation system must satisfy seven key criteria; Comprehensive, Flexible, Holistic, Consistent, Comparable, Affordable and Actionable. There are a number of useful tools that can help businesses understand the possible barriers between them and their older customers, but none satisfies all of the criteria for success.

CHAPTER 9

Evaluating age-friendliness

The previous chapter established the need for companies to adopt age-friendly practices that will help them satisfy the needs of older customers. This chapter explains how they can start.

The immediate barrier that companies face when trying to formulate their age-friendly strategy is the lack of business metrics to drive their decisions.

First, companies require a way to measure their existing age-friendliness and that of their competitors. Second, the output from research must be a simple and actionable roadmap with clear-cut actions.

What is the best way of feeding the vast amount of complex research about physical ageing into a methodology that provides practical guidance to business leaders who are unlikely to have doctorates in gerontology?

This chapter begins by describing a simple test to assess a business's age-friendliness. Then it will introduce and explain a tool that the authors created: the AF (Age-Friendly) Audit toolset.

Is your company age-friendly?

Throughout this book we have emphasized the importance of assessing the entire customer journey to determine whether the brand experience is age-friendly.

Answering the six questions in Table 9.1 gives an indication of whether a company is operating in an age-friendly way.

Score each of the following questions 1, 2 or 3, where 1 = never and 3 = always, and add the total.

You can also do this test online at www.age-friendly.com/quickcheck.

These very basic questions provide an indication of the consideration given to the experience of older customers throughout the purchase journey.

Table 9.1 A simple test to determine a company's age-friendliness

Age-friendly quick-check	Score 1 = never 2 = seldom 3 = always
1 We develop advertising that uses creative techniques that we have tested with older customers.	
2 We include the needs and behaviours of older people in our social networking strategy.	
3 We regularly test our website to ensure it provides an online experience that is easy for older people to navigate and understand.	
4 The particular needs of our older customers are reflected in our retail store presence, product placement and ambience and the training of our customer contact staff.	
5 We design products and services that include the particular needs of older people without overtly referencing age.	
6 We ensure that sales and support call centres and their staff are designed to respond to the needs, concerns and frustrations of older customers.	
Your total score =	
Total possible =	18

Here's what your score means

Score = >15

Good job! You seem to understand the impact of physiological ageing, but don't be complacent; the real test is to understand if your older customers agree with your opinion.

Score = 10–14

Trouble looms. Although you seem to have some understanding of the impact of physiological ageing on older customers, you are at risk of losing customers to more age-friendly competitors. Would alienating your older customers be detrimental to your business? If so, you should conduct a more thorough assessment of age-friendliness and take corrective action.

Score = <9

Serious risk. You may be upsetting older customers to the point where they are leaving for more age-friendly competitors. If you are not monitoring the business your older customers contribute, you should. You urgently need to reassess your business practices and take corrective action to make the customer experience age-friendly.

As explained in Chapter 8, if a process is to provide a comprehensive, accurate and practical evaluation of age-friendliness it must meet seven criteria:

1. Comprehensive – it must reflect all of the major physiological effects of ageing and all the common touchpoints that might influence consumer behaviour.
2. Flexible – it must be applicable to all types of products and services, regardless of the industry.
3. Holistic – it must be capable of evaluating all touchpoints along the entire customer journey.
4. Consistent – it must minimize subjectivity and apply objective measures wherever possible.
5. Comparable – it must employ a standard scoring method that will enable the data to be combined, analysed and compared.
6. Affordable – it must be accessible to companies of all sizes and applied by researchers on a large scale without the need for onerous specialist training.
7. Actionable – it must distil the research and science into a process that will generate metrics that are practical and actionable by business leaders.

The quick checklist of questions might give a simple insight into a company's age-friendliness but it fails to satisfy most of these criteria, as do most of the current forms of evaluation such as MIT's age-suit, mystery shopping, usability studies and so on.

In 2010, the authors concluded that there were no tools that satisfied all the criteria and decided to create one that did – the AF Audit toolset. The rest of this chapter describes the development and refinement of a process that delivers actionable results for any type of business and that has been used to evaluate over 50 customer journeys.

The AF model

The essence of an age-friendly audit is simple.

The different variants of the customer journey are divided into a sequence of unique touchpoints. Then, each touchpoint is evaluated to understand how it might be affected by the customer's sensory, physical and cognitive ageing.

AGE-FRIENDLY

The authors began by defining the set of physiological effects that need to be considered. A detailed explanation of these is provided in Chapters 5, 6 and 7. Medical doctors and gerontologists could probably identify many more effects of ageing but we were anxious to use only those that affected consumer behaviour and that could be resolved by practical business remedies.

The model for understanding customer experiences was described in Chapter 4 and involves grouping the experiences into five areas of business. These 'CORPS' experiences were defined as:

Communications – all forms of marketing communications, including advertising, PR, sponsorship, events, etc.
Online – the experience of using search engines, the brand and corporate website and supporting help and e-commerce microsites.
Retail – all aspects of the physical retail shopping experience.
Product – preparing to use and using the product and all of the supporting materials, including packaging.
Sales support – the physical aspects of selling and supporting the product, including face-to-face and phone communications.

Before these customer experiences can be measured, they need to be broken down into their constituent parts.

The customer experience hierarchy

The authors exploded the five CORPS experiences into the next level of detail – the sub-experience. This is the point at which the experience connects with the customer. For example, the packaging is a sub-experience of the product experience.

However, to measure age-friendliness it is necessary to expand the sub-experience into the next level of granularity, the touchpoint.

Table 9.2 shows how the product 'experience' is divided into a hierarchy of factors. At the touchpoint level, it is possible to incorporate the physiological effects of ageing.

Table 9.2 Example showing how the graphics touchpoint is linked to the product factor in the CORPS experiences

Experience categories of the customer journey	Sub-experience intersection between the business and the consumer	Touchpoint the specific point being measured
• Communications • Online • Retail • **Product** • Support		
	• Assembly • Design • **Packaging** • Pricing • Warrant	
		1. **Graphics** 2. Handling and carrying 3. Information 4. Opening and closing 5. Text

The authors discovered that it was necessary to expand the CORPS customer experiences to over 200 touchpoints to achieve the level of granularity needed to construct an age-friendliness model that satisfied all of the seven evaluation criteria.

It requires only a few applications of the model to real-life situations to reveal that the relationship between companies and their customers invariably creates unique touchpoints that have to be measured. The rule for measuring an additional touchpoint was that it would be included if it could result in a significant impediment to the customer's experience and could be solved by a practical business remedy.

To accommodate this requirement, the AF Audit toolset had to be capable of accommodating customer-specific changes and inclusions.

Tracing the AF customer journey

Having defined the customer touchpoints and the physiological effects of ageing, the two had to be combined into a single model.

To achieve this, the authors considered each of the 200 touchpoints and determined the physiological effect(s) of ageing that were dependent on that touchpoint for an acceptable customer experience.

Table 9.3 Hierarchy of customer experiences and the effect of ageing that could impair the quality of experience

CORPS experience	Sub-experience	Touchpoint	Associated effect of ageing
Communications	Direct mail	Physical format	Dexterity
Communications	Advertising creative	Colours	Eyesight (clarity)
Product	Assembly	Access	Flexibility
Online	Website	Comparison	Cognitive (complexity)

Table 9.3 shows how the hierarchy of the customer experience is connected to the factor of ageing that could impair its quality.

Many of the touchpoints involve multiple effects of ageing. For example, among the many touchpoints involved in a website, the quality and quantity of animation can create major problems for older people. Animated images may actually improve the functionality of the site or, on the contrary, may distract to the point that they make the experience more complex, difficult and annoying. This problem arises because of cognitive ageing.

Animated menus may aid operation of the website or, as is often the case, require excellent pointer–eye coordination that frustrates website navigation for older users. The loss of dexterity causes this problem.

There are touchpoints that involve two of more physical effects of ageing. Examples of these are shown in Table 9.4.

Many of the relationships between touchpoints and ageing seem to be obvious and easy to define. Some are, but many are much more complicated than they appear on first inspection.

Most people are aware of the connection between age and font size but fewer people understand the problems caused by insufficient illumination. This is an issue that most designers of lifts appear to have overlooked. Trying to read the floor buttons in the darkened space within a lift is a common problem that older people encounter.

Unlike the tangible effects of ageing, such as eyesight, hearing and dexterity, some are much harder to observe but are associated with multiple touchpoints. The different types of cognitive ageing affect all of the CORPS experiences.

The process of associating the ageing effects with each touchpoint is not simple but it forms the foundation of any tool to evaluate age-friendliness. This was one of the most challenging tasks in constructing the AF Audit toolset.

Table 9.4   Examples of touchpoints involving multiple effects of ageing

Consumer touchpoint	Physical effect
Reading a newspaper advertisement	Eyesight (clarity) *and* Comprehension
Navigating a website	Dexterity *and* Complexity
Assembling a product for use	Strength *and* Complexity *and* Eyesight (clarity)
Telephone call to a service representative after buying a product	Hearing (clarity) *and* Hearing (volume) *and* Comprehension *and* Complexity

Measurement and scoring

The specification of a touchpoint and its associated ageing effect is of little use unless there is a way of quantifying how effectively it has been implemented to overcome the problems older consumers might encounter.

To be of use, each touchpoint must have a measureable and comparable metric.

The difficulty is that many of the touchpoints have no established conventions of measurement. These are some examples of the issues the authors encountered and the measurement solutions that resulted:

Shelf height – what is the appropriate product shelf height in a retail store? As people's heights differ by age group and by geographic region, it is necessary to score on the basis of the average height for males and females in the particular country in which the audit is being conducted.

Lighting – what is the ideal lighting level in a retail store? Available research provides guidance on suitable lumen levels. Based on these metrics we determined the ideal lumen readings for packages, store shelf labels and signs taken at specific distances.

Colour contrast – at what point does low colour contrast render a printed piece of marketing collateral or a website difficult to read? To determine the minimum acceptable level of contrast between colours we used the Luminosity Contrast Ratio algorithm, suggested by the World Wide Web Consortium[1] (W3C).

Seating – does the store provide seating that is suitable for older people? Seats that are too low can cause difficulties in sitting and in raising the body. The ideal height is when the thighs are parallel to the ground or higher than the knees – this was calculated using average height data for each country. Equally important, seating needs to have arms for leverage.

Web search – how easy is it to find information about a company's product online using a search engine? Since Google accounts for over 80 per cent of global web searches, it is used for the test. For Chinese-speaking countries, Baidu would also be used. As Google's search page layout becomes more complex, it can be confusing (and annoying) for older people to search for a specific company or product. Often the required URL is preceded by numerous other references. The authors determined that ideally the required listing should appear as a paid ad or among the top five organic URLs.

Setting such criteria enables auditors (people conducting the assessments) to score more accurately and their results to be more comparable.

As is evident from the above examples, there are cases in which established industry conventions can be adopted or adapted, such as in determining colour contrast and acceptable lighting levels. Where no such conventions existed, the authors created them.

Conducting a comprehensive audit of age-friendliness requires the rigorous application of a sequence of these types of questions and tests for all of the touchpoints associated with the customer journey.

Furthermore, to derive metrics from the process, each touchpoint needs to be 'scored' and, for this purpose, the authors used the established 'one-to-five' scoring method. On the AF Audit scale, a score of '1' means 'unacceptable' whereas '5' means 'perfectly age-friendly'. On this basis, a score of 4 or above qualifies as 'age-friendly'.

To ensure consistency in the scoring it is necessary to have clear guidelines for the measurement of each touchpoint. These were developed for AF Audit questions and are illustrated in Table 9.5.

These examples show how touchpoints are defined to the auditor – first by explaining the issue being examined, then by providing specific guidance for how the touchpoint should be measured.

Table 9.5 Examples of the questions that measure the effectiveness of the touchpoint for the older person

Touchpoint	Issue	Question/test
Printed advertising creative	How easy is it to read the text used in the printed advertising?	Use a micrometer to measure point size of body text. 10-point type is considered the minimum and scores 3. Because serif typefaces are known to be more difficult to read, they are deducted a point.
Website language – use of jargon	Does the site use language or expressions that make it difficult to understand?	If the website employs clear language appropriate for all ages it is scored 5. However, if the site uses jargon, complex technical language and overtly youth-oriented expressions it achieves the lowest ranking of 1.
Retail ambience – lighting	Is the light in the store sufficient for you to easily see the product on display and the packaging?	Using a light meter, measure the lumen reading at a distance of 2 metres. >800 = 5 <750 = 4 <700 = 3 <650 = 2 <600 = 1
Retail ambience – visual	Does the visual noise of the store make the shopping experience difficult and confusing?	A disciplined and orderly display that makes the merchandise easy to see and select scores 5. But cluttered and disorderly displays that make the shopping experience confusing or difficult to navigate are scored 1.

Through the procedure outlined above, it is possible to match the relevant physiological effects of ageing to each touchpoint and then to apply a consistent scoring technique to ensure consistency and reliability of the resulting data.

Later in this chapter we will explain how smartphone app technology helps in undertaking many of the tests.

Not all touchpoints can be linked to a specific physiological effect. For example, there are no quantifiable factors for testing a product design to ascertain whether it reduces the chance of error or accident, or for evaluating the sales support personnel for their knowledge about the product. Both these instances are relevant and important to age-friendliness.

We call such cases 'sensory independent' – touchpoints that are independent of specific physiological effects. Roughly one-third of all questions in the AF Audit are 'sensory independent'.

Customizing the audit

Having created the questions to evaluate each of the touchpoints there were three issues that remained to be solved before the AF Audit questions were complete. How could the questions be adapted to account for the following?

1. Issues that were specific to a company, such as the need to focus on a particular *stock-keeping unit* (SKU) in a particular retail store type or location? A specific piece of communication or website? A specific phone helpline?
2. The particular company's industry or sector. For example, the different emphasis and importance of the touchpoints of a fast-moving consumer goods business compared with a financial services company.
3. Different ages of 'older' people. For example, if the customers were exclusively aged 50–60 the importance of the effects of ageing would be different from if they were over 75 years old.

Ultimately, the system had to be capable of handling this level of sophistication and flexibility, yet remain readily usable by auditors without the need for technical training.

The best, and possibly only, solution to these problems was to employ the Cloud and tablet computing technology.

The AF technology platform

The complexity of the AF Audit model could not be implemented using conventional techniques such as paper checklists and spreadsheets. There were too many questions that were regularly being edited, the total volume of data was too great and there was too much scope for the introduction of human error.

These demands for a more sophisticated mode of processing were apparent when conducting a single audit but were multiplied tenfold when multiple auditors conducted audits simultaneously in multiple locations and countries.

There was a need for a more sophisticated mode of data collection and processing.

The computing architecture that was selected to implement the AF Tool had two components: a processing 'engine' to manage the administration functions and an iPad app that enabled auditors to collect the touchpoint data.

The AF Engine

The processing engine that manages the AF Tool is a cloud-based web application that is:

- Flexible, enabling audits to be customized for individual company and industry requirements.
- Scalable, providing central management of potentially hundreds of simultaneous audits.
- Complex, enabling data analysis and comparison across industries, companies, their subsidiaries and competitors.
- Interactive, allowing real-time monitoring of all the audits.
- Secure, providing multiple levels of user privileges and the firewalls to protect company confidential data.

The AF Engine is used to set up and customize an audit to reflect the specific needs of a company and industry.

Figure 9.1 shows the question-management screen of the AF Engine. This shows how the multiple levels of customer experience, which were discussed earlier in the chapter, are implemented in the computer model.

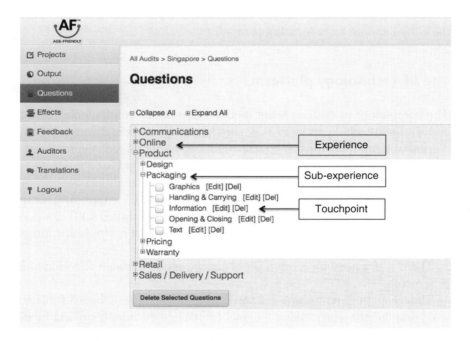

Figure 9.1   The AF Engine screen that is used to manage customer experiences

From this screen, unnecessary questions are removed and company-specific images and links to their advertising, product and website are added, along with imagery and information about the retail channels to be assessed.

During the initial set-up of an audit the AF Engine prompts the user to edit those questions that need to be customized to reflect the peculiarities of the company and the industry.

Once the auditors have evaluated the age-friendliness of a customer journey and the data has been uploaded the AF Engine is used to manage the input.

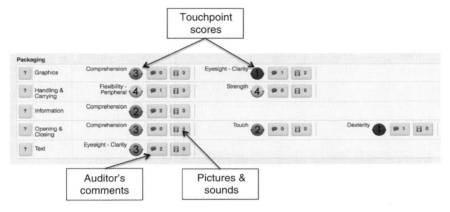

Figure 9.2   The AF Engine input-management screen

Figure 9.2 shows the AF Engine screen where scores, image files and contextual comments can be reviewed and edited.

Once the audit inputs have been received and project editing done, the AF Engine is used for analysing and graphing the information and generating outputs in chart and data format. The charting functionality is discussed later in the chapter.

This is a very short description of what is a complex module of software. There is a video at www.age-friendly.com/videos/AF_engine that gives a more detailed explanation of the tool.

The AF iPad app

A customer journey might include over 200 touchpoints that have to be evaluated. The auditor, the person undertaking the evaluation, needs a simple and portable way of:

- Reading the question explaining what needs to be measured.
- Recording their score and any associated comments.

- Recording images and sounds to substantiate their scores.
- Instantly transmitting their input for analysis.

The Apple iPad was the ideal technology platform to achieve these requirements.

The AF iPad application is a custom-built, licence-only tool (not available on iTunes) containing the specific audit parameters and questions defined via the AF Engine. Auditors are guided through questions and tests for each touchpoint. Figure 9.3 shows a screen image of the functionality to complete a touchpoint test.

The Apple iPad enables the capture of images and sound recordings, both of which are needed to conduct a comprehensive audit.

The ability to record images is needed when evaluating the retail environments, pack labels, displays and other visual references to explain why scores were applied and to add context and specific recommendations on how the touchpoint's age-friendliness can be improved.

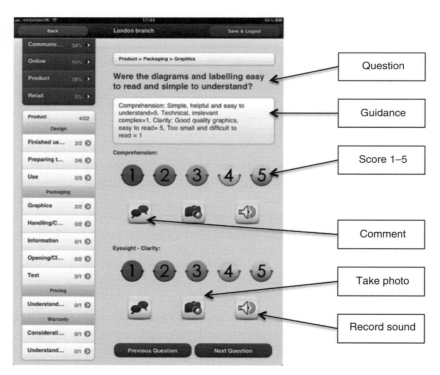

Figure 9.3 The AF iPad app screen that is used to test a touchpoint

Sounds files are often recorded in the process of measuring ambient noise levels and to demonstrate other audio issues identified during the assessment. All of this multimedia data and auditor comments can be reviewed using the AF Engine, as was shown in Figure 9.2.

The importance of precision, when evaluating touchpoints, was discussed in the 'Measurement and scoring' section of this chapter. Apple's iPad offers numerous third-party apps that provide precise measurements of environmental factors. These are robust commercial-quality products and are inexpensive.

The third-party applications that are currently used by the AF iPad app are detailed in Table 9.6. Because there are so many new iPad apps being created, this list will undoubtedly grow.

The final reason the iPad was used as the platform for data collection was its ability to instantly transmit and connect with the AP Engine and upload the auditor's scores, comments and multimedia files.

This is a very short description of the AF iPad app. There is a video at www.age-friendly.com/videos/AF_app that gives a more detailed explanation.

Analysing the results

Once the touchpoint audit is complete, the AF Engine analyses the data and presents results. There are numerous ways this analysis needs to be done. For example, comparing audits for the same company across different locations; how the touchpoint scores have changed over time and compared with audits of competitors' age-friendliness.

Table 9.6 The third-party apps that are currently being used by the AF iPad app

Tool	Measure	Example of use
Micrometer	Measurements as small as I point to as large as the iPad screen	Font sizes on printed or digital matter, including pack labels and signs. Package closures
Pedometer	To measure distances	Distances people are expected to walk – for instance, from car park to retail store
Audio meter	To measure ambient noise levels	Background music levels in a retail or other service environment
Light meter	To measure lighting	Overall lighting levels plus reflected light from store labels and signs

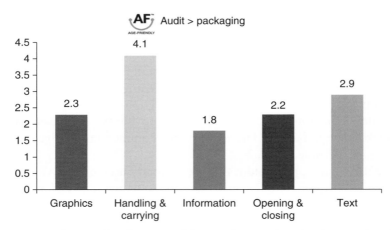

Figure 9.4 The graphical scores of the product and packaging section from auditing a yogurt container

Figure 9.4 illustrates the detail of the output that is required to conduct a thorough age-friendly audit and shows the scores for each touchpoint from the 'product – packaging' experiences of using a container of yogurt.

The chart shows that poor graphics, information and opening & closing mechanism would all create difficulties for the older consumer.

These scores were given because of poor colour contrast on the label (Score = 2), confusing technical information in the instructions (Score = 2) and a difficult-to-grasp opener (Score = 2).

The handling and carrying element of the packaging was good (Score = 4) because consideration had been given to making the bulk-pack easy to grasp. The size and colour contrast of the text was satisfactory (Score = 3).

The touchpoint auditing requirements of multinational companies can be complex. These are the requirements of one of our clients:

- Multiple audits of the same customer journey in different retail environments.
- Audits in different countries for the same customer journey to buy the same product.
- Comparison of the quality of the journey with the primary competitors in different countries.
- Measurement of how the quality of customer experience had changed from the previous audit.

Figure 9.5 illustrates this complexity, showing the summary output of an audit conducted for the same product in Singapore and the UK.

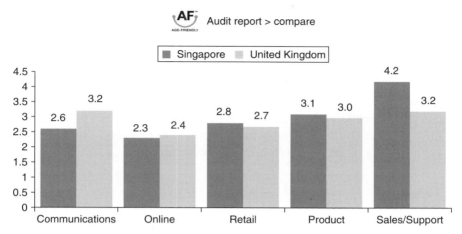

Figure 9.5 Comparing scores of the CORPS experiences for an AF Audit conducted in Singapore and the UK

What is evident from this output is that the online experience in both locations was not age-friendly (2.3/2.4). The only CORPS experience that scored as being age-friendly was the after-sales support in Singapore (Score = 4.2).

Interestingly, although the retail experience is generally something that manufacturers don't control, in this example it scored higher, in both countries, than some of the more controllable aspects of the brand.

In the future, as our database of touchpoint audits grows, it will be possible for companies to see how their performance compares with the norms in their industry. This will provide management with further metrics to help decide their investment priorities.

Although the numeric scores and resulting data are powerful, richness of information is also derived from the comments, photos and sound files captured by the auditor during the process.

This helps management understand why certain elements, particularly negative ones, were scored in a particular way.

Examples from actual audits

How is it possible that one accountant can uncover flaws among the multitude of numbers in a company's accounts or for a pilot to complete all of the flight checks before an aircraft flies? The answer, of course, is that both follow disciplined checklists in a consistent, replicable way, based on an accumulated body of knowledge.

The same applies to the AF Audit. A forensic interrogation of the customer experience, through the prism of physiological ageing, allows the auditor to identify possible flaws in the brand experience for older customers. Equally important, the process may reveal issues that management can transform into competitive business advantages. The following are examples of the types of issues the audit can reveal.

TV controller

The AF Audit toolset was used to assess the usability of the remote controller for a cable TV service. The audit revealed that the device did not generate any audio feedback when the control buttons were depressed. Audio feedback, as with tactile and visual feedback, provides important reassurance to older users. Although it is currently absent from most TV remote devices, this feature is common on mobile phones.

Unlike TV controllers being sold in other geographies, the one being evaluated could not be adapted to help people with touch and flexibility problems. The size of the keys was on the threshold of acceptability. In total, the audit identified five significant problems with the device. Similar numbers of issues were found in the other CORPS experiences.

Hotel

Applying the audit for a multinational hotel company identified numerous touchpoints that were below the satisfactory score:

- Different factors of the lighting and signage scored poorly.
- The reception area provided insufficient seating.
- The illumination of the lift controls was so bad that even young people found them difficult to see.
- There were numerous issues with navigation and colours used on the website.
- The phone handset in the room was totally unsuitable for older people.
- There was no anti-slip surface on the wet-floor in the bathroom and there were no rails or handles to steady somebody with poor balance.

Needless to say, it was impossible to read the shampoo, conditioner and body lotion labels without wearing glasses.

The most important lesson to be taken from this example is that the hotel had just been redecorated and refurbished. It would have been possible to avoid all of the problems that the audit identified, without spending any additional money, just by doing things differently and taking account of age-friendliness.

Bank branch

The audit revealed that the area reserved for premium customers was uncomfortably cold. As discussed in Chapter 7, older people are more sensitive to cold temperatures and this environment was well below the comfort threshold of 23 degrees.

Furthermore, the low level of illumination made reading and writing difficult. The ambient music was clearly designed for younger ears, both in style and volume. As cognitive filtering becomes more difficult with age, this music created a distraction and made the conversation with the bank representative more difficult than it should be.

Added to all this, the youth of the bank representatives and their manner of speaking could easily create a barrier between them and their older customer.

Why these audit results are particularly important is that over the course of a day approximately 70 per cent of the people using the premium area of the branch were at least 50 years old and probably half were over 60 years.

Fast moving consumer goods product

The package closure had not evolved since the product was first launched. Although the brand remains popular among older adults, it retains a decades-old package design involving a small foil tab. Both dexterity and strength of ageing fingers were challenged in the basic task of opening this product.

The colour contrast on the packaging was just at the threshold of acceptability but for a customer aged 75-plus it would create problems.

It was very difficult to identify the salt and sugar contents of the product and there was no reference made to recommended daily consumption. In most geographies, this information is becoming increasingly important to healthiness-conscious older people.

It takes one auditor roughly three to four days to evaluate all of the touch-points along a customer journey. The exact time is totally dependent on the complexity of the journey.

The time and effort needed to conduct the complete age-friendliness audit depends on the number of audits, the degree of customization, the complexity of the analysis and the number of geographies being studied.

Before embarking on an age-friendliness project, we always stress that the audit is just the beginning. The challenge for management is what to do with the results.

The results of an AF Audit are potentially transformational. Insights and implications revealed across the consumer journey are likely to impact the entire organization. For this reason, top management must be 100 per cent committed to, and supportive of, all age-friendly initiatives.

Chapter at a glance

→ The immediate barrier that companies face when trying to formulate their age-friendly strategy is the lack of business metrics to drive their decisions. First, companies require a way to measure their existing age-friendliness and that of their competitors. Second, the output from research must be a simple and actionable roadmap with clear-cut actions.

→ A simple test comprised of six questions gives an indication of whether a company is considering the needs of its older customers throughout the purchase cycle. To provide the level of information that enables management to make decisions requires a much more complex model.

→ The essence of an age-friendly audit is simple. The different variants of the customer journey are divided into a sequence of unique touchpoints. Then, each touchpoint is evaluated to understand how it might be affected by the customer's sensory, physical and cognitive ageing. The devil is in the detail of how this process is structured and conducted.

→ The absence of a methodology that could satisfy all the criteria required to rigorously evaluate the age-friendliness of a business lead the authors to create the AF Audit toolset. This business tool uses an iPad application and cloud-based technology to evaluate how 24 physiological effects of ageing are satisfied or frustrated at each of around 200 customer touchpoints across the customer journey.

➔ Auditing a company's age-friendliness is just the beginning. The challenge for management is what to do with the results. The results of an audit are potentially transformational and likely to impact the entire organization. For this reason, top management must be 100 per cent committed to, and supportive of, all age-friendly initiatives.

CHAPTER 10

Creating an age-friendly strategy

This book describes why companies should adopt an age-friendly approach to their customers and how they can achieve it. We believe the default option is to engineer the company's processes to become age-friendly. There will be instances when this is not the case but they are rare. Not everybody agrees with this assumption.

Some senior executives argue that because their organizations are not targeting older consumers they do not need to become age-friendly. We believe this logic is incorrect.

This chapter explains why the changes in the demographic profile of the world's industrialized nations compel businesses to become age-friendly regardless of their strategic intent to include or exclude targeting older consumers.

Similarly, we would argue that if you adopt age-friendly policies and accommodate the needs of ageing consumers, you would improve everybody's customer experience.

It is essential to make the distinction between age-friendly as a *tactic* and age-friendly as a *strategy*.

A *tactic* is a short-term, opportunistic manoeuvre whereas a *strategy* is: 'gaining a position of advantage over adversaries or best exploiting emerging possibilities'.[1] The relentless ageing of the world's population must be viewed as an 'emerging possibility'.

Understanding population ageing and how it can be exploited is of little value if 'age-friendly' is relegated to the status of a *tactic* or merely a dormant addendum to the title of some junior executive.

The decision to adopt age-friendly business practices is most definitely a strategic issue and, as with any corporate strategy, embedding it within the corporate culture is a necessary condition for its success.

The difficulty of identifying the age-related barriers within the customer journey can be small compared with the obstructions en route to gaining acceptance in the company boardroom. Without the 'buy-in' and active support of internal stakeholders, particularly the top management, this strategic initiative, as any other, will fail.

Too often when discussing the ageing population, demographic evolutions are quoted 20, 30, even 50 years into the future, well beyond the work-span of most senior managers. This, plus management's focus on more traditional concepts of business growth and short-term 'wins', goes a long way to explaining the lack of urgency that has historically been attached to this issue.

At the beginning of this book we explained the myths and stereotypes that are often used as excuses for inaction against the inevitable impact of consumer ageing. To combat these excuses and apathy, senior management must drive their business teams to understand the special needs of ageing consumers and operational departments must collaborate seamlessly to deliver an age-friendly experience, throughout the entire customer journey.

The tipping point?

The business world is full of uncertainties and unpredictable events that can rapidly change a company's trajectory. So when offered a polished crystal ball, it would be foolish not to glimpse and take advantage of its predictions. Yet some 50 years ago it was clear that the world was experiencing a demographic change, generated in the aftermath of World War II, that is now resulting in a rapid increase in the older population. Since then, demographers and marketing pundits have exploited the Baby Boom phenomenon and responded with products and services appropriate for these consumers as they progressed through different life stages. Clearly, demographics do not lie, so as we look to the immediate future we can predict with absolute certainty (excluding cataclysmic events) that in most economies there will be a rapid increase in the balance of older people to younger people – something that is 'unparalleled in the history of humanity'.[2]

The impact on business is also clear. In Chapter 1 we referred to a study that indicated 65 per cent of business leaders expect the proportion of revenue they derive from older customers to increase during the next five years. Importantly, however, only 13 per cent of the sample thought themselves highly effective in understanding the needs of older customers.

In 2006, AARP conducted a multinational survey of opinion leaders in Asia and Oceania.[3] The majority of opinion leaders, in all eight countries surveyed, considered population ageing to be an important issue that must not be ignored. The leaders also recognized that the population ageing will deliver challenges and opportunities, including the creation of new markets for products and services targeted at older people as well as the potential availability of older people to contribute as productive members of the workforce.

Yet despite these irrefutable facts, many companies are still slow to take specific action. It seems there is always something more pressing that pushes this issue lower on the priority scale–perhaps understandably so in difficult economic times when the focus is sometimes on mere survival. Another factor that may explain this apparent apathy is the intense share-holder scrutiny of share price movement, which drives chief executives and marketing executives to concentrate on short-term, quick wins, at the expense of broader, longer-term strategic certainties.

By way of comparison, back in the late 1960s and early 1970s the world started thinking about the environment. By the late 1980s, satellite data showed measurable ozone depletion. Yet it was not until 2006, almost 40 years later, when a former US vice president and some clever film-makers presented alarming data about the planet, that the issue rocketed to the top rungs of national and corporate debate. Eco-friendliness became crucial to relationships between governments and their citizens, companies and their customers, and companies and their employees.

The documentary *An Inconvenient Truth*[4] is credited with energizing the environmental movement and creating the tipping point that placed environmental concern on the agenda of most corporations.

The Carbon Disclosure Project, a not-for-profit group, polls many of the world's largest corporations and grades them according to their attempts to tackle climate change. Drinks giant Diageo was among the top-ranked companies and their CFO had this to say; "Our focus is less on payback periods and more on targeting environmental investments to be 'value positive.'"[5]

Sceptics who doubt the need to consider and adapt their business to the ageing population should reflect on the speed with which environmental issues leaped to the top of the corporate agenda.

A similar story can be told about the way that an arcane technology, developed for the American defence industry in the 1960s, evolved in the last decade to reshape companies and industries. This of course refers to the internet.

Leaders who had the foresight to anticipate the impact of the digital revolution and the importance of sustainability were able to achieve competitive advantage. They managed to implement progressive change to their organizations and in so doing avoided the need for sudden capital expenditure once consumers, competitive pressure or government legislation demanded it.

The tipping point for embracing the changes demanded by the ageing consumer is upon us. Companies have a unique window of opportunity to take the lead and adopt an age-friendly strategy. Or they can wait and play an expensive game of 'catch-up'.

Strategic options

As mentioned at the beginning of this chapter, the decision for a company to adopt age-friendly principles is independent of the decision to actively pursue the older customer with age-related products and services, in much the same way that being eco-friendly does not compel a business to develop and market products for environmental protection.

The authors argue that every business should become age-friendly because there are few organizations now, and there will be even fewer in the future, with which older people will not somehow interact, whether as customers for themselves, for their children or for their grandchildren.

On the other hand, only select companies may take the strategic decision to actively pursue older consumers and allocate capital to develop specific products or services and to invest in marketing support. The decision to target the ageing consumer will depend on the relevance of the company's core competencies in terms of products and channels, among many other considerations. Creating the best buying experience for all customers and overtly targeting older people are very different issues and should not be confused.

The strategies that companies adopt can be summarized by the following three options, which are illustrated in Figure 10.1:

- Be passive and do nothing.
- Become age-friendly and remain relevant to older customers.
- Be age-active and actively pursue the ageing consumer with specific marketing initiatives.

Experience tells us that there will be many who adopt the passive approach of doing nothing. For this group, there are lessons to be learnt from the tale of the frogs that are happy swimming in cold water. Slowly the water is heated – they become comfortable with their environment and keep swimming. They only discover their error when the water is too hot for them to escape.

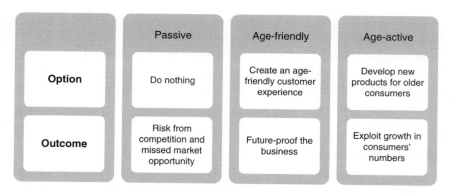

Figure 10.1 The three strategic options for responding to the ageing consumer

The way that the customers of companies are ageing – slowly, but continuously – is like the change in the water temperature. The sooner companies respond to this change the better, before they become the equivalent of *Cuisses de Grenouille* (cooked frogs' legs).

There are seven issues that senior executives should be discussing to build their understanding of why adopting an age-friendly strategy makes sound business sense.

- The size of the prize and the risk of inaction.
- The susceptibility to competitive threat.
- The earlier the adoption of age-friendliness the better.
- The voice of the older consumer will be loud.
- The benefits of first-mover advantage.
- Why future-proofing a company is a wise decision.
- Why becoming age-friendly = becoming customer-centric.

The size of the prize and the risk of inaction

Most of the global management consulting companies have published papers dramatizing the spending power of the ageing consumer. Some of their findings are covered in more detail in Chapter 2.

In Asia Pacific alone, MasterCard predicted that by 2015, people over 65 years of age would have annual spending power of US$2 trillion.[6]

Furthermore, when considering the importance and urgency of responding to the growing number of older consumers, companies also need to be mindful of the shrinkage in younger consumer segments and its impact on their business.

Table 10.1 compares the age composition of key regions of the world in 2011. This shows dramatic differences in their age profile. The centre of gravity of Africa's population is in the early 20s; in Europe it is closer to 45. This presents very different challenges and opportunities.[7]

The consequence of changes in the relative numbers of younger and older customers is illustrated by a company the authors advised in Japan. The company concerned is a well-known global brand whose entire business and marketing strategy is aligned to the youth market. At a business planning meeting for the Japan division, it targeted sales growth of 6–8 per cent annually over the coming decade. However, its calculations did not incorporate the absolute shrinkage of the youth market population by around 14 per cent during that same period.

Figure 10.2 further illustrates this change in generational balance, detailing how in Japan, in the period 2010–20, the relative sizes of the age groups change.

In the course of a decade, companies will have to manage a significant shrinkage in the number of potential young customers and find ways of satisfying rapidly increasing numbers of older people – especially those over the age of 75.

Table 10.1 World population in 2011, showing the age composition of key global regions

	AFRICA	ASIA	EUROPE	LATIN AM.	N. AMERICA	OCEANIA
0–14	40%	25%	15%	27%	19%	23%
15–24	20%	18%	12%	18%	13%	15%
25–44	25%	30%	28%	29%	26%	27%
45–59	9%	16%	20%	15%	20%	17%
60–74	4%	8%	14%	7%	12%	10%
75+	2%	4%	11%	4%	10%	7%

1–14	2010	–6%	2020
15–24		–8%	
25–44		–17%	
45–59		+7%	
60–74		–1%	
75+		+33%	

Figure 10.2 Change in size of age groups in Japan 2010–20[8]

Needless to say, in a shrinking market, served by mature and savvy local and international competitors, growth among the diminishing pool of younger customers will be extremely difficult to achieve.

All companies that adopt a passive (do-nothing) approach should be aware of how their sales are affected by demographic change.

The authors use a simple metric to illustrate the magnitude of this change when talking to clients – the age multiplier factor (AMF).

To demonstrate how this works we take the example of a company with revenues in Japan, in 2010, of $10,000,000.

The steps to calculating the AMF are shown in Table 10.2:

- Column 1 is the company's sales in 2010 divided into the six age groups.
- Column 2 shows the sales in age range 0–44 and 45–75+.
- Column 3 is the sales in 2020, assuming the same unit sales per person but accounting for the change in the numbers of people in each age group (Column 4).
- Column 5 shows the summary of sales by age group in 2020.
- Column 6 shows the absolute change in the revenues generated from the two age groups.

The AMF is the change in the amount of revenue from the two age groups as a percentage of the 2010 revenue. In this example, over 11 per cent of the company's revenue will have to be generated from different age groups. This is a measure of the challenge that results purely from demographic change.

Table 10.2 Age multiplier factor for a company with sales in 2010 of $10,000,000 in Japan. Column 4 has been rounded to the nearest whole number

	1	2	3	4	5	6
	2010		2020			
0–14	$1,000,000		$941,000	−6%		
15–24	$3,000,000	$7,000,000	$2,755,000	−8%	$6,201,000	−$799,000
25–44	$3,000,000		$2,505,000	−17%		
45–59	$2,000,000		$2,145,000	+7%		
60–74	$500,000	$3,000,000	$493,000	−1%	$3,302,000	$302,000
75+	$500,000		$664,000	+33%		
			Total change in revenue			$1,101,000
			Age multiplier factor			11%

You can calculate the AMF for your own company at www.age-friendly.com/downloads/Chapter10_AMF.xlsx, where you can download a template with the latest population data and forecasts for 2015, 2020 and 2030 covering the USA, Japan, India, China and Northern Europe. There is also a link to the appropriate section of the United Nations website, where specific country data can be retrieved.[9]

The AMF provides a simple measure for understanding the revenue implication of adopting a passive strategy. It also provides a basis for quantifying the 'size of the prize' for companies that adopt the age-friendly strategic option that will be more likely to build loyalty among their ageing customers and so offset the effects of demographic shifts. Companies that choose the age-active option, by actively exploiting changing demographics, have the most to gain from the changing demographic landscape.

This simple model makes no assumptions about the variation in the disposable incomes of the age groups. The recession in Europe and the USA has reduced the economic prospects of many young people. When these changes are figured into the calculation, they increase the value of the AMF.

Susceptibility to competitive threat

A weakness of the AMF measure is that it cannot account for competitive activity. Needless to say, competitors with effective age-friendly practices will capture the business of older customers.

In Chapter 8 we identified Apple as an example of how age-friendliness can become a competitive advantage. Apple is very protective about the demographics data of its customer base, but anecdotal evidence suggests that in the past three years the brand has attracted increasing numbers of older customers. The intrinsic age-friendliness of the iPad and iPhone partly explains this success and the company's advertising has been a casebook example of being age-neutral.

What is important to note here is that Apple does not (yet) manufacture or market products specifically for older consumers. Its products are age-neutral and, because of the company's obsession with the quality of the customer experience, delivered in an age-friendly way – a combination that appears to work well.

Companies that are category leaders and are tempted to adopt a passive approach should consider the Apple example and its implications. Without overtly adopting an age-friendly strategy, the company appears to be highly successful – just think of the outcome if it adopted an age-active strategy.

The earlier the adoption of age-friendliness the better

In many businesses, periodic renewal or refurbishment is necessary. In such cases, age-friendly principles could be applied with minimal additional expense by embedding their adoption into the process of specifying capital expenditure investments.

Take the example of the hotel industry. According to our discussion with industry experts, hotels undertake refurbishments of their rooms and common areas approximately every seven years and major structural refurbishment every 15 to 20 years. A five-star hotel with around 300 rooms might spend upwards of $30 million for a major upgrade. Replacing potentially dangerous baths with more easily accessible showers, applying non-slip surfaces, positioning shelves for easy access, installing electronics that are intuitive and easy to operate, providing appropriate lighting in the rooms and food and drink outlets … If age-friendliness is part of the design specifications, it results in zero or minimal additional costs.

During the period of amortizing this expense, the median age of hotel guests is almost certain to increase. But if these kinds of changes are made retrospectively, they are likely to be less effective and the costs will probably escalate.

In the automotive industry, the cost of retooling for a new car is astronomical, which probably explains why many car companies – including Honda, Ford, Nissan and Toyota – already use age simulators in the design phase of their new model development. It costs no more to be age-friendly at the design phase.

The same principle applies to other forward-looking investments in product or service R&D, retail design and so on. Any capital expense where cost amortization is likely to run over a decade should be sanctioned only after considering the needs of the future consumer and the limitations that physiological ageing may inflict on them.

The voice of the older consumer will be loud

Beginning with the Vietnam War protests, Baby Boomers have become famous for their outspoken behaviour. Unlike generations before them, they were prepared to protest when things didn't seem right, proper and fair.

This age group will not stop its revolutionizing tendencies as it enters its 60s and 70s.

In the two years to 2011, social networking use among internet users aged over 65 in the USA grew 150 per cent. In the same period, use among the 50–64-year-old age group doubled, from 25 to 51 per cent.[10] The digital voice of older people will be loud and they will not hesitate to use it if they believe companies are not recognizing their needs.

Word-of-mouth as a source of product information is important to older people. Consider this in relation to recent research showing that 82 per cent of consumers would share a bad customer service experience.[11]

Companies that track blogs and social comment sites report that although younger people contribute comments more frequently, older people tend to write longer, more thoughtful compliments or criticisms – possibly because they have more time at their disposal. Companies that fail to meet the needs of their older customers or aggravate them because of non-age-friendly practices are likely to find themselves on the receiving end of an increasing volume of highly visible, negative publicity.

The benefits of first-mover advantage

It is simply a matter of time before all companies respond to the inevitabilities outlined in this book. As the passive ponder, the bold have the opportunity to gain a competitive lead on their rivals.

As Apple has demonstrated, being a first-mover among older consumers can translate into business success. Apple's competitors now face the daunting task of dislodging the loyalty Apple has stealthily generated among this segment. This also demonstrates that being age-friendly does not necessarily mean shouting about it from the rooftops. It may simply be one of the corporate values the company adopts. Older customers will feel more comfortable interacting with a brand that better meets their needs and will reward it with their custom at the expense of competitors that are slow to act.

Future-proofing a company is a wise decision

As we have witnessed with the evolution of the sustainability cause from mere chants of a vocal minority to strictly enforced legislation, issues of global concern that touch people's lives inevitably find their way into law.

In many countries, accessibility requirements for the physically challenged are already entrenched in regulatory conditions. As the social impact of ageing moves up the political agenda, it is inevitable that legislation will follow. As a sign of the times, in 1998 Australia's Department of Health and Family Services changed its name to the Department of

Health and Aged Care and is today known as the Department of Health and Ageing. Most governments of the developed economies, the World Health Organization and the United Nations have specialist departments focused on ageing issues.

As the institutional forces become more vocal, the corporate sector will have to become age-friendly, like it or not.

This transformation does not have to be done as a sudden, dramatic and possibly expensive change. As illustrated in Figure 10.3, once the strategy is set the operational changes can be phased over time.

Like most changes in strategic direction, the starting point is gathering the basic data to inform decisions, followed by consistent application throughout the organization. The strategy will have succeeded when it is seen as the only way of doing things.

Companies and their shareholders should be reassured by the thought that the early adoption of these principles is not only based on sound business principles but is also socially responsible and helps to future-proof the business.

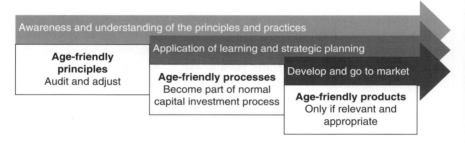

Figure 10.3 Phased implementation of an age-friendly strategy

Becoming age-friendly = becoming customer-centric

The adoption of an age-friendly strategy is more about a cultural shift than a shift in spending priorities. To continue the analogy with sustainability, reduced use of paper, use of recyclable materials, reduced energy consumption and so on result from a culture change in the organization. However, the similarity between these issues ends here because eco-friendly corporate behaviour rewards employees and customers with a sense of altruism but delivers little commercial benefit in return.

An age-friendly strategy will ultimately affect the relationship between a company and its customers, of all ages. This will translate into better-satisfied, loyal customers and commercial rewards in the form of increased competitiveness.

Becoming an age-friendly company means becoming customer-centric to the needs of older customers. For decades, glossy annual reports have professed customer devotion, claiming 'the customer is king' and other such slogans. Too many shopping experiences prove that many companies just pay lip service to this concept. The price for this customer neglect can be high. Some studies now suggest that failing to deliver a high-quality customer experience can result in a staggering erosion of a company's customer base – a loss of as much as 50 per cent over a five-year period.[12]

A study of product and service companies in the USA and Europe found that truly customer-centric businesses outperformed industry peers two-to-one and generated profit margins 5 to 10 per cent above their competitors'.[13] A separate study from the UK reveals 53 per cent of consumers are likely to spend more with companies with excellent customer service.[14]

Developing an age-friendly strategy

Once an audit of a company's touchpoints has been completed, using one of the models described in Chapter 9, it will reveal all of the weaknesses and the changes that need to be made along the customer journey. The next stage is to assign priorities to the required changes.

Companies need to know which items will have an immediate and critical impact on older customers and which things may be an irritant but are not likely to materially change behaviour.

To help establish these priorities, two other inputs are required in addition to the audit results. What are the expectations and priorities of older customers? Which of the required changes to the touchpoints reinforce or negate the company's brand and corporate values? The interrelation of these three inputs is shown in Figure 10.4.

Customer expectations

The results of an audit must be contrasted with insights from actual customers. This applies whether the audit is a simple spreadsheet checklist or the computerized measurement of hundreds of customer touchpoints made with the AF Audit Tool that was described in Chapter 9.

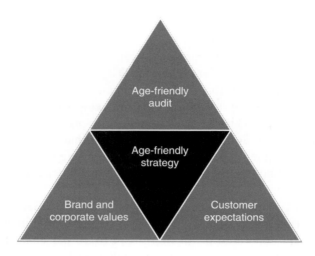

Figure 10.4   The three inputs that determine the priorities for an age-friendly strategy

There is little point investing time and money in initiatives that older customers think are of little merit.

The authors have conducted many assignments researching older people's opinions and have observed that, irrespective of the research technique employed, care needs to taken to:

- Discount the instinctive response of respondents who refuse to admit that age creates any physical impediments.
- Use physical examples of the touchpoints being tested rather than asking them to respond to a conceptual question.
- Use simple language to speak to the respondent, with no marketing or design jargon.
- Pose questions at a product category level rather than about a specific brand. In this way it is possible to identify the competitive factors that might cause the customer to switch brands.

Ideally, the customer research questions should be aligned with the audit model to allow direct correlation and analysis.

Company or brand values

The customer experience must ultimately align with the values of the brand or company, unless this creates a significant conflict.

For example, corporate values might dictate that the company use leading-edge technology. However, an age-friendly assessment and customer feedback might suggest that the advanced automated response helpline being deployed by the company annoys older customers, who often prefer more personalized 'human' support. The company will need to reconcile this conflict between its values and the customer experience.

Executives need to judge the importance of each audited consumer touchpoint according to their sense of the corporate values and business goals. This can be done using a five-point scale of importance or another similar scoring method that allows input from multiple executives to be combined and sorted.

Using the method described above, it is possible to map the age-friendly assessment results, at a touchpoint level, relative to the priorities deduced from the customer research. Once they have been weighted with the company or brand priorities, it is then possible to see the issues' relative importance.

The example in Figure 10.5 is taken from work the authors completed for a mobile phone client and shows how the three inputs from the audit, customer and company can be combined.

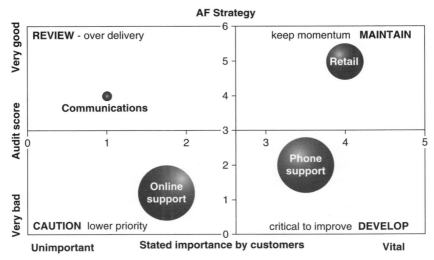

Figure 10.5 Matrix showing a combination of the AF Audit and customer research scores. The bubble size indicates the importance assigned by the company to the touchpoint

In this case the 'phone support' touchpoint is considered important by customers, scoring 3.5, and receives an unsatisfactory score of 2.0 from the audit. Clearly, this element should be improved as a priority, whereas online support scored very badly in the audit (1.0) but is of lower importance to the customer (2.0).

The company believes that excellence in both touchpoints is important, so the circles are of equal size.

'Communications' is of low importance to customers and the company but receives a high score from the audit. 'Retail' scores well in the audit and with customers and is of moderate importance to the company.

Once the mapping is complete and analysed, the final determinant of strategic priorities is the opportunity cost and return on investment (ROI) considerations.

Implementing an age-friendly strategy

As described earlier in this chapter, there are three strategic approaches that companies can adopt to population ageing – passive, age-friendly and age-active.

The authors think it is safe to assume that readers who have committed to the passive (do-nothing) approach will have abandoned reading this book so it is not necessary to say anything more about this option.

The business benefits of pursing the age-active option and developing and marketing specific products and services for older consumers depend on numerous factors, most importantly the company's core competencies. Providing advice on the suitability of this as an option is outside the remit of this book. What is certain, however, is that if this route is pursued then achieving a high degree of age-friendliness is vital.

For companies wishing to adopt an age-friendly strategy, to remain relevant to their ageing customers and to build loyalty with them, we offer some basic advice on how to begin the process.

Chapter 9 contains a simple checklist that helps determine the extent of a company's age-friendliness. This can be modified to illustrate the connection between strategic intent and operational actions when a company commits to becoming age-friendly. Table 10.3 shows this connection between strategy and operations.

Embarking on a venture of this magnitude is not a trivial undertaking. There is a large body of research that has identified the key things that make projects of this magnitude succeed or fail. Although the following actions appear to be basic business common sense, it is worth

Table 10.3   Translating the strategic intent of achieving age-friendliness into operational actions

	Strategic intent	Operational actions
Communications	To develop advertising that uses creative techniques that are tested with older customers. To ensure that all marketing collateral is physically suitable for and understandable by older people.	**Awareness** – appoint a board-level executive to drive the initiative throughout the company. Ensure the leadership team is aware and enthused. **Scoping** – have a clear action plan to measure age-friendliness across all disciplines.
Online	To include the needs and behaviours of older people in the social networking strategy. To regularly test websites and apps to ensure they provide a consistent online experience for all ages.	**Prioritization** – devise a way to correlate the age-friendliness assessment with customer opinion and with corporate/brand values. **Training** – recognize that team members will need to be trained to understand the
Retail	To ensure the retail store location, product placement, ambience and sales staff address the needs of older customers.	needs of ageing customers. **Testing** – implement a process that ensures that any major capital expenditure and development project is vetted for age-friendliness at the earliest stage.
Product	To design products/services that include the particular needs of older people without overtly referencing age.	**Monitoring** – regularly evaluate the quality of the touchpoints to measure progress. Also consider evaluating competitors' performance.
Support	To ensure that sales and support call centres and their staff are designed to respond to the needs, concerns and frustrations of older customers.	

emphasizing them, because companies continue to fail to understand their importance.

- Appoint a champion at board level.
- Persistence in implementation and compliance.
- Communications and training.

Appoint a champion at board level

Not only will this provide the necessary seniority to ensure integration of the principles across departments, but it also signals the importance management place on the initiative. The person must not just be a 'figure-head' but must have the time and knowledge to undertake the role.

Persistence in implementation and compliance

Depending on the company size and history, old habits can take a long time to break down. A realistic expectation needs to be set that a change in corporate culture of this type will take years to achieve fully. In the short term, systems must be established that require all major capital expense items to be scrutinized to ensure they comply with age-friendly philosophies.

Communications and training

Smart managers will want to thoroughly understand the rationale and goals driving the changes they are being asked to implement. Given the general lack of understanding about the ageing consumer, specific training and communications programmes will be needed to help educate, persuade and influence the teams concerned.

The ultimate goal is to embed age-friendly thinking into the fabric of an organization. Only a few people can lead this initiative but many must be convinced of its benefits.

The evidence of the relentless change in the age composition of consumers in the world's industrialized societies is overwhelming. Viewed from this perspective there is no option but for companies to adopt an age-friendly strategy. The question senior managers must answer is whether they will do this proactively or when forced by competitive pressure. The costs of the first option are small compared with the second approach. This is one of very few business decisions where the answer is blatantly obvious.

Chapter at a glance

➜ There are few certainties in business. One of them is that in the industrialized countries there will be more older and fewer young consumers. Companies can be proactive in their response to this change or be forced to respond by competitive and regulatory pressures. That is the strategic decision that managers have to make.

→ The decision to focus corporate resources on older consumers is totally different from that of making a company age-friendly. The first approach depends on a company's core competencies and strategy. The second is a rational response to the changing structure of the market.

→ Early adopters of age-friendly strategies will enjoy multiple benefits and minimize capital-intensive retrofits. Incorporating high standards of sustainability into capital investments is a default decision; the same will apply to age-friendly design.

→ The initiative must have board-level leadership with cross-functional mandates. If age-friendliness becomes a marketing 'project' or is assigned to the corporate social responsibility (CSR) group it will flounder.

→ A business that is truly customer-centric will already be adopting many of the principles of age-friendliness. Unfortunately, there are many companies that profess to be customer-centric but very few that have developed the concept beyond a PR tagline. Companies that are committed to making their customer touchpoints age-friendly achieve the added bonus of improving the customer experience for all ages.

CHAPTER 11

Age-friendly employers and governments

The focus of this book has been on why the ageing bodies, minds and senses of consumers will change the way they interact with the companies that market to them. This change in the relationship is not in doubt – the only questions are when and by how much.

The effects of physiological ageing are not just limited to our role as consumers. Older consumers are older workers, older citizens and older patients. Most of the vertical markets will have their own variants of the journey. This chapter considers the impact of physiological ageing on these other parts of our lives. We will illustrate how the age-friendly principles and tools that we have already discussed will be vital in designing the workplaces and urban environments of the future.

The ageing employee

In Chapter 2 we outlined the macro-economic consequences of population ageing and identified the factors that could have the greatest impact on gross domestic product (GDP) growth:

- Fewer people in the workforce to pay taxes and fund public expenditure.
- Rising taxation levels needed to fund healthcare and pensions, resulting in a reduction in the disposable incomes available to buy goods and services.
- Falling demand, which affects employment levels and the amount of tax collected.
- Falling savings levels as older people use their wealth to fund retirement and the young have insufficient income to invest.

None of these outcomes is certain. Government policies will determine whether population ageing results in a downward spiral of economic hardship or an exciting opportunity to stimulate growth.

So far, the most common policy response to population ageing has been to extend the retirement age of workers. This has been the policy in many OECD countries. Figure 11.1 shows that most countries allow their citizens to collect their pensions from the age of 65.

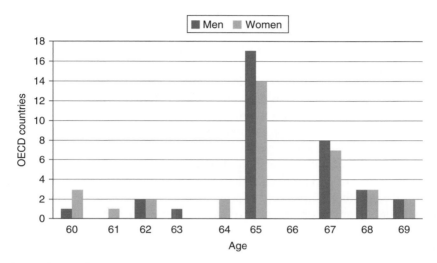

Figure 11.1   Retirement age

Italy and Denmark plan to link pension age to life expectancy, a policy that is being considered in the UK.[1] The UK will lift the pensionable age from 65 to 66 by 2020 and from 66 to 67 by 2026–28, both much earlier than originally planned. It has yet to be seen what the final repercussions of the European and USA debt crisis will be for pension age but the most likely outcome will be to accelerate the rate at which it is extended.

France has recently **reduced** the age of retirement from 62 to 60. This was an election promise of the incoming socialist government, a policy driven by the difficulty young people have finding jobs in a weak economy and the naïve rationale that this is exacerbated by older people working longer.

Globally, the proportion of people in the working-age population who are 50 years of age or older will grow from 20 per cent in 2010 to 30 per cent by 2050. It is clear that companies need to adapt to having an older workforce.[2]

Recently, a popular question with the think tanks in Europe and the USA has been 'What to do with older workers'. There have been numerous ideas about encouraging 'Boomer entrepreneurs' to start new businesses and government and charity-funded ideas such as the UK's 'National Retirement Service', which would mobilize a large group of older volunteers.[3] So far, most of these ideas have failed to make the transition from the conceptual stage to large-scale implementation.

The thing that we know for certain is that all types of people will have to work longer. Although some may do so to pursue a passion or simply to remain engaged, many older workers will be compelled to continue working out of financial necessity.

In the USA and in Europe, many people in their 50s and early 60s are financially unprepared for retirement – irrespective of when governments say they can and should stop work.

The burden of debt among Americans is reflected in their intention to work past retirement age. Figure 11.2 shows the results of a poll conducted in the USA that shows 63 per cent of non-retired USA adults plan to work either full time or part time when they reach retirement age. The same study also revealed that 42 per cent of the respondents were 'very concerned' about not having enough money to live comfortably in retirement.[4]

With more people remaining employed, well into their senior years, it is inevitable that the age profile of the workforce will change. Just as companies must adapt to the changing needs of their ageing consumers, they will also need to adapt to the changing capabilities of their ageing employees.

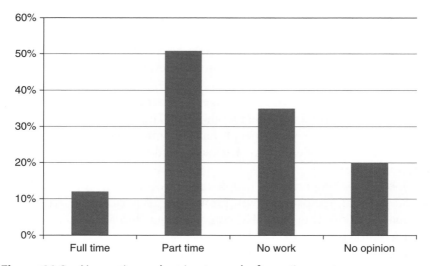

Figure 11.2   Non-retirees planning to work after retirement

Despite the irrefutable evidence that there will be increasing numbers of older workers, the response from companies, with a few exceptions, has been muted.

Those enlightened companies that have proactively encouraged the recruitment of older people believe they have tangible advantages over younger workers. The most often cited is their:

- Accumulated knowledge, experience and skills gained from years of employment.
- Strong commitment to their jobs and tendency to stay in the same job for longer.
- Flexibility in terms of work hours and pay.
- Judgement and problem-solving abilities and interpersonal skills.
- Ability to empathize with older customers.

This list of attributes does not mean older employees are better than younger ones. All ages have different skills and attributes. Ideally a company is looking to optimize its workforce with a mix of ages and their associated skills.

B&Q, the home-improvement store, is a much-quoted example of a company that has successfully incorporated older people into its workforce. Currently 21 per cent of the company's 37,000 workforce are aged over 50 and 7 per cent are over 60.[5]

To put B&Q's employment rate of older workers into perspective, in 2006 none of the following companies had more than 5 per cent of their employees over the age of 55 – Barclays Bank, Thomas Cook, Microsoft, Vodafone, KMPG and the BBC.

In the USA, the 'Best Employers for Workers Over 50' is the highest-profile venture to encourage companies to adapt to the realities of an ageing workforce. This annual event is run by AARP, the lobby group and membership organization, with the aim of recognizing US and international organizations that have implemented innovative policies and best practices in the management of older workers.

AARP's 2011 awards were given to 15 international and 50 US companies and institutions. Interestingly, few of the winners were consumer marketing companies.[6]

The factors AARP considers when judging whether a company is a good employer of older people include:

- Recruiting practices.
- Opportunities for training, education and career development.

- Workplace accommodation.
- Alternative work options, such as flexible scheduling, job-sharing and phased retirement.
- Employee health and pension benefits.
- Benefits for retirees.

These are excellent criteria to judge the working practices of companies. However, we believe that viewing workers in the same way as consumers and constructing an 'age-friendly employee journey' will add an additional level of insights.

The age-friendly employee journey

Chapter 4 demonstrated that understanding the effects of physiological ageing, on each of the customer touchpoints, improves the customer journey for older consumers.

The authors believe that the same advantages will accrue if the employee journey is imagined in the same way. If such a journey were constructed, it would be likely to have the following five types of employee experience.

Commute

The location of a business, including its proximity to public transport and convenient car parking, is an important consideration for older workers.

If public transport is an important component in how employees attend work, then it must accommodate their mobility needs, destinations and schedules, and be affordable. One challenge for older workers can be the mismatch between available commuter services and services needed to match their work hours.

As was illustrated in Figure 11.2, working part-time is how most older people would prefer to extend their employment, which means they are more likely to travel outside peak commuting times. Although these flexible commute times have the benefit of avoiding the crowds and the cost and inconvenience of peak-hour travel, some commuter services may run less frequently or not at all during off-peak periods.

Companies need to consider the approach to the workplace once their staff reach the public transport station or car park. For example, if the distance or waiting time is long there may be a need to provide shelter or rest areas.

Workplace

Just as retail environments must adapt to accommodate older consumers, the ergonomics and accessibility of the workplace must adapt to the same physiological changes.

Elements such as the temperature and humidity of the work environment, levels of sound and illumination, provision of amenities and the proximity of reasonable food outlets need to be included in any assessment.

The automaker BMW is an excellent example of how workplace productivity can be enhanced by using older workers.

In 2007, anticipating an increase in the average age of production workers, BMW staffed a pilot production line with workers with an average age of 47. This represented the predicted age of their employees in 2017.

The workers were invited to suggest changes they felt would make their jobs easier and their work better. What they suggested was revealing and simple to implement:

- Wooden flooring, rather than concrete, to reduce knee strain and exposure to static electricity jolt.
- Barbershop chairs to enable short breaks and alternating physical strain (workers can stand or sit).
- Orthopaedic footwear to reduce strain on feet.
- Angled monitors to reduce eyestrain.
- Magnifying lenses to reduce eyestrain and minimize sorting errors.
- Adjustable worktables to ease physical strain and facilitate personnel rotation during shifts.
- Large-handled gripping tools to reduce strain on arms.
- Stackable transport containers to ease physical strain and facilitate personnel rotation during shifts.
- Larger typeface on computer screens to reduce eyestrain and minimize sorting errors.
- Manual hoisting cranes to reduce back strain.

As a result of these modifications there was a 7 per cent productivity improvement within one year. By June 2009, absenteeism had dropped below the plant average. The capital investment for the project amounted to just € 20,000.[7]

Readers will notice that each of the suggested production line modifications relates to one or more of the 24 effects of ageing discussed throughout this book. Equipped with an understanding of the physiological effects presented in Chapters 3 to 7, many of the suggested modifications could have been anticipated. More important, if the production line were exposed to a rigorous audit using the data and tools discussed in this book, how much more could productivity have been improved?

Work task

Some companies may have the scale and flexibility to switch older workers to less physically demanding jobs; however, this will not always be the case.

When evaluating whether an older worker remains physically capable of performing a physically demanding work task, for prolonged periods of time, it will be valuable to consider the potential risks to their health and personal safety. Some of the risks and mitigating factors include:

- **Task variation and task repetition.** Consider the physical functional capacity to lift and carry, including the possibility of sudden peak loads, awkward work and repetitive work. This will tax both aerobic capacity and body flexibility.
- **Frequency of rest breaks.** Work and jobs should be designed so that workers are able to vary the timing of their own rest breaks to match their individual needs.
- **Noise levels.** The use of sound protection should ensure that the work tasks do not exacerbate age-related hearing loss. The volume and frequency of machine controls need to be audible.
- **Temperature levels.** These may need to be altered due to age-related changes to workers' sensitivity to hot and cold conditions.
- **Lighting.** Make sure there is enough light to eliminate the chance of manual accidents or falls.
- **Workstation design.** Consider vibrations and slippery or uneven surfaces that increase the risk of falls and disorientation. Also consider the postural demands placed on the older worker's body.
- **Equipment design.** Supply instrumentation that can be readily seen without eyestrain and manipulated with declining hand strength.

Companies should be careful not to create risks for other people in the workplace out of their enthusiasm to be an age-friendly employer – for example, by overloading a younger worker in an effort to reduce the heavy manual tasks for an older worker. Employers should also be aware of the potential risk levels of their older workers experiencing increased levels of ill health.

Not all older workers will be engaged in physically demanding work. In the office environment, good safety procedures and ergonomics are important in keeping workers, of all ages, safe and healthy. Certain ergonomic factors will become more important as the age of the workforce increases:

- A well-designed ergonomically correct workstation to optimize posture and motions.
- Increased lighting or reduced glare to diminish the impact of age-related visual problems.
- Lower computer monitor height or the use of single-vision 'computer glasses' to reduce musculoskeletal problems that bifocal wearers may develop from tilting their head back to see out of the bottom of the lens.

In addition to ergonomic considerations, a thorough assessment of an age-friendly workplace would need to include work organization, emergency procedures and health advice programmes that are tailored to older bodies.

Knowledge

The issue of the knowledge and experience of older employees raises two questions:

- Is there a need to retrain them to keep them productive and motivated?
- Does the potential retirement of the employee result in a loss of knowledge that needs to be captured during their continuing employment?

Training

Despite the stereotypes, older people are often keen to learn new skills. A common complaint is that older people receive less training because employers perceive it as 'wasted' on people who are at the end of their career and about to retire.

Older workers sometimes prefer to train at their own pace and, for this reason, companies should provide training materials in a variety of formats to accommodate different learning styles and speeds.

The format of their training needs to take account of the fact that their style and speed of learning will be different from those of younger people. The age-related changes in cognitive skills are explained in Chapter 6.

Knowledge transfer

As a company's longest-serving members of staff retire, the organization can experience a haemorrhaging of knowledge. This affects not just technical skills, but also the knowledge and rapport established with customers and the understanding of how companies really function, which might be very different from the theoretical approach explained by the formal processes, procedures and organization charts.

For example, a problem in the telephone and large-scale computer infrastructure systems industry is the difficulty finding qualified service technicians for legacy systems. The USA company Lockheed Martin Space Systems responded to this issue over a decade ago by instituting a project to identify and assess employees' skills to prepare for the time they retire.[8]

As the number of older people leaving their employer accelerates, it is hardly surprising that a poll of employers, conducted by the AARP, showed that 72 per cent of human resources managers stated that the loss of talented older workers was a current or potential problem.[9] The same research revealed that many US organizations are largely unprepared for the situation when older workers leave the company.

Figure 11.3 illustrates the popularity of various strategies organizations have taken, ranging from increasing training (45 per cent) to offering part-time positions (24 per cent).[10]

All the evidence suggests that an assessment of training and knowledge transfer is a vital element in evaluating a company's employment age-friendliness.

A useful reference for the development of age-friendly training and communications materials is the section of Chapter 9 that analyses the customer touchpoints involved in marketing communications.

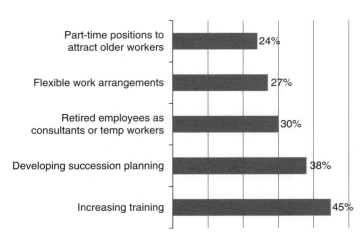

Figure 11.3 Actions organizations have taken to prepare for the loss of talented older workers

Compliance

Despite the demographic evidence and business logic showing why preparing for an older workforce is necessary, there will be many companies that will be slow to react. The increasing body of anti-age-discrimination legislation might provide the needed catalyst to persuade these companies to change.

The Citizens Advice Bureau of the UK puts it succinctly: 'Your employer isn't allowed to treat you worse than other colleagues at work because of your age, or the age they think you are, unless they've got a very good reason.'[11]

Clearly, evaluating how a company complies with relevant labour laws is an essential part of any review of a company's age-friendliness.

The 'carrot' to accompany the legislative 'stick' is that some governments are already developing initiatives and incentives for businesses to employ or retain their older workers. The challenge for national governments is to align the interests and abilities of mature adults with the interests and requirements of employers.

Another aspect of compliance is how embedded the age-friendly principles are into the corporate culture. An age-friendly company needs to actively promote this philosophy to its entire staff. This is becoming more important to counter the sometimes vitriolic media ranting that older employees are stealing younger people's jobs.

Simplistic generalizations about how different generations approach their work should be applied with caution, because they can be viewed as ageist stereotypes.

However, there is little doubt that conflict can arise between the value systems and opinions of people separated by many years of age and experience. Otherwise parents and children would coexist in perfect harmony, which is seldom the case.

Companies need to encourage the benefits of combining the skills of older and younger workers to create an effective workforce.

There are many similarities between a customer journey and an employee one, as is shown in Table 11.1. However, as is the case with the customer journey, the devil is in the detail of defining the touchpoints and the criteria that enable their conformance to be measured.

To properly evaluate an employee journey, it is necessary to account for the variations in company size, industry and the legislative environment in which the business operates. For instance, there will need to be different touchpoints for managerial office work from those for factory manufacturing jobs. However, some of the touchpoints will be common to all types of employee.

Table 11.1 The age-friendly journey for customers and employees

Age-friendly journeys

Customer		Employee	
Experience	**Touchpoints**	**Experience**	**Touchpoints**
Communications	All forms of marketing communications, including advertising, PR, sponsorship, events, etc.	Commute	Transport access and approach to the workplace, including provision for off-peak travel.
Online	The experience of using search engines, the brand and corporate website and supporting help and e-commerce microsites.	Workplace	Physical structure of the workplace, including accessibility, signage and amenities.
Retail	All aspects of the physical retail shopping experience.	Task	Physical demands of the work tasks.
Product	Preparing to use and using the product and all of the supporting materials, including packaging.	Knowledge	All aspects of acquiring knowledge (re-skilling) and the transfer of knowledge.
Sales support	The physical aspects of selling and supporting the product, including face-to-face and phone communications.	Compliance	Compliance with law and industry standards, including corporate culture and feedback.

The mechanism for auditing customer and employee journeys is exactly the same as that defined in Chapter 9 'Evaluating age-friendliness'. There must be a mechanism for managing the auditing process, a way of collecting the audit data and a way of reporting the results.

When defining the architecture for the AF Audit Tool, the authors realized that the only thing that differs between customer, employee and citizen age-friendliness is the database of touchpoint questions.

There is now the possibility of constructing an objective measuring tool to evaluate age-friendly employment. All that is required is management will to use it.

The ageing citizen

Two of the mega-issues that will most affect life in the future are ageing and urbanization. Their combined effect results in an urgent need to make cities and towns capable of supporting an ageing population.

In the same way as companies need to respond to the ageing of their customers and employees, governments have exactly the same challenge with their ageing citizens.

Rapid urbanization creates strains on the citizens who live in the rapidly growing cities, the government that plans their growth and the institutions that govern their workings. The magnitude and speed of the migration of the population to cities is difficult to comprehend. As detailed in Chapter 2, by 2050 an additional 100 million Americans will be living in cities[12] and an **additional** 350 million people will be added to China's urban population by 2025.[13]

A dramatic example of the ageing of cities is illustrated by Shanghai, which has the largest percentage of older people of all Chinese cities. At the end of 2008, it had over 3 million registered citizens aged 60 and above. This represents 21.6 per cent of Shanghai's population, twice the national average. Of the 3 million, 17.8 per cent were in their 80s and 90s, a 6.4 per cent rise on the previous year. About 20 per cent of the 534,400 people aged above 80 needed daily care services.[14]

The huge numbers of older people who will soon be living in Chinese cities pose tremendous challenges for the governing authorities.

The two things that authorities can do to improve the quality of life for the urban old are help them extend the period of healthy and active ageing as long as possible and ensure that the buildings and infrastructure of cities are designed for their ageing bodies.

Beyond mere altruism, governments have a financial interest in the active ageing and wellbeing of their ageing citizens because the longer they remain active and engaged, the more tax they pay and the smaller their demands of the health and care support services.

The next two sections of this chapter describe how to audit the infrastructure and services that enable active ageing in the urban environment.

Active ageing

In the USA in 2002, the over-65s comprised 13 per cent of the American population but consumed 36 per cent of the total expenditure on personal healthcare services.[15] In the UK, this age group consumes 43 per cent of the NHS's total budget.[16]

Throughout this book, we have stressed that a person's lifestyle can influence the extent and timing of their decline in functional capacity. This refers to body functions such as cardiovascular capacity and muscular strength. The rate at which these body functions decline is greatly determined by lifestyle factors, such as smoking, the level of alcohol consumed, the healthiness of the diet and the amount of regular physical exercise.

The World Health Organization (WHO) has shown that it is possible for older people to delay the decline of their functional capacity by adopting a healthy lifestyle. The WHO's advice was published in a document called a *Life Course Approach to Active Ageing*.[17]

The WHO's conceptual model of how the decline in functional capacity can be delayed is illustrated in Figure 11.4.

Most governments accept that positive interventions, through an active ageing programme, can delay the point at which an older person enters the disability threshold zone. This saves medical costs for individuals, families and the public purse. It is important to note, however, that there are marked differences in functional capacity profiles between countries.

Active ageing is officially defined as: 'The process of optimizing opportunities for health, participation and security in order to enhance quality of life as people age.' The WHO has even published recommended levels of physical activity for people 65 years and above, which include:

- At least 150 minutes of moderate-intensity aerobic activity; or
- 75 minutes of vigorous-intensity aerobic physical activity throughout the week.

The recommendations also include muscle-strengthening activities, two or more days a week.[18]

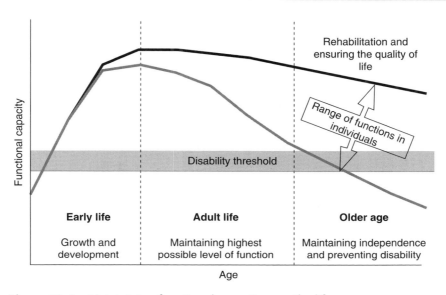

Figure 11.4 Maintaining functional capacity over the life course

Governments and regional bodies have been adopting the WHO active-ageing guidelines with varying degrees of enthusiasm. To help bring focus onto the importance of active ageing, 2012 has been determined the European Year for Active Ageing and Solidarity between Generations. It is too early to determine if this has had any success.[19]

Participating governments and institutions would be well advised not to confuse the social goal of active ageing with its use as a slogan for communication with the intended participants. Older people will generally not wish to be labelled as being in the process of 'active ageing' or attending an 'active ageing' training programme. Ireland provides a good example of how to separate the objective of the initiative from its branding. Its Go for Life programme is a people-friendly, local adaptation of the WHO active-ageing initiative.[20]

Clearly, the need for active ageing facilities, or whatever they are called, is an ongoing requirement. It should be relatively simple to adapt the question database used to measure consumer and employee age-friendliness to evaluate active ageing initiatives.

The WHO has already done much of the work in defining the experiences and some of the touchpoints of active ageing. As the 24 physiological effects of ageing are constant, all that would be required, to extend this checklist into a detailed auditing tool, would be to complete the list of touchpoints and to define how they could be measured.

Table 11.2 The age-friendly journey for customers and for the active ageing of citizens

Age-friendly journeys			
Customer		**Active ageing**	
Experience	**Touchpoints**	**Experience**	**Touchpoints**
Communications	All forms of marketing communications, including advertising, PR, sponsorship, events etc.	Economic determinants	Schemes to reduce poverty at all ages. Social insurance programmes and employment opportunities.
Online	The experience of using search engines, the brand and corporate website and supporting help and e-commerce microsites.	Health and social services	Life course programmes that focus on health promotion, disease prevention and access to quality primary healthcare.
Retail	All aspects of the physical retail shopping experience.	Behavioural determinants	Education to combat the myth that it is too late to adopt healthier lifestyles in the later years.
Product	Preparing to use and using the product and all of the supporting materials, including packaging.	Personal determinants	All aspects of acquiring knowledge (re-skilling) and the transfer of knowledge.
Sales support	The physical aspects of selling and supporting the product, including face-to-face and phone communications.	Physical environment	Safe, accessible environments for both urban and rural dwellers.
		Social determinants	Social support, opportunities for education and lifelong learning and protection from violence and abuse.

Table 11.2 shows a greatly summarized version of the determinants of active ageing, as prescribed by the WHO, in the age-friendly journey format that is used to analyse customers.

Age-friendly living

The effectiveness of active ageing programmes is greatly enhanced if a city's buildings and infrastructure are designed to cope with the physical limitations of older people.

Accommodating the needs of ageing citizens is not the unique domain of big cities or the more affluent strata of societies. Governments must ensure that their age-friendliness plans apply to smaller towns and villages and all socio-economic groups.

Governments are responding with a variety of measures to better understand and accommodate the needs of their older citizens. In Manitoba, Canada, there is a longitudinal research study that has been running since 1971 to track physical and mental wellbeing.[21] Elsewhere, there are small-scale ventures, such as the one funded by the Australian Department of Health and Ageing to create a national public toilet map.[22]

Without doubt the most expansive initiative to improve the age-friendliness of cities is the WHO Age-Friendly Cities programme.

The WHO defines an age-friendly city as one that 'adapts its structures and services to be accessible to and inclusive of older people with varying needs and capacities'.[23] This requires the city to have the policies, services, structures and support to allow older people to age safely and actively.

The WHO has created a model that details eight areas of activity that need to be addressed if a city is to improve its age-friendliness. Table 11.3 shows how these areas of activity can be viewed in the format used for the customer journey.

The WHO's Age-Friendly Cities guide provides a comprehensive checklist of touchpoints for city officials to consider. However, by its own admission, the features checklist is not a system for ranking one city's age-friendliness against another's. It is a tool for a city's self-assessment and a map to chart progress.[24]

As there are no metrics or standards applied in the guide, evaluations are likely to be largely subjective. From our experience, developing and using the customer AF Audit Tool the best results are obtained by devising objective questions to evaluate the touchpoints.

Table 11.3 Comparing the customer journey with the citizen journey using the WHO Age-Friendly Cities touchpoints

Customer Experience	Age-friendly journeys	
	Citizen – as defined by the WHO	
	Experience	Touchpoints include
Communications	Respect and social inclusion	Respectful and inclusive services, public images of ageing, public education, community inclusion, economic inclusion.
	Civic participation and employment	Volunteering and employment options, training, accessibility, civic participation, entrepreneurship, pay.
Online	Housing	Affordability, design, modifications, maintenance, ageing in place, community integration, housing options, living environment.
Retail	Community support and health services	Service accessibility, offer of services, voluntary support, emergency planning and care.
Product	Communication and information	Oral communication, printed information, plain language, computers and the internet.
Sales support	Outdoor spaces and buildings	Environment, green spaces and walkways, outdoor seating, pavements, roads, traffic services, buildings, public toilets.
	Transportation	Affordability, reliability and frequency, age-friendly vehicles, priority seating, safety and comfort, information.
	Social participation	Accessibility of events and activities, affordability, range of events and activities, facilities and settings, promotion and awareness of activities.

We share the view of McKinsey, which states: 'Benchmarking relative to peers and best-in-class performers can provide city officials with invaluable information on how other cities around the world have tackled the problems they face.'[25] McKinsey's Urban Performance Index benchmarking tool is designed to assess a city's performance across a range of economic, social, sustainability, financial and governance issues.

The authors believe that a more rigorous, objective approach to evaluating the age-friendliness of urban environments would have merit – an AF Audit Tool for citizens.

In creating such an auditing tool, it would be necessary to create touchpoints and associated questions that could be tailored according to:

- **Size.** The touchpoints and scope for a village will be different from those for a major metropolis. However, there should be some common elements to enable countrywide comparisons.
- **Budget.** The scope of an audit and the number of touchpoints evaluated would depend on the available budget. This means there would need to be the facility to prioritize the touchpoints being evaluated.
- **Development.** Mature cities with effective but dated infrastructure will find it more disruptive and costly to adapt. Cities that are in the early stages of their development can incorporate age-friendly principles from their inception.
- **Profile.** The proportion of older residents will dictate the urgency of evaluation and transformation. Small rural towns that are unlikely to be repopulated with young people will face greater challenges as the median age of their residents increases.

In Chapter 10, it was shown that the costs of achieving age-friendliness in buildings and large-scale developments, such as public transport systems, is greatly reduced if they are part of the design specification. The most costly way of achieving age-friendliness is to do it as a dedicated project. These rules apply to the corporate sector just as they do to large infrastructure projects funded by the government.

It is financial lunacy if the cities of the future, being built today, do not incorporate the best-of-breed age-friendly principles.

Chapter at a glance

➔ With more people remaining employed, well into their senior years, it is inevitable that the age profile of the workforce will change. Just as companies must adapt to the changing needs of their ageing consumers, they will also need to adapt to the changing capabilities of their ageing employees. Few companies are prepared.

→ Understanding the effects of physiological ageing, on each of the customer touchpoints, improves the customer journey for older consumers. A similar approach can be employed to understand and improve the 'employee journey'. The employee experiences involved in such a journey include the commute, workplace, work task, employee knowledge and the employer's compliance with regulations.

→ The mechanism for auditing customer and employee journeys is exactly the same. There must be a mechanism for managing the auditing process, a way of collecting the audit data and a way of reporting the results. To properly evaluate an employee journey, it is necessary to account for the variations in company size, industry and the legislative environment in which the business operates.

→ There is an urgent need to make cities and towns capable of supporting an ageing population. In the same way as companies need to respond to the ageing of their customers and employees, governments have exactly the same challenge with their ageing citizens.The same conceptual model of age-friendliness that applies to customers and employees applies to citizens.

→ The two things that authorities can do to improve the quality of life for the urban old are help them extend the period of healthy and active ageing as long as possible and ensure that the buildings and infrastructure of cities are designed for their ageing bodies. Governments have a financial interest in the active ageing and wellbeing of their ageing citizens. The longer they remain active and engaged, the more tax they pay and the smaller their demands of the health and care support services.

CHAPTER 12

The future

In 1962, executives at the Decca Recording Company reportedly rejected the Beatles, saying, 'We don't like their sound, and guitar music is on the way out.' Thomas Watson, the chairman of IBM, is said to have predicted: 'I think there is a world market for maybe five computers.' *Business Week* magazine reported in 1968 that 'With over 50 foreign cars already on sale here, the Japanese auto industry isn't likely to carve out a big slice of the US market.'

The one thing that you know when predicting the future is that you are almost certain to be wrong.

In the case of the ageing consumer, there are things we know with some certainty and things that are difficult to predict. Inevitably, there are eventualities we have yet to even imagine.

Despite all of these difficulties, this chapter provides a view of what the future holds for business and the ageing consumer, using the information and opinions already discussed in the book.

How will companies approach the adoption of age-friendly practices and how will consumers respond? What does the future hold for business and governments in relation to their ageing employees and citizens?

How are things likely to develop between now and 2020? By 'things' we mean the way that business adapts to the reality of the ageing bodies of their customers. What will influence the future – what are the different types of future that might emerge? What do the authors think is the most likely trajectory of the corporate and government adoption of age-friendliness?

Trying to understand the forces that determine how the story of age-friendliness might unfold better equips us to create the future we desire.

Questions to the oracle

A good starting point for any forecasting project is to define the key questions that, if answered, would most improve the chances of accurately predicting the future.

To assist in writing this final chapter of the book, these are the questions the authors would ask if they could spend five minutes with the oracle at Delphi:

- How long does it take companies to fully embrace age-friendliness into their corporate culture? For years, sustainability was something that companies discussed and studied but it has only recently become integral to how they do business. How long will it take age-friendliness to make this transition?
- What industries and global regions will lead the way? Will the rapid economic growth of the economies of Asia Pacific enable them to leap-frog over the debt-ridden economies of the USA and Europe and set the standards for implementing age-friendliness?
- Will there be a tipping point or a gradual realization that change is inevitable, necessary and profitable? The media coverage about the 'ageing issue' is increasing. But, will the accumulated effect of this be to prompt companies to take action or provide the excuse that it is too big an issue for them to solve?
- What factors, internal and external to companies, are the largest barriers and drivers to change? There are obvious and significant reasons why companies have been slow to react. But, are these the most important barriers or is the reluctance to change deeply embedded in corporate culture?
- What actions would make the transition from age-indifferent to age-friendly faster and easier to achieve? Are there any 'magic bullets' to speed the transition or is it solely a matter of time?
- What will be the collective response of older people as their bodies age? The Baby Boomers have a reputation, deserved or undeserved, for changing society's rules. As their bodies succumb to the effects of ageing, will their response be materially different from that of their parents' generation?

Unfortunately, an audience with the oracle could not be arranged.

To visualize the future, the authors are forced to rely on what they know and to hazard a guess at what they don't.

Knowns, unknowns and unknown unknowns

The future evolution of age-friendliness will be determined by a few things that are almost certain, some that can be forecasted by extrapolating current trends and some that haven't been imagined.

Knowns

In the next decade, other than a catastrophic event, we can be certain that the following will occur:

- Demographics – the population of much of the planet will age and the support ratio, of young to old, will continue to decline.
- Physiological ageing – consumers' bodies, senses and minds will continue to age in the way the book has described.
- Urbanization – the populations of most countries will continue to migrate to large urban centres.
- Wealth – in the USA and Europe, older people will be the primary owners of wealth and be significant drivers of consumer expenditure.
- Corporate inertia – the large majority of companies will remain slow to adapt to external events unless forced to change by a crisis.
- Consumers and ageing – older people will continue not to 'feel old' until the reality of their ageing cannot be ignored. This emotion conditions much of their purchasing behaviour.
- The sandwich generation – people in their 50s and 60s will remain emotionally and financially squeezed by the demands of their children and parents.

Unknowns

These factors determine how fast and to what extent companies embrace the concept of age-friendliness and adapt their culture and business strategy. They are a disparate group of issues with one thing in common. There is great uncertainty about how they will evolve:

- Global financial instability – the USA and Europe need to reduce national, corporate and personal debt, realign their economies to the migration of economic power to Asia Pacific and manage the financial consequences of their ageing populations. Nobody knows if these can be done without rupturing the global stability of the financial markets.
- Financial effect of ageing – in one scenario, population ageing results in financial Armageddon. In another, it creates a 'demographic divided' as older people extend the period during which they contribute to society. The reality will be somewhere between the two extremes.

- Obesity and Alzheimer's – on the current trajectory, the emotional and financial costs of these two conditions are horrific. The first condition is avoidable; the second might be curable, or at least delayed. It is certain that both conditions will distort demand for resources in the health and care systems. To what extent and for how long is difficult to predict.
- Pressure from older consumers – a basic rule of business is that companies respond to consumer pressure. What is unknown is how much pressure older consumers will exert to change the way companies cater for their needs. There are numerous examples of consumer pressure being organized and extended by social networking mechanisms. Will the Baby Boomers employ these techniques or remain silent and meekly accept the products and touchpoints created for their children and grandchildren?
- CSR versus business operations – will companies view age-friendliness as a 'CSR issue' or see it as something that affects all parts of the business operations? Perhaps it will follow the route of sustainability and have a period residing in CSR before rocketing up the list of corporate priorities.
- Ageing= disability? Will legislators think it is possible to provide for the needs of older people by extending the regulations and laws that apply to those with disabilities?
- Silo syndrome – the issues of age-friendliness span most of the operational functions within a company. It is not just a 'marketing issue'. How well will companies be able to manage its adoption and coordination over multiple functional silos?

Unknown unknowns

The mistake that most forecasters make is to assume the future is little more than an aggregation of extrapolating existing trends. The golden rule of forecasting should be that: 'Trends go on until they stop.'

Donald Rumsfeld, a past United States Secretary of Defence, is famous for saying that 'There are also unknown unknowns – there are things we do not know, we don't know.'

Who could have predicted that the self-immolation of a Tunisian street vendor over police abuse would ignite a revolution that would bring down governments across the Arab world? Who could have imagined that after decades of evidence and lobbying, the environmental debate would achieve mass consciousness because of a documentary film presented by a former vice president of the USA?

By definition, it is impossible to speculate about what we don't know, but that doesn't stop us opening our minds to the type of events that could distort the logical evolution of age-friendliness:

- Unfortunately, there are far too many events that could radically change corporate priorities, ranging from war to terrorist attack to a cataclysmic financial instability resulting in civil unrest.
- The double-digit growth of the BRIC countries could stop, or at least be interrupted, with horrible implications for economies in the rest of the world.
- The much-discussed issue of intergenerational conflict could evolve from its current low level of media and think tank whingeing and griping to a coordinated chorus of actions and events that prompt politicians into action. This could disrupt companies investing in changes that are perceived as favouring one generation more than another.
- Will pharmaceutical, electronic and genetic engineering game-changing technological developments alter the economics of ageing? It is already possible for devices to use face recognition software to compute the age and gender of the user and adapt accordingly. What other wonders will be available in 5-10 years time?
- Rapid changes in the fertility rate, up or down, would have repercussions on the demand for retaining older workers.

These factors, of varying degrees of certainty, will determine how, by 2020, businesses will respond to their ageing customers. Beyond this date, the difficulty in forecasting geometrically increases but one factor remains certain – the world's population will continue to age. So, in the final analysis, the issue is not if companies will adapt their culture and priorities, but when.

What do the experts think?

The authors are not the only people considering and discussing the implications of ageing. The following are very vocal and influential in forming public and business opinions about ageing and the evolution of age-friendliness:

- Demographers.
- Economists.
- Politicians.
- CEOs.

Of course, each group contains a range of opinions but it is possible to identify some dominant themes and opinions.

Demographers

In mid-2012 the worldwide community of demographers was asked to consider what they thought would be the most important population issues during the next 20 years. Figure 12.1 shows the resulting ranking of issues.[1]

Africa was the only region that didn't consider population ageing the most important issue. This is not surprising considering the age profile of the African population and the high incidence of HIV/AIDS.

Economists

Economists have been very good at describing the multiple implications of population ageing but rarely venture into prescribing the policy options that governments should take to ensure the outcome is positive rather than negative. The work of Professor David Bloom at Harvard, described in Chapter 2, is an exception. His view is that demographics are not destiny and politicians have the power, and the duty, to take the necessary policy decisions. The major strategic consultancies echo this opinion and

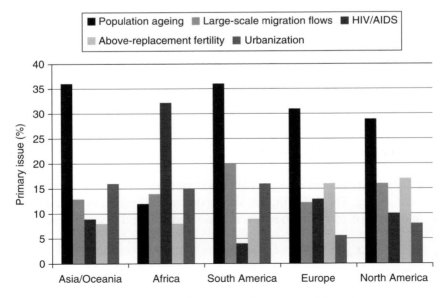

Figure 12.1 The primary population issue by geographic region

although they are aware of the potential dangers they also see the many upsides. A paper by Booz & Co called *Demographics Are Not Destiny* is representative of their views.[2]

Politicians

Politicians are politicians. If they need to act, but the policies do not bring demonstrable benefit during the electoral cycle, then they will invariably find reasons why inaction is the best decision. The only time they ignore this rule is during a crisis.

Because the actions necessary to prepare for population ageing can always be delayed, seemingly without any apparent downside, they are. This is a cynical view of the political class but seems to be substantiated by their actions (or lack of them).

The reality is that the longer decisions are delayed, the more expensive the consequences. There is a long list of issues needing reform but few countries are taking the necessary actions. Policies to cope with the ageing population are needed to reduce the cost of public sector pensions, to redesign the health and care systems and to prepare for the haemorrhaging of retiring skilled workers. Few countries have begun to address these issues.

CEOs

Most companies understand that the ageing of their customers necessitates change. However, few have transformed this 'need' into a strategy, let alone an operational plan, outlining how it can be used for competitive advantage. In an interview with the BBC, the CEO of Coca-Cola identified population ageing as one of the five 'mega trends' affecting his company.[3] The other trends were urbanization, consumer power, the rising power of the middle class and sustainability. It was unclear how Coca-Cola would react to the ageing trend other than: 'employ more focused marketing and greater reliance on home delivery'.

As discussed in Chapter 2, in the *Economist* survey of companies there was a strong awareness about the importance of population ageing and a realization about its importance to business but this was not matched by plans to do anything about it.

The experts are of one mind about the importance of population ageing. Its implications have been endlessly analysed, reported and debated. What has been less well discussed is how companies and governments need to act – there are fewer ideas, even less agreement and only the sketchiest of details.

Barriers and drivers

How fast and to what extent companies and governments incorporate age-friendliness into their culture and operations are determined by two opposing sets of forces. These forces, the drivers and barriers to age-friendliness, are listed in Figure 12.2.

Listing the forces is simple. What is difficult is quantifying their relative strength and likelihood, and then calculating how these disparate forces combine so as to determine the future.

Unfortunately, there is no formula that can resolve how these forces interrelate. The value of this listing is to highlight the forces that companies need to combat and those they need to encourage.

The secondary value of this analysis is to help describe the different scenarios that might occur.

Possible futures

There are four ways that companies might adopt and implement age-friendliness. Each of these results in very different views of the future.

Do nothing unless forced

Organizations do the minimum necessary to fulfil the regulations and legislation pertaining to age-friendliness. This 'non-strategy' results from believing there are more immediate priorities requiring attention or from management's lack of strategic vision. Probably both reasons apply.

Evolve slowly

There is a grudging acceptance that it is necessary to adapt the customer touchpoints and product mix to reflect customers' changing age profile. This is implemented by a series of one-off projects that are unlikely to be coordinated. Companies are not driven by a common vision of what it means to adopt age-friendly business principles. Through a zigzag route of trial and error, companies transform their business processes. This is an inefficient, slow and high-cost strategy.

Follow the route of sustainability

There are two ways that this future can evolve.

In the first instance, age-friendliness is defined as the responsibility of CSR and is merged with accessibility and disability initiatives. It is perceived

Drivers		Barriers
Scale – global increase in numbers of older people	→←	**Corporate inertia** – inherent resistance to change
Intensity – increasing median age of population	→←	– organizational structures (CSR and corporate silos)
Awareness – increasing media coverage of population ageing (good and bad)	→←	**Consumer pressure** – not wanting to admit to physical ageing
Financial – older demographic aggregate purchasing power and wealth ownership	→←	**Financial** – global deleveraging resulting in lower funds for investment
– diminishing economic power of the young	→←	– assigned a low priority because of the austerity conditions in the USA and Europe
Visibility – obvious results of physiological ageing	→←	– large number of older people being perceived of diminishing financial importance
Consumer pressure – to prolong existing habits and lifestyle	→←	**Sensitivity** – to inter-generational fairness of favouring one age group over another
– to have access to age-relevant products	→←	
Austerity – growth opportunities of ageing population	→←	
Global issue – ageing of China becomes a mainstream issue	→←	

Corporate adoption of age-friendliness

Figure 12.2 The drivers and barriers that determine the speed and extent of companies' incorporation of age-friendliness into their culture and operations

as a 'good thing to do' rather than a 'vital thing to do'. Companies adopt this option when the CSR group is used to manage those issues that need to be implemented without materially changing the operations of the business.

The second approach is the route that was adopted by companies that understood that sustainability would become a dimension of competition. These companies rapidly appreciate the immutable logic that incorporating age-friendliness into the specification of capital investments costs nothing. Adapting the customer touchpoints is perceived as essential to delivering a winning customer experience. In a world that is desperate for growth opportunities, the potential for age-friendliness to result in new innovative products is too difficult for these companies to ignore.

Divide into those that 'get it' and those that don't

The universe of companies divides into those that 'get it' and those that don't. One dimension of this divide is determined by geography. The economic problems of Europe and the USA deplete most companies' funds and energy for rapid change and adoption of age-friendliness.

Change is more likely to occur in Asia Pacific because of the experience and solutions that Japan is forced to create, as it enters a phase of 'ultra-ageing' and because of the demographic and economic necessity for China to manage its ageing population.

Europe and the USA become followers rather than leaders in the adoption of age-friendly business practices. There is an analogy with the way that Africa jumped a generation of technology and went straight to mobile e-commerce.

There is another divide between companies that value adaptability and competing on the quality of the customer experience and those that don't. Companies that have the culture and vision to be continuously adapting their customer experience will naturally adopt the principles of age-friendliness. These companies are experienced in implementing change and breaking down silo boundaries.

Most likely future

There will be companies that inhabit all four of these future scenarios and all the variants and combinations of these futures that can be imagined and some that cannot. It seems likely that the most common stance will be a combination of 'those that get it and those that don't' and 'follow the same route as sustainability'.

The authors believe that age-friendliness will follow the same route as sustainability. Because the financial benefits that result from embracing age-friendliness are faster to materialize and easier to predict, its potential as a competitive factor will be more quickly appreciated.

According to a 2010 Accenture global survey of CEOs, 81 per cent claim they have already fully embedded sustainability into their businesses strategy; in 2007 this figure was just 50 per cent.[4] If we are correct in our assumption, then the rate of adoption of age-friendliness will be faster.

We believe the companies that will most readily adopt age-friendliness are those that are already committed to maximizing the quality of their customer engagement. In a paper about ways of improving customer engagement, McKinsey said: 'Companies must move beyond their function-by-function view of customer engagement and to improve the coordination of activities across the broad range of touch points they must care about.'[5] Companies have exactly the same challenge with age-friendliness. Solve one of these problems and you have solved them both.

Finally, we believe the drive for change is most likely to come from Asia Pacific. Many of the countries in this region are aware of their ageing population issues and appear to have the financial strength and resolve to act. Often, the national government also has the levers of control to initiate change faster than in Europe and the USA.

China is rapidly urbanizing and these expanded and new cities will soon have to house a rapidly ageing population. China has a pressing need to act.

Companies operating in Asia Pacific will need to respond to their governments' demands for age-friendly solutions. This domestic demand will equip companies to take the lead in delivering age-friendly solutions to the USA and Europe, where government and corporate change is slowed by economic malaise.

Chapter at a glance

→ The future evolution of age-friendliness will be determined by a few things that are almost certain, some that can be forecasted by extrapolating current trends and some that haven't been imagined. We know a lot about the effects of demographics, physiological ageing, urbanization and the wealth profile of consumers. There are many unknowns about the repercussions of the financial instability of Europe and the US and how older consumers will exert their purchasing power. And then there are events that will determine the future that we cannot even speculate about.

→ The experts and thought leaders all agree about the magnitude of the ageing population issue. Economists have been very good at describing the multiple implications of population ageing but rarely venture into prescribing the policy options that governments and companies could adopt. Politicians are politicians. If they need to act, but the policies do not bring demonstrable benefit during the electoral cycle, then they will invariably find reasons why inaction is the best decision. Most companies understand that the ageing of their customers necessitates change. However, few have transformed this 'need' into a strategy, let alone an operational plan, outlining how it can be used for competitive advantage.

→ The authors believe that age-friendliness will follow the same route as sustainability. Because the financial benefits that result from embracing age-friendliness are faster to materialize and easier to predict, its potential as a competitive factor will be more quickly appreciated. We believe the companies that will most readily adopt age-friendliness are those that are already committed to maximizing the quality of their customer engagement. Finally, we believe the drive for change is most likely to come from Asia Pacific. Many of the countries in this region are aware of their ageing population issues and appear to have the financial strength and resolve to act. This domestic demand will equip companies to take the lead in delivering age-friendly solutions to the USA and Europe, where government and corporate change is slowed by economic malaise.

Notes

Introduction

1. Median age calculated from http://scholar.lib.vt.edu/theses/available/etd-12098-13236/unrestricted/CHAP2-3.PDF and https://www.cia.gov/library/publications/the-world-factbook/geos/us.html.

Chapter 1

1. Pew Research Center, Tablet and E-book reader Ownership Nearly Double Over the Holiday Gift-Giving Period, 23 January 2012.
2. Nielsen Survey: New US Smartphone Growth by Age and Income February 2012.
3. IPA Agency Census 2011.
4. Interview with Dick Stroud, The 50-Plus Market.
5. *World Population Prospects, the 2010 Revision,* http://esa.un.org/unpd/wpp/index.htm.
6. Pensions in Asia Pacific, http://www.oecd.org/dataoecd/2/18/46260941.pdf.
7. http://www.saga.co.uk/newsroom/saga/media/Content%20Editors%20Library/Newsroom/quarterly%20reports/Saga%20Quarterly%20Report%20%20Q4%202011.ashx.
8. We are the 99% movement. http://en.wikipedia.org/wiki/We_are_the_99%25.
9. Advertising to the 50-plus market, Jo Rigby (OMD) and Dick Stroud, Warc, November 2007.
10. Age and Sex Composition: 2010, US Census Bureau, http://www.census.gov/prod/cen2010/briefs/c2010br-03.pdf.

Chapter 2

1. A Nielsen Report, The Global, Socially-Conscious Consumer March 2012.
2. http://www.csreurope.org/pages/en/demographicchange.html.
3. http://data.un.org/Default.aspx and http://esa.un.org/unpd/wpp/unpp/panel_indicators.htm.
4. The financial impact of longevity risk, IMF April 2012, page 6.
5. Source: Population Division of the Department of Economic and Social Affairs of the United Nations Secretariat.
6. BostonConsulting Group 2011. http://www.bcg.com/media/PressReleaseDetails.aspx?id=tcm:12-93373.
7. Megatrends CNBC in Cooperation with the Economist http://www.cnbc.com/id/46683669/.
8. McKinsey Preparing for China's Urban Billion.

9. World Urbanization Prospects, the 2011 Revision, http://esa.un.org/unpd/wup/Documentation/press-release.htm.
10. Mapping Regional Demographic Change and Regional Demographic, Rostock Centre for the Study of Demographic Change.
11. http://www.imf.org/external/pubs/ft/fandd/2009/09/blanchardindex.htm.
12. http://www.federalreserve.gov/newsevents/speech/bernanke20061004a.htm.
13. Standard & Poor's Analyst report. http://www.standardandpoors.com/ratings/articles/en/us/?articleType=HTML&assetID=1245328578642.
14. NHS A Recipe for Care – Not a Single Ingredient. http://www.dh.gov.uk/prod_consum_dh/groups/dh_digitalassets/@dh/@en/documents/digitalasset/dh_065227.pdf.
15. The Graying of Global Population and Its Macroeconomic Consequences, David Bloom.
16. New Waves of Growth: Unlocking opportunity in the multi-polar world. http://www.accenture.com/SiteCollectionDocuments/PDF/Accenture_Institute_High_Performance_New_Waves_of_Growth_Executive%20Summary.pdf.
17. DWP, The Macroeconomic Impact from Extending Working Lives, 2011.
18. McKinsey, Meeting the 2030 French Consumer – How European-wide trends will shape the consumer landscape.
19. Where Will the Jobs Come From? The journal of high-performance business, Accenture.
20. Global Ageing, How companies can adapt to the new reality, Boston Consulting Group (BCG).
21. The charmed generation: the last of the lucky ones *Dick Stroud, Market Leader*, Quarter 4, 2009, pp. 45–7.
22. A silver opportunity? The Economist Intelligence Unit and Axa http://longevity.axa.com/pdf/AVIVA_Axa_Longevity_GB_Web.pdf.

Chapter 3

1. http://www.ons.gov.uk/ons/dcp29904_266798.pdf.
2. Strehler, B. (1962). *Time, Cells and Aging: New York and London*, Academic Press.
3. http://www.bbc.co.uk/news/health-18176017.
4. *The 50 Plus Market, Dick Stroud.*
5. http://www.worldfoodscience.org/cms/?pid=1005427
6. Access Economics 2007 Painful realities report.
7. http://www.nytimes.com/2010/08/31/health/research/31muscle.html#.
8. http://ageing.oxfordjournals.org/content/39/4/412.full.
9. P&G longitudinal study of the age related changes to female hair. http://www.pgbeautygroomingscience.com/assets/files/8%20Year%20Longitudinal%20Hair%20Aging%20Study.pdf.
10. Mintel report on the European Anti-Ageing marketing 2011 http://www.mintel.com/press-centre/press-releases/684/no-worry-lines-for-european-beauty-retailers-as-anti-ageing-market-lift.
11. Size of the market for menopause treatments http://seekingalpha.com/article/146717-women-s-health-after-whi-what-s-the-potential-market-size.
12. Nutrition – Ageing and Longevity, Jean-Pierre Mihel, Geneva Medical School and University Hospitals, Switzerland.

13. http://www.prweb.com/releases/nutraceuticals/dietary_supplements/prweb4563164. htm.
14. http://www.nhs.uk/conditions/Incontinence-urinary/Pages/Introduction.aspx.
15. Women's health: U.S. Markets for Urinary Incontinence Management Products, Life Science Intelligence, 2010.
16. http://www.medtechinsight.com/ReportA408.html.
17. http://www.bloomberg.com/news/2012-05-09/elderly-at-record-spurs-japan-stores-chase-1-4-trillion.html.
18. Sexual Function in Men Older Than 50 Years of Age: Results from the Health Professionals Follow-up Study, Annals of internal medicine.

Chapter 4

1. http://accessibility.sky.com/news/age-ok-award–29 April 2009.
2. http://accessibility.sky.com/.
3. Forrester: Competitive Strategy In The Age Of The Customer, June 2011.
4. Welcome The Age Of The Customer, Forrester Blog, 8 August 2011, http://blogs.forrester.com/william_band/11-08-08-welcome_the_age_of_the_customer_look_at_processes_from_the_outside_in.
5. BCG Global Aging. How companies can adapt to the new reality–December 2011.
6. Mystery Shopping Providers Association (USA).
7. http://agelab.mit.edu/agnes-age-gain-now-empathy-system.
8. Global age-friendly cities and communities. World Health Organization. http://www.who.int/ageing/age_friendly_cities_guide/en/index.html.
9. International Best Practices in Universal Design: A Global Review. August 2007, Canadian Human Rights Commission.
10. The Digitally Excluded Consumer–Options for Marketers, *Journal of Direct Marketing*, vol. 14 no. 1 pp. 5–17.
11. http://www.dailymail.co.uk/news/article-1050195/Tesco-reveals-Britains-pensioner-friendly-supermarket--magnifying-glasses-seats-trolleys.html.
12. http://www.sciencedirect.com/science/article/pii/S0022103112001126
13. *ConsumerReports* magazine: July 2011: What's wrong with customer service?.

Chapter 5

1. What do Mature Consumers Want? AT Kearney for the Global Business Policy Council.
2. Visual Field Loss Increases the Risk of Falls in Older Adults, The Salisbury Eye Evaluation.
3. Vision Problems in the U.S., by the National Eye Institute and Prevent Blindness America, 2008.
4. http://www.patient.co.uk/health/Age-Related-Macular-Degeneration.htm.
5. http://www.rnib.org.uk/eyehealth/eyeconditions/eyeconditionsdn/pages/glaucoma.aspx.
6. National Eye Institute http://www.nei.nih.gov/health/diabetic/retinopathy.asp.
7. Consumer Superbrands Volume VI, July 2004, Superbrands, http://www.brandrepublic.com/analysis/470346/Superbrands-case-studies-Specsavers/.

8. Vision Council of America 2006; Jobson Research 2005; Johnson and Johnson Study 2006, https://www.mesvision.com/includes/pdf_Broker/MESVision%20Facts%20 and%20Statistics.pdf.

9. Lighthouse International Statistics of Visual Impairment, http://www.lighthouse.org/ research/statistics-on-vision-impairment/prevalence-of-vision-impairment/.

10. Vision Problems in the USA – Prevalence of Adult Vision Impairment and Age-Related Eye Disease in America, 2008, update to the fourth edition.

11. http://www.w3.org/TR/2007/WD-WCAG20-TECHS-20070517/Overview.html.

12. http://www.cibse.org/content/documents/SLL/2009%20Code%20&%20 Application%20Standards.pdf.

13. http://www.visionloss.biz/statistics/refractive-error.html.

14. http://medical.presslib.com/vision/869084.htm.

15. http://www.lifeactivated.com/.

16. Connecting with Older Consumers, *Market Leader, Q1, 2011, Dick Stroud.*

17. National Institute on Deafness and Other Communication Disorders.

18. Guidance for employers on the Control of Noise at Work (HSE), http://www.hse. gov.uk/pubns/indg362.pdf– Multiple sources including A Guide to Noise Control in Minnesota.

19. World Health Organization, Grades of Hearing Impairment, http://www.who.int/pbd/ deafness/hearing_impairment_grades/en/index.html.

20. Hearing Loss Prevalence and Risk Factors Among Older Adults in the United States, *Journal of Gerontology.*

21. Prevalence of Hearing Loss and Differences by Demographic Characteristics Among US Adults, Archives of Internal Medicine.

22. Background music on BBC programme deemed to be too loud http://www.radiotimes. com/news/2011-03-14/background-music-cox-up-wonders-of-the-universe,-say-irate-viewers-.

23. Thornbury and Mistretta, 1981.

24. *The Cambridge Handbook of Age and Ageing*, p. 128.

25. Effects of ageing on touch, M. M. Wickremaratchi, Postgrad Medical Journal 2006.

26. http://www.averygilbert.com/Downloads/Gilbert%20et%20al.%20-%20Psychosom %20Med%201991.pdf.

27. Taste Perception with Age: Generic or Specific losses in Threshold Sensitivity to the Five basic Tastes? http://www.ncbi.nlm.nih.gov/pubmed/11555480.

28. The US Department of Health and Human Services-NIH 2000 Report entitled: Oral Health in America: A Report of the Surgeon General.

Chapter 6

1. Mental Capital and Wellbeing: Making the most of ourselves in the 21st century. UK Government Office for Science.

2. Cattell, R. B. (1971). *Abilities: Their structure, growth, and action.* New York: Houghton Mifflin. ISBN 0-395-04275-5.

3. Age-related Top-down Suppression Deficit in the Early Stages of Cortical Visual Memory Processing, Adam Gazzaley, Department of Neurology and Physiology, University of California, PNAS, 2 September 2008.

4. http://www.wired.com/wired/archive/4.02/jobs_pr.html.

5. http://news.stanford.edu/news/2005/june15/jobs-061505.html.

6. Effects of regulating emotions on cognitive performance. Susanne Scheibe, *American Psychological Association*, 2009, Vol. 24, No. 1, 217–223.

7. Article appearing in AdAge, September 2012 http://adage.com/article/news/inside-brain-a-boomer-cash-rich-demo-sees-ads/237089/.

8. University of Iowa, http://www.frontiersin.org/Decision_Neuroscience/10.3389/fnins.2012.00100/full#h4.

9. Major Issues of Cognitive Ageing, Timoty Salthouse, Oxford Psychology Series.

10. What Is the Age of Reason? Center for Retirement Research at Boston College, based on research by Timothy Salthouse.

11. Center for Retirement Research, Boston College. Data based on research by Timothy Salthouse.

12. http://www.bmj.com/content/344/bmj.d7622. Timing of Onset of Cognitive Decline: results from Whitehall II prospective cohort study.

13. The Effects of Aging on Brand Attitude Measurement, Rama Jayanti, *Journal of consumer marketing*, Vol. 21, No. 4.

14. The 50 Plus Market, Dick Stroud.

15. Connecting with Older Users, Dick Stroud, *Market Leader*, Q11 2011.

16. Everyday Memory Errors in Older Adults, *Aging, Neuropsychology and Cognition*, 2012.

17. Taken from USA Today. http://health.usnews.com/health-news/news/articles/2012/03/22/obesity-linked-to-poorer-mental-skills-in-seniors.

18. http://www.emaxhealth.com/11306/coffee-reported-ward-dementia.

19. http://www.emaxhealth.com/1020/new-information-shows-tai-chi-does-good-things-aging-brains.

20. https://www.cobra.com/detail/cobra-tag.cfm.

21. http://www.bloomberg.com/news/2011-07-14/google-searches-may-influence-what-people-forget-test-finds.html.

22. Alzheimer's Society website.

23. New Data on the Prevalence of Dementia, Summary of Key Findings, Dementia. UK.

24. The Key to Improving the Lives of People with Dementia, UK All Party Parliamentary Report on dementia, July 2012.

25. The Silver Book: Neurological Disease.

26. http://www.alzheimer-europe.org/Research/European-Collaboration-on-Dementia/Cost-of-dementia/Cost-of-illness-and-burden-of-dementia.

27. http://www.alz.org/alzheimers_disease_facts_and_figures.asp.

Chapter 7

1. http://www.sciencedaily.com/releases/2012/08/120821212511.htm.

2. http://www.everydayhealth.com/longevity/physical-health/body-gets-better-with-age.aspx?xid=tw_womenscancer_20120113_longevity.

3. http://web.mit.edu/tkd/stretch/stretching_3.html.

4. The role of physical activity in healthy ageing. The Finnish Centre for Interdisciplinary Gerontology. 1998.

5. http://www.betterhealth.vic.gov.au/bhcv2/bhcarticles.nsf/pages/Ageing_muscles_bones_and_joints.

6. http://www.cdc.gov/arthritis/data_statistics/arthritis_related_stats.htm.
7. Centers for Disease Control and Prevention. USA.
8. http://www.cdc.gov/arthritis/data_statistics/arthritis_related_stats.htm.
9. Falls Prevention and Healthy Aging. Public Health Agency of Canada.
10. https://select.bestinvest.co.uk/fund-factsheets/jpmglct/jpm-global-consumer-trends-a/portfolio.
11. Worldwide survey of fitness Trends for 2010 by Walter R. Thompson, PhD.
12. The Aging Hand and Handling of Hearing Aids: A Review, p. 267. Under the subheading 'Hand muscles'.
13. Increased Age Leads to Decreased Dexterity: is it really that simple? Jason Martin,University of Birmingham.
14. Dr Alaster Yoxall, Packaging Accessibility, Sheffield Hallam University.
15. http://www.aaos.org/news/aaosnow/nov10/research7.asp.
16. Smart Features for Mature Drivers. AAA. © 2008.
17. http://hseb.gtri.gatech.edu/images/Glove%20Instructions.pdf.
18. 'Yours' Magazine Packaging Survey, 2004.
19. UK Department of Trade and Industry, 1997.
20. Age UK, TNS Consumer Omnibus.
21. ICM survey for Age UK, April 2009.
22. http://www.crowncork.com/products_services/orbit_closure.php.
23. Amazon Frustration Free Packaging, http://www.amazon.co.uk/b?ie=UTF8&node=514254031.
24. Villeroy & Boch. NewWave.
25. Microsoft Kinect development website http://www.microsoft.com/en-us/kinectforwindows/.
26. Hosam Kamel, Sarcopenia and Aging, *Nutrition Reviews*, 61(5): 157–67, May 2003.
27. Designing for Older Users, Felicia Huppert, University of Cambridge.
28. Physical Activity in Later Life. Health Education Authority UK, ISBN 0-7521 1573-1.
29. Voorbij and Steenbekkers.
30. Matthew Delmonico et al., Alternative Definitions of Sarcopenia, Lower Extremity Performance, and Functional Impairment with Aging in Older Men and Women, *Journal of American Geriatrics Society*, 55:769–74, 2007.
31. Be Smart, Exercise your Heart: exercise effects on brain and cognition, http://www.sappa.sa.edu.au/documents/events/Neuro_Articles/NRN_Exercisereview.pdf.
32. Hospitalizations due to falls in older people, Australia 2008–9.
33. http://www.bbc.co.uk/news/business-18503627.
34. BBC interview with the CEO of Coca-Cola http://aging.senate.gov/crs/aging3.pdf.
35. World Health Statistics 2012. WHO.
36. World Health Statistics 2012. WHO.
37. International Union of Nutritional Sciences, http://www.iuns.org/.
38. IASO. Overweight Obesity in the EU, 27, 2008.
39. http://hpi.georgetown.edu/agingsociety/pubhtml/obesity2/obesity2.html.
40. http://www.worldometers.info/weight-loss/.
41. Incidence and Prevalence of Stress Urinary Incontinence, Ananias C. Diokno, MD.
42. National Continence Management Strategy, September 2006.
43. http://www.bladderandbowelfoundation.org/bladder/bladder-problems/frequency.asp.
44. http://www.hhc.rca.ac.uk/2988-3008/all/1/Out-of-Order.aspx.
45. http://www.nutrition.tufts.edu/research/modified-mypyramid-older-adults.

46. Eight-year Longitudinal Hair Ageing Study, P&G Beauty & Grooming.
47. Oxidative Stress in Ageing of Hair, Ralph M. Trüeb.
48. http://www.epa.gov/sunwise/uvandhealth.html.
49. http://www.skincancer.org/skin-cancer-information/skin-cancer-facts#aging.
50. http://www.prweb.com/releases/2009/02/prweb2021254.htm.
51. http://www.nia.nih.gov/health/publication/menopause.
52. http://www.sciencedaily.com/releases/2012/06/120623144944.htm.
53. Sexual Function in Men Older Than 50 Years of Age: Results from the Health Professionals Follow-up Study. It is in the 5 August 2003 issue of *Annals of Internal Medicine*, 139 (161–8). The authors are C. G. Bacon, M. A. Mittleman, I. Kawachi, E. Giovannucci, D. B. Glasser, and E. B. Rimm.
54. National Center for Family and Marriage Research at Ohio's Bowling Green State University, 2012.
55. http://www.webpersonalsonline.com/demographics_online_dating.html.
56. http://www.evaluatepharma.com/Universal/View.aspx?type=Story&id=235291.
57. http://www.futuramedical.com/content/products/erectile_dysfunction.asp.
58. King' College London, and Thomas's Hospital London, in the Student British Medical Journal. Author; Dr Ranjababu Kulasegaram.

Chapter 8

1. http://www.unfpa.org/swp/2007/english/introduction.html.
2. http://www.seniorsbc.ca/documents/pdf/afbc_evaluation_report.pdf.
3. What Do Mature Consumers Want? Martin Walker, Xavier Mesnard, A. T. Kearney, Inc.
4. Age UK and TNS in November 2010.
5. Nottingham University for the UK Department of Trade and Industry, 2003.
6. http://www.mcknights.com/nursing-home-residents-use-ipad-to-vote-in-house-primary-election/article/216327/.
7. MetaFacts Research (USA 2006).
8. http://www.informationweek.com/news/196601642.
9. http://www.macrumors.com/2012/03/15.
10. http://www.eng.cam.ac.uk/inclusivedesign/index.php?section=introduction&page=ex-oxo.
11. Pew Research Center's Internet and American Life Project, January 2012.
12. 2010 J. D. Power Auto Offline Media Report, Winter.
13. http://www.who.int/ageing/age_friendly_cities/en/index.html.
14. http://agelab.mit.edu/agnes-age-gain-now-empathy-system.

Chapter 9

1. http://www.w3.org/WAI/bcase/soc.html#older.

Chapter 10

1. Wikipedia.
2. United Nations Population Report.

3. Aging in Asia and Oceania. AARP Multinational Survey of Opinion Leaders 2006.
4. http://an-inconvenient-truth.com/.
5. Global 500 Climate Change Report 2012. Carbon Disclosure Project.
6. *The Glittering Silver Market: The Rise of the Elderly Consumers in Asia*, Yuwa Hedrick-Wong, John Wiley & Sons, 2007.
7. http://esa.un.org/unpd/wpp/unpp/panel_indicators.htm.
8. Data provided by Global Demographics.
9. http://esa.un.org/unpd/wpp/unpp/panel_indicators.htm.
10. http://pewinternet.org/Reports/2011/Social-Networking-Sites.aspx.
11. Cognito & YouGov Plc, April 2012.
12. Accenture: How to Make Your Company Think Like a Customer, 2012.
13. Booz Allen Hamilton, Smart Customization: Profitable Growth Through Tailored Business Streams, November 2003.
14. Cognito & YouGov Plc. April 2012.

Chapter 11

1. OECD Pensions Outlook 2012.
2. Global Aging. How companies can adapt to the new reality, BCG.
3. http://www.gulbenkian.org.uk/press/press/234-Lord-Wei-calls-for-a-National-Retirement-Service--.html.
4. USA Today/Gallup poll, 9–11 June 2006.
5. The New Agenda on Ageing, Sinead Shannon, Research Manager, Ageing Well Network.
6. http://www.aarp.org/work/on-the-job/info-09-2011/aarp-best-employers-winners-2011.html.
7. C. H. Loch, F. J. Sting, N. Bauer, and H. Mauermann (2010), How BMW Is Defusing the Demographic Time Bomb, *Harvard Business Review*, 99–102.
8. http://www3.cfo.com/article/2012/6/training_baby-boomers-retirement-hiring-managing-older-workers-knowledge-transfer.
9. SHRM-AARP Survey – conducted February 13–March 12 2012.
10. SHRM-AARP Survey – —conducted February 13–March 12 2012.
11. http://www.adviceguide.org.uk/england/work_e/work_discrimination_e/age_discrimination_at_work.htm.
12. World Urbanization Prospects, The 2011 Revision. http://esa.un.org/unpd/wup/index.htm.
13. http://www.cnbc.com/id/46683669.
14. http://english.people.com.cn/90001/90782/90872/6633932.html.
15. The High Concentration of U.S. Health Care Expenditures, http://www.ahrq.gov/research/ria19/expendria.htm.
16. http://www.dh.gov.uk/prod_consum_dh/groups/dh_digitalassets/@dh/@en/documents/digitalasset/dh_065227.pdf.
17. Kalache and Kickbusch, 1997.
18. Global recommendations on physical activity for health, ISBN 978 92 4 159 997 9 World Health Organization 2010.
19. http://europa.eu/ey2012/ey2012main.jsp?catId=971&langId=en.
20. http://ageandopportunity.ie/go-life/.

21. Aging in Manitoba (AIM) Longitudinal Study. http://umanitoba.ca/centres/aging/research/funded_projects/1068.html.
22. http://www.toiletmap.gov.au/.
23. Global Age-friendly Cities: A guide, World Health Organization 2007, ISBN 978 92 4 154730 7.
24. Global Age-friendly Cities: A guide, World Health Organization 2007. ISBN 978 92 4 154730 7.
25. Urban World: Cities and the rise of the consuming class, McKinsey Global Institute, June 2012.

Chapter 12

1. What Is on a Demographer's Mind? A worldwide survey, Hendrik p. van Dalen, Demographic Research, 26(16), 363–408, published 3 May 2012.
2. Demographics Are Not Destiny, http://www.strategy-business.com/media/file/00091-Demographics-Are-Not-Destiny.pdf.
3. http://www.bbc.co.uk/news/business-18503627
4. A New Era of Sustainability, http://www.unglobalcompact.org/docs/news_events/8.1/UNGC_Accenture_CEO_Study_2010.pdf.
5. https://www.mckinseyquarterly.com/Marketing/Strategy/Five_no_regrets_moves_for_superior_customer_engagement_2999.

U

UK
dementia, 103–4
Department of Trade and Industry, 121
divorce rates of older people, 33
GDP growth, 25
healthcare expenditure, 23
hearing assistance devices, usage of, 73
Internet usage, 53
Office for National Statistics, 19, 33
quality of life, 9, 10
uncertainties, of population ageing, 22
GDP growth, 24–6
healthcare costs, 23–4
Unilever, 55, 144
United Nations (UN), 8–9, 194
universal design, of age-friendliness, 153
unknown factors, of age-friendliness, 223–4
unreadiness, for retirement, 9–11
urbanization, 21, 223
Urban Performance Index, 219
urge incontinence, 43, 139
urinary incontinence (UI), and ageing, 43–4, 138
business opportunities, 141
people affected, 139
science, 138–9
touchpoints, effects on, 139–41
USA
birthrate in, 19, 20
brand preferences and age, 6
budget deficits, reduction of, 21
consumer spending, 27
demographic transition, 18
divorce rates of older people, 33
eyesight problems, people affected by, 64
financial convulsions, 1
growth levels, 25
healthcare expenditure, 23

hearing assistance devices, usage of, 73
housing values, fall in, 11
intergenerational equity, 25
Internet usage, 53
life expectancy, 19, 20
marketing communications, 7
National Institute on Aging, 146
older people, wealth owned by, 9
optical industry, 68
quality of life, perception of, 9
recession in, 191

V
vascular dementia, 103
Viagra, 44, 149
Villeroy and Boch, 123, 124
Vision Council of America, 64
vision impairments, in ageing, 62–3
Vodafone, 205

W
Watson, Thomas, 221
wealth, 9, 223
weight
and ageing, 40
control
devices, 137–8
exercise, 137
foods, 137
Wolfe, David (*Ageless Marketing*), 14
Wolff Olins, 8
World Health Organization (WHO), 51, 72, 133, 152, 194, 214, 215, 217
World Wide Web Consortium (W3C), 66

Z
zeitgeist effect, 13
'zero-sum fallacy,' 25